Television, AIDS and Risk

D1546233

Other titles in the series

Australian Television
Programs, pleasure and politics
Edited by John Tulloch, Graeme Turner

Australian Television Culture
Tom O'Regan

Communication and Cultural Literacy
An Introduction
Tony Schirato, Susan Yell

Dark Side of the Dream
Australian Literature and the postcolonial mind
Bob Hodge, Vijay Mishra

Fashioning the Feminine
Girls, popular culture and schooling
Pam Gilbert, Sandra Taylor

Featuring Australia
The Cinema of Charles Chauvel
Stuart Cunningham

From Nimbin to Mardi Gras
Constructing community arts
Gay Hawkins

From Pop to Punk to Postmodernism
Popular music and Australian culture from the 1960s to the 1990s
Edited by Philip Hayward

High Culture, Popular Culture
The long debate
Peter Goodall

Making it National
Nationalism and Australian popular culture
Graeme Turner

Myths of Oz
Reading Australian popular culture
John Fiske, Bob Hodge, Graeme Turner

National Fictions
Literature, film and the construction of Australian narrative
Graeme Turner

Out West
Perceptions of Sydney's western suburbs
Diane Powell

Public Voices, Private Interests
Australia's media policy
Jennifer Craik, Julie James Bailey, Albert Moran

Racism, Ethnicity and the Media
Edited by Andrew Jakubowicz

Resorting to Tourism
Cultural policies for tourist development in Australia
Jennifer Craik

Stay Tuned
The Australian broadcasting reader
Edited by Albert Moran

Temptations
Sex, selling and the department store
Gail Reekie

AUSTRALIAN CULTURAL STUDIES
Series editors: John Tulloch and Terry Threadgold

Television, AIDS and Risk

A cultural studies approach to health communication

John Tulloch and Deborah Lupton

ALLEN & UNWIN

First published in 1997 by
Allen & Unwin Pty Ltd
9 Atchison Street, St Leonards, NSW 2065 Australia
Phone: (61 2) 9901 4088
Fax: (61 2) 9906 2218
E-mail: frontdesk@allen-unwin.com.au

National Library of Australia
Cataloguing-in-Publication entry:

Tulloch, John, 1942– .
    Television, AIDS and risk: a cultural studies approach to
    health communication.

    Bibliography.
    Includes index.
    ISBN 1 86448 224 9.

    1. Television in health education—Australia. 2. AIDS
    (Disease) in mass media—Australia. 3. Health risk
    communication—Australia. 4. AIDS (Disease)—Australia—
    Prevention. I. Lupton, Deborah. II. Title.

614.5993

Set in 11/12pt American Garamond by DOCUPRO
Printed by SRM Production Services Sdn Bhd, Malaysia

10 9 8 7 6 5 4 3 2 1

Other titles by John Tulloch

J. Tulloch (ed.), 1977, **Conflict and Control in the Cinema**, Macmillan, Melbourne

J. Tulloch, 1980, **Chekov:** *A structuralist study*, Macmillan, London

J. Tulloch, 1981, **Legends On The Screen:** *the narrative film in Australia 1919–1929*, Currency, Sydney

J. Tulloch, 1982, **Australian Cinema:** *Industry, narrative and meaning*, Allen & Unwin, Sydney

J. Tulloch and M. Alvarado, 1984, **Doctor Who:** *the unfolding text*, Macmillan, London

J. Tulloch and A. Moran, 1986, **A Country Practice:** *'Quality Soap'*, Currency, Sydney

J. Tulloch and G. Turner (eds), 1989, **Australian Television:** *Programs, pleasures and politics*, Allen & Unwin, Sydney

J. Tulloch, 1990, **Television Drama:** *Agency, audience and myth*, Routledge, London

J. Tulloch and H. Jenkins, 1995, **Science Fiction Audiences:** *Watching Doctor Who and Star Trek*, Routledge, London

Other titles by Deborah Lupton

Lupton, D., 1994, **Medicine as Culture:** *Illness, disease and the body in western societies*, Sage, London

Lupton, D., 1994, **Moral Threats and Dangerous Desires:** *AIDS in the news media*, Taylor and Francis, London

Chapman, S. and Lupton, D., 1994, **The Fight for Public Health:** *Principles and practice of media advocacy*, British Medical Journal Publishing, London

Lupton, D., 1995, **The Imperative of Health:** *Public health and the regulated body*, Sage, London

Lupton, D., 1996, **Food, the Body and the Self**, Sage, London

Petersen, A. and Lupton, D., 1996, **The New Public Health:** *Health and self in the age of risk*, Allen & Unwin/Sage, Sydney and London

Series Editor's Foreword

Cultural Studies as a phenomenon can be located at the intersection of a number of productive debates and historical tensions between and among disciplines. Among the many characterising features of its current metalanguages and methodologies are its interdisciplinarity and a poststructuralist vocabulary that has emerged from a powerful critique of, and the struggle for self-definition against, dominant disciplinary formations. If you want to construct different realities, if you want to challenge ways of knowing and being that have been institutionalised through specialised modes of 'professional vision' (Goodwin 1994), including specialised discursive practices, then you cannot, or so we have argued in Cultural Studies, continue to use the same professional languages. This process of critique and of 'deconstruction' has inevitably produced new vocabularies. The meta-language of poststructuralist discursive analysis is one example, with its regular use of the terms *discourse, intertextuality, knowledges, narrative, genre, subjectivity, positioning, reading formations, embodiment*—to name just a few. These processes have also increased immeasurably our cultural studies understandings of the complexities and unpredictabilities of the processes of embodiment, textual practice and the social process which constitute this thing we call 'culture'.

At the same time, the languages we have developed to talk among ourselves have become in turn a 'professional vision', institutionalised and now largely impenetrable (without goodwill and the desire to negotiate) to many of our colleagues in other fields whose work might find the insights we have arrived at invaluable if only they knew what we were talking about. There is a crucial need for translation on our part and for a willingness to engage with the complexities of what we have to say on theirs. At the same time, this may also be the moment to begin to re-think the metalanguages we have arrived at so slowly and with such labour. We need to try to remember the now institutionalised process of forgetting whereby we rejected ethnography, textual analysis and quantificational analysis of 'data' (a word we have also stopped using) to name just a few. We need to try to translate those rejected concepts too into forms that may again be useable for a Cultural Studies which has set itself some very demanding analytical and social and political goals.

This book, in various ways, addresses all of these very current and important issues. Tulloch and Lupton argue that Cultural Studies may gain a lot by going back to approaches like quantitative data analysis or ethnography, acknowledging the critique that rejected them but rewriting them self-reflexively as still productive social science methodologies within Cultural Studies. On the other hand they demonstrate that the tools that cultural studies does have as a contextualised textual practice, as a practice for understanding and theorising reading, writing and visual practices in complex sites like television production, are potentially of enormous value to professions and communities who have not necessarily been trained to know about them or to use them.

In the terms of this book the health communication profession, television production and the advertising industry are all professional communities at issue. The book's primary argument is that health communication, which uses the resources of television and advertising as a pedagogy to deal with 'risk' culture, must have more sophisticated Cultural Studies derived tools if it is to begin to deal effectively with matters of life and death such as AIDS advertising. Tulloch and Lupton do an excellent job of showing just why and how past programs of AIDS advertising in a number of countries have missed their readership or failed to communicate the messages they were intended to communicate. Part of their agenda here is to show just why the new Cultural Studies vocabulary matters, why it matters that there are *knowledges*, and therefore differences in knowing, at stake in the making of AIDS advertisements or in the making of soap opera around AIDS themes.

They use the methodology of exploring the intertextual histories of AIDS ads and the performance studies methodology of analysing the production, the process of the making of soap opera, rather than, in each case, looking only at made texts. This is invaluable in demonstrating the sheer complexity of the collaborative efforts, the intersection of differences—in training, in discipline, in discursive resources, in attitude, in *lived bodily experience*—that need to be understood, self-reflexively, by the professions working in these contexts if they are to protect populations at risk. The body matters in these places of production just as it matters in the places where the advertisements and the messages of a soap opera episode may or may not be 'taken up', 'signed for' by very different audiences. In using contemporary work on the body Tulloch and Lupton are acknowledging the absence of the body in the health communication theories they critique. Bryan Turner (1995) has argued that there is no adequate sociology of ageing precisely because there is no adequate sociology of the body. Tulloch and Lupton, particularly in their references to questions of desire and psychoanalysis, but throughout the book in their attention to the audiences of/for AIDS materials and in their analysis of the habitual refusal of certain kinds of explicit sexual and homoerotic messages by those who make the advertisements, point to the absence of a theorisation of the body as a significant lack in current attempts to deal with the problem of AIDS.

The final Cultural Studies methodology explored in the book is audience research. The focus is on the very complex relationships between genre, intention of health care message, and cultural meanings. This is the context in which they exlore the relationship between quantitative and qualitative modes of analysis. They are also able to show here the potential effectiveness of working inductively from the perceived needs and understandings of the audience towards AIDS health communication messages rather than working from government policy and 'expert' knowledges out towards an ill-defined and often conceptually homogenised audience.

This book, then, makes a valuable and important contribution to the field of health communication using Cultural Studies methodologies. At the same time it suggests timely ways of extending and re-working the methodologies themselves and it engages productively with current debates within Cultural Studies about the most appropriate means of engaging from within the academy with issues of risk, ethnography, textual practices and policy. The work the book does *matters*, and it matters precisely because AIDS advertising and health communication *is* a matter of life and death. It is a matter of life and death which depends on effective communication: but the first step towards effective communication and towards understanding how to use the mass communications media for and as pedagogy is to begin to understand the complexities involved. It seems to me that one of the major accomplishments of the theoretical conjunctions which have produced Cultural Studies has been an understanding of these complexities, not in order to stop trying to make sense, but to know that we have to try all the harder. The message of this book is comparable to Derrida's response to Searle and Habermas:

> Exposed to the slightest difficulty, the slightest complication, the slightest transformation of the rules, the self-declared advocates of communication denounce the absence of rules as confusion. And they allow themselves then to confuse everything in the most authoritarian manner. (Derrida 1988: 158)

Less polemically, but with equal enthusiasm, Tulloch and Lupton are asking their health care colleagues to listen to some Cultural Studies complexity, to understand some different methodologies, in order to try to deal more effectively and with greater understanding with matters that are, after all, matters of life and death.

Terry Threadgold,
English Department, Monash University.

References

Derrida, J., 1988, *Limited Inc.*, trans., S. Weber, Evanston, Ill.: Northwestern University Press

Goodwin, C., 1994, 'Professional Vision', *American Anthropologist* 96, 3:606–33

Turner, B.S., 1995, Ageing and Identity: Some reflections on the somatisation of the self. In M. Featherstone and A. Wernick, *Images of Ageing: Cultural representations of later life*. London: Routledge, 245–62

CONTENTS

Foreword   vii
Tables   xiii
Figures   xiii
Abbreviations   xiv
Acknowledgments   xv

I   Television, AIDS and cultural analysis

    1 Introduction   3

    2 Interpreting television   14
       Conceptualising 'health communication': towards a
       cultural studies perspective   15
       Analysing television: empirical research approaches   19
       Concluding comments   25

II AIDS on television: text and context

    3 Advertising aids   29
       Cultural aspects of health campaigns   29
       AIDS advertisements in the United States and Britain   34
       Australian AIDS advertisements   39
       Concluding comments   48

    4 The 'AIDS body' in television drama   50
       AIDS drama in the United States and Britain   50
       AIDS in Australian television drama   56
       The 'Sophie' episodes   58
       Concluding comments   70

III Making AIDS television: expert cultures/production cultures

    5 AIDS advertisements: the state/marketing interface
       The state/marketing interface   75
       Constructing the message and audience   79
       Concluding comments   94

6 The 'three waves' of AIDS: intertexts and expertise   96
Ethnographies of production   96
The 'three waves' of AIDS   98
Writing the 'Sophie' texts   106
Script editing   111
Concluding comments   113

7 Pastoral space and commercial time: 'Sophie' in
image, music and sound   114
Lighting 'the dark side'   115
'A kind of menace': sounding 'Sophie'   120
Sequencing AIDS: time coordinates   124
Concluding comments   128

IV Viewing AIDS television: audience response

8 Reading the 'Grim Reaper'   133
General responses to the 'Grim Reaper'   134
The HIV test study   137
The AIDS education study   142
Concluding comments   146

9 Reading the 'Testimonials' and 'Vox Pop Condom'   149
The 'Testimonials' audience research   149
The 'Vox Pop Condoms' audience research   168
Concluding comments   174

10 Reading 'Sophie'   176
Measuring responses to production meanings   176
The 1990 audience research   177
Concluding comments   201

11 Response in context: television and AIDS education   202
The communication context of HIV/AIDS education   203
Bridging the information gap   205
Concluding comments   213

Conclusion   216
References   224
Index   231

TABLES

9.1 Major messages identified for each 'Testimonial' subject 155
9.2 Emotional responses to the 'Testimonial' advertisements 157
9.3 Signs of HIV/AIDS discerned in 'Testimonial' subjects 165
9.4 Perceived social class of 'Testimonial' subjects 166
9.5 Topics of discourse in the 'Vox Pop Condom' advertisement 172

FIGURES

9.1 Semantic differentials—'Laura' 161
9.2 Semantic differentials—'Emma' 161
9.3 Semantic differentials—all 'Testimonial' subjects 162
9.4 One student's suggested AIDS images 171
10.1 Semantic differentials—'Paul' by different 'Sophie' tapes 189
10.2 Semantic differentials—'Sophie' 195
10.3 Semantic differentials—'Debby' 196
10.4 Semantic differentials—'Paul' and 'Chris' 197

ABBREVIATIONS

ACP	*A Country Practice*
AMA	Australian Medical Association
AZT	azidothymidine
CARG	Commonwealth AIDS Research Grants
DCSH	Department of Community Services and Health (Commonwealth of Australia)
HIV/AIDS	Human Immunodeficiency Virus/Acquired Immunodeficiency Syndrome
IV	Intra-Venous
IVDU	Intra-Venous Drug User
KAB	Knowledge–Attitude–Behaviour (model of communication)
NACAIDS	National Advisory Council on AIDS
NH&MRC	National Health and Medical Research Council
STD	Sexually Transmissible Disease

ACKNOWLEDGMENTS

Findings from five separate funded research projects are drawn upon in this book. In 1989 the National Health and Medical Research Council (NH&MRC) funded a project by Simon Chapman and John Tulloch, 'The mass communication of news on AIDS: journalistic intent, messages and audiences'. Two projects were funded by the Commonwealth AIDS Research Grants (CARG) committee: 'The communication context of school-based HIV/AIDS education: impact, effects and meanings' (awarded to John Tulloch and Deborah Lupton in 1992) and 'Reasons for requesting an HIV antibody test: risk perception in its socio-cultural context' (awarded to Simon Chapman and Deborah Lupton in 1993). Two other projects were conducted as consultancies. One was carried out in 1994 for the New South Wales Family Planning Association: 'The heterosexual men's campaign' by John Tulloch with Sue Venables. The other was for the Commonwealth Department of Community Services and Health: 'Review of issues and methodologies in national AIDS education campaigns' (John Tulloch with Sue Kippax and June Crawford), funded in 1990. We are grateful to these organisations for supporting our research.

Because so much of the research depended on access to media and educational institutions, we owe a very great debt of thanks to many people. Contractual agreements with the New South Wales Department of Education (which we thank for giving us research access to schools) prevent us from nominating individual institutions. But principals, staff and students at many schools in New South Wales gave us their time and support during both the NH&MRC and CARG research and we should like to thank them profoundly for this. We thank too the participants in our other research. Major thanks are also due to James Davern and the *A Country Practice* production team, at both JNP Films and Channel 7, Sydney, for allowing John access to their full range of production activities, without which chapters 6 and 7 could not have been written. Many producers, directors, editors, writers, actors and other staff gave generously of their time in being interviewed in relation to the production study. John particularly thanks James Davern, Forrest Redlich, Bruce Best, Tony Morphett, Judy Colquhoun, Stephen Measday, Bill Searle, Leigh Spence, Bob Meillon, John Norton, Bob Miller, Steve Muir, Howard Fricker, Rhys Rees, David Alley, Graeme Andrews, Katrina Sedgwick, Shane Porteous, Di Smith and Virginia Foster.

Special thanks are due to Sue Venables who was not only an extraordinarily effective interviewer for the school-based CARG project but also a research colleague involved in the construction of the surveys as well as contributing ideas to the project. Similar thanks are due to Julie Crittle who was research assistant in the school-based section of the NH&MRC project. Mary Abrams and Scott Gazzard contributed important research assistance to the CARG schools study. Thanks are due to Anton Tulloch for ideas relating to the design of the questionnaires for the school students, and also to students from Bathurst High School and Glenbrook High School on feedback and advice about constructing the questionnaires out of the focus group data. Important clerical assistance for part of this book has been provided by Jennifer Newton and Janice Lamb. Finally, Deborah thanks Gamini Colless and John thanks Marian Tulloch for their continuing support of their work.

A version of some of the audience research material in chapter 10 has been published by John Tulloch under the title 'Using TV in HIV/AIDS education: production and audience cultures' in *Media Information Australia*, no. 65, 1992.

PART I

TELEVISION, AIDS AND CULTURAL ANALYSIS

1

INTRODUCTION

We want to start with two anecdotes about communication, culture and HIV/AIDS. Soon after we had begun working on this book, one of us noticed painted on the side of a commuter train near Sydney the graffiti: 'AIDS RULES, OK?'. We don't know who wrote this message, nor what bodily (or other) risk the writer took in executing it. We can, though, make some observations about this particular form of mass communication. One observation is about language, power and the resistant conventions of young people, where generic graffiti like 'ARSENAL RULES, OK?'—almost always written in public places—relate to an assertion of ownership that is generally denied in the real world. Another is to do with the mode of communication itself, with 'vandalism' and graffiti as mass communication strategies which are unofficial, written at night and operate in the very interstices of official mass communication forms. Both of these observations relate to issues of control: to the fact that the person who wrote 'AIDS RULES, OK?' controls neither the dominant modes of communication nor the systems of knowledge and power that those dominant modes uphold. This person did not, for example, have the opportunity to write Australia's first and best-known AIDS television advertisement, the 'Grim Reaper'. Nor is she or he likely to have been a member of a government-funded organisation set up to conduct HIV/AIDS policy. Instead the graffiti writer used the site of communication that was most available and 'useable' at the time—the commuter train—to speak and be seen widely.

Our second anecdote is about a sequence of events that occurred around the time of the first to-air transmission of the 'Grim Reaper' advertisement. Soon after it was shown, a fifteen-year-old Aboriginal girl one of us knew travelled to Kings Cross (Sydney's red-light district) and according to her own account had unprotected sex there. We are not, of course, suggesting any kind of direct causal link between the final hectoring warning, 'Always use condoms, always' in the advertisement and her totally contrary sexual behaviour. What we can consider, however, is the meaning of her comment 'condoms are chicken' (that is, 'cowardly') when we subsequently asked her about her response to the 'Grim Reaper'. We may understand a little more about that comment if we examine her socio-cultural background. She was young (and in and out of remand homes), female, black and working-class, so in four ways she was among the powerless and underprivileged. She mixed with other young, underprivileged people (both black and white) who stole fast cars, enjoying the police chases, and some of her group were at one time in court on a charge that related to knocking over older women for their handbags. Risk was, it seems, deeply embedded in her culture—in its economics as well as in its 'leisure' time. For someone who enjoyed stealing, fast cars and police chases, using condoms might indeed seem 'chicken'. Her group was one among the many in contemporary society which takes pleasure in risk activities. Hence, perhaps, we may understand her visit to Kings Cross to engage in unprotected sexual activity.

Our point is that it is a mistake to think of the two people in our anecdotes as simply 'irrational', as people who may be changed (in attitude and behaviour) by the appropriate transmission of 'knowledge'. In their own context they take risks as rational actors; rational, that is, in terms of their economic, social, cultural and cognitive schemas. Both people deliberately engaged in activities that are defined by the dominant culture as 'risky', and both did so in part because they take pleasure in a kind of empowerment that works in the spaces between 'normal' behaviour and convention. It would also be foolish to think of either of these two people, or the groups to which they belong, as simply marginal or 'deviant'. There are many people in contemporary western societies who derive pleasure and leisure from risk activities, and there are many more who deliberately put themselves at risk as part of a 'calculated' process. To take a group at the other end of the socio-economic privilege spectrum, consider, for instance, those much more affluent people who live surrounded by timber and trees in areas of Sydney and the nearby Blue Mountains region that are prone to devastating bushfires. Although we are much less likely to refer to these people as a 'group' or 'sub-culture', they too take what others see as 'irrational' risks. Among them there prevails a mixture of class-based aesthetics (surrounding the house with native trees rather than a lawn and concrete backyard), 'lifestyle' choice (timbered homes rather than red brick), assessment and avoidance of high-risk factors (clearing the gutters of leaves, moving the woodpile from under the house, installing sprinkler systems), fatalism (waiting each year for the high-risk summer months), and, in the last resort, uncertain trust in the experts (when should one abandon the house when fire is imminent?).

As a growing number of writers have commented, people in the late modern world are constantly faced with risks as phenomena that must be negotiated in order to live a 'reasoned' and 'civilised' life (see, for example, Giddens 1991; Beck 1992; Douglas 1992; Lash et al. 1996). The contemporary emphasis on risk is part of 'a social surge of individualisation' (Beck 1992, p. 87), in which people have become compelled to make themselves the centre of the conduct of life, and where dangers, threats or crises are frequently seen as individual problems rather than socially-based. Unlike in previous times, when misfortunes were often attributed to something out of individuals' control such as the gods or fate, the concept of risk assumes human responsibility to act to prevent misfortune. Thus, for example, calamitous events like the mass shootings at Dunblane in Scotland and Port Arthur in Australia in March and April 1996 generated public debate that 'something must be done' about gun laws, violence in the mass media, identifying 'perverts' and 'the mentally ill' and so on to prevent further tragedy and protect the 'innocent' from society's 'deviants'. In such debates, risk is used to distinguish between self and other, to project anxieties and cast moral judgements and blame upon marginalised social groups (Douglas 1992). As this suggests, the way that certain events, phenomena, individuals, actions or activities are singled out and named as 'risks' is an inextricably socio-cultural process.

Part of the discourses of 'risk society' is the uncertainty of expert knowledge systems and yet the continuing need to trust in expert solutions. This ambivalence, in the days of Chernobyl and HIV/AIDS, is fundamental to the play between risk management and personal identity, rationality and fatalism that characterises anxiety about risk in our time (Giddens 1991; Beck 1992). It also relates to the 'AIDS RULES, OK?' graffiti and the pleasures associated with risk of our earlier anecdotes. This mix of scepticism about expert knowledges and yet continuing need for expert solutions establishes commonalities of experience in the 'risk society' of the late twentieth century. It establishes a context in which medical and public health knowledges, for example, are both frequently taken up as solutions to anxieties around bodily health and are rejected in favour of other solutions (see Lupton 1995; Petersen & Lupton 1996). Theorists of risk, however, often over-emphasise common experience and fail to 'deal satisfactorily with difference and structural location' in relation to the ways that people respond to and understand risks (Scott & Freeman 1995, p. 165). There are profound differences in the classed and gendered response to risk 'calculation' and fatalism between, for example, the fifteen-year-old Aboriginal girl and the professional middle-class 'bush' dwellers we have described that must also be understood. While the tendency towards individualisation evident in discourses of risk suggests a high level of choice, it is important to recognise that some people have greater access to choice and have greater authority over the ways that 'risks' are identified and managed than do others.

This need to work between an understanding of both the commonalities and differences in constructing, understanding and experiencing risk in contemporary western societies applies also to an analysis of HIV/AIDS risk and the media. In matters of life and death like HIV/AIDS, we often depend on kinds of mass communication that we do not understand very well and cannot fully control. Even those of us with close access to the dominant media forms do not fully understand how mass communication works and the ways through which the media convey their meanings—witness the endless academic and public debate about the 'effects of television violence'. It is clear that the popular media have become important sites for the production and circulation of a proliferation of knowledges and experiences about health risks. It is vital, therefore, that we are able to understand better the processes by which the mass media convey meanings about risks and how these meanings are taken up, negotiated or ignored by audiences in the differentiated contexts in which they experience and act in their everyday lives. Some individuals (particularly various 'experts' including doctors, academics, health bureaucrats and media professionals) have close access to defining risk and constructing strategies to deal with risk, in many cases using the mass media to do so. Yet even these experts find themselves dealing with forms of communication they do not fully understand and the impact of which they cannot fully control. Public health professionals tend to confine themselves to particular models of behaviour, even while they recognise that media campaigns often seem not to 'work' in the ways they intended. In academic writings, too often our debate about these matters of communication and risk gets lost across what seem like incommensurable theoretical paradigms and methods of empirical research. These professional/paradigm boundaries *matter*, because issues of risk matter, and also because our boundaries and our quests for cultural authority tend to prevent us from taking enough factors into account in our conceptualisation of the problem, and in our strategies to use our research findings.

It is because there are differences between ways of thinking about and dealing with risks between sub-cultures that we use the term 'knowledges' in this book. 'Knowledge' seems such a neutral word. In at least one dominant paradigm in communication theory it conveys the sense that if only experts can transmit knowledge about HIV/AIDS effectively and transparently enough to members of the general public, then the latter will deal with sexuality and the risk of HIV very differently. 'Knowledges', on the other hand, suggests the idea that there are many different forms of bounded and differentially located 'expertise'. We need access to as many as possible of the cultural meanings that these different forms of expertise represent if we are to understand media communication better. 'Knowledges' suggests also the multiple boundaries that exist—physically, conceptually, and in terms of access and power—between these different cultures of expertise. It suggests that these different competences are conveyed in training, in intellectual discipline, in attitude and in lived bodily experience (whether as a young Aboriginal woman or a middle-aged, white, male public health bureaucrat).

Our use of the word 'knowledges' also points to our reflexivity as academic writers; our awareness, as far as possible, of our own boundaries, paradigms and prejudices as 'cultural authorities'. The concept of reflexivity incorporates the understanding that researchers are not producing objective 'truths' when engaging in research, but rather are constructing a particular version of a phenomenon, in which the politics, interests and particular viewpoints of their position as researchers are inevitably implicated. As Ang has pointed out, 'It is not the search for (objective, scientific) knowledge in which the researcher is engaged, but the construction of *interpretations*, of certain ways of understanding the world, always historically located, subjective, and relative' (1989, p. 105, original emphasis). Reflexivity involves critically interrogating one's professional position as a researcher, the ways in which one uses and produces knowledge and the power relations inherent in one's claims to truth (Smith 1990, p. 4). It incorporates a poststructuralist ambivalence about the progressive claims of knowledge and its socio-political contingency, and a recognition of the multiple forms of discourse that constitute the subjectivity of both researcher and researched (Foucault 1984, p. 73).

Even as we begin this book with two examples of the 'powerless', and as we privilege 'below-up' against 'top-down' HIV/AIDS campaigns, we are perhaps running close to the tendency of cultural studies academics who seek, in their methodology as much as in their research subject matter, some kind of 'authenticity' by identifying with the 'oppressed'. As Walkerdine says, we need to take 'the important step beyond assertions that academics should side with the oppressed, that film-makers see themselves as workers or that teachers should side with their pupils' since such rhetoric may represent little more than our 'wish-fulfilling denial of power' (1986, p. 191). Our political position can never fully be separated, of course, from our theoretical stance. But it can blind us to important debates and issues in other fields. We feel that too often cultural studies (and of course every other communication paradigm) imposes its own cultural boundaries. Thus, we want to suggest that cultural studies needs to reconsider approaches it has forgotten how to use (such as quantitative analysis) and also needs to offer approaches that it can use well (such as textual analysis and ethnographic research methods) to people working in the public health field. We hope too that this book will be useable among the people in the public health and media professions whose voices and practices we discuss here, as well as to students and academics interested in cultural studies, media studies and health communication research.

This book addresses the ways in which meanings and images of HIV/AIDS are communicated via television. We argue that in contemporary western societies, the particular media form of television significantly contributes to a heightened awareness of risk, danger and uncertainty. Through news reporting of crime, accidents, hazards, diseases, upheavals, natural disasters, wars and environmental pollution, through public health advertisements that are intended to provoke awareness of health risks, through talk shows that discuss the effect on 'real' people's lives of family breakdown, addiction and 'deviant' sexual desires, and via fictionalised portrayals of all these issues, television constructs a world in which danger and risk are ever present. One such risk is that threatened by HIV/AIDS, a condition that is associated with sexual activity (particularly gay sexuality) and injecting drug use. Prurient portrayals of gay male sexuality, graphic representations of the bodies of people ill with the final stages of AIDS-related illnesses and apocalyptic visions of the virus spreading throughout society have all been a feature of television and other mass media coverage of HIV/AIDS since its emergence in the early 1980s.

Judith Williamson once stated that 'Nothing could be more meaningless than a virus. It has no point, no purpose, no plan; it is part of no scheme, carries no inherent significance' (1989, p. 69). It is through culture, as well as via sensual embodied experience, that a virus such as HIV and an illness such as AIDS take on meaning. This production of meaning has taken place, and continues to be redefined, via the representation of HIV and AIDS in television texts, amongst other socio-cultural texts and practices. That is not to say that HIV/AIDS does not exist outside society and culture—quite patently there is a biological entity that may cause serious illness and death which has been labelled HIV/AIDS—but is to assert that it is through society and culture that we make sense of this phenomenon, understand it and experience it. We argue, as does Treichler (1993, p. 167), that televisual (and other media) representations of HIV/AIDS serve not simply to 'depict' or 'reflect' but indeed to constitute HIV/AIDS both as a socio-cultural phenomenon and as a 'reality', intertwined with medical and scientific discourses and practices. It was through the mass media, even though coverage was sparse and sporadic to begin with, that most people in western countries came first to hear about the new syndrome that was eventually to be called AIDS (and is now commonly referred to as HIV/AIDS). Television is a cultural product and culture is integral to our approach. In this book, as the title suggests, we continually point to the need to understand the role of culture when analysing the ways in which television portrayals of HIV/AIDS, sexuality and injecting drug use are constructed and interpreted.

The term 'culture' as we use it here draws on usage in the field of cultural studies, which brings together textual and social research into the production and interpretation of culture. Culture, for us, is not simply a collection of practices and artefacts that stands outside the individual, but incorporates the discourses, meanings and everyday practices through which people construct their sense of self and their understandings of reality. Culture is both symbolic and embodied, expressed and reproduced through human bodily actions. Culture encompasses the ways in which we interact both with other people and with non-human phenomena. When we speak of 'culture' we refer not only to elite cultural products, such as the opera, literature or fine art, but to all artefacts, experiences and institutions of social life, including the popular mass media, education, the law, science, medicine and public health, social movements, religion and the consumption of such commodities as food, drugs, clothing, cars and other technologies. The field of cultural studies, thus, analyses the development, reproduction and uses of the meanings and practices around these artefacts, experiences and institutions. Writers in cultural studies are interested in exploring and bringing to the fore the assumptions, tacit understandings and belief systems that underlie social structures and social actions. They generally take a critical stance, seeking to highlight the ways in which factors integral to individuals' sense of self and their life-course such as gender, race, ethnicity, degree of socio-economic and cultural privilege, sexual preference and age are both constructed and mediated in and through socio-cultural processes.

One way to adopt an approach that is more conversant with socio-cultural theory is to focus attention upon discourse as a source of meaning. We use the term 'discourse' here to describe a system of knowledges and practices, including speaking and writing about or visually representing social or material phenomena, that serves to shape and constitute individuals' perceptions of reality and the self. There exist contrasting and competing discourses and orders of discourse that are open to struggle, conflict and contestation (Fairclough 1992). Developments in textual analysis over the past decade or so have drawn upon poststructuralist theory, including discourse theory and analysis, to analyse the meanings of texts. Such approaches highlight the importance of language, as well as non-verbal sounds (such as incidental music) and visual images combining in television texts to produce meaning.

Other exciting theoretical developments during this time have paid close attention to issues around the human body (see, for example, Featherstone et al. 1991; Turner 1992; Scott & Morgan 1993). This literature argues that bodily experiences and sensations and bodily practices are inextricably shaped through social and cultural practices. The mass media, it may be argued, provide one forum for reproducing integral assumptions and understandings about the conduct, shape and size of the body. Through the mass media, inter alia, notions of the 'normal' and 'attractive' body, including the importance of the 'disciplined' body, the 'slim' body, the 'clean' body, the 'healthy' body and the 'civilised' body, for example, are conveyed to audiences through language, image and sound. These notions are invariably associated with moral meanings and distinctions between self and Other (see Crawford 1994; Lupton 1995; Gilman 1995). Public health professionals who attempt to convey health risk messages to audiences via television constantly draw on these notions of the 'normal' body. Health communication practices themselves, therefore, have contributed to the ways in which we perceive and live our bodies in the context of health and illness. The construction of a certain type of ideal body in health promotional and medical discourses and practices, the binary oppositions constantly articulated therein between self/other, masculine/feminine, healthy/diseased and normal/deviant, are central to our understandings of our bodies.

We share an interest with other researchers in the field of mass communication in the way that certain representations of a health issue (in this case, HIV/AIDS) are depicted in a popular medium (specifically, television) and how these representations are understood by audiences. We do not so much have an interest in 'getting the "right" message across' about AIDS to the public, however, but rather in the network of meaning formation that takes place in the interstices between the production of a text about AIDS by public health and media professionals and its reception by audiences. The following questions are central to our book: which particular discourses and meanings have circulated in television representations of AIDS? How have these discourses and meanings been constructed through the professional cultures of television production and government health promotion agencies? How have audience members 'made sense' of these discourses and meanings in the context of other, competing discourses and meanings around AIDS and sexuality? We therefore examine culture as it is produced and reproduced at a number of sites related to television products: the television product itself, the texts and sites of professional television production and health promotion, and audience sub-cultures. We use a number of analytical approaches to address these questions, including the methods of textual analysis, one-to-one interviews, participant observation, focus group discussions and self-administered questionnaires.

We focus here upon two major genres of AIDS television texts: health promotion advertisements and soap opera. One reason for this focus was purely pragmatic: we had, separately and together, conducted several research projects over the past few years around these forms of television, and the data were available to us to conduct an in-depth and synoptic analysis. Another reason is our observation that analysis of these types of AIDS texts have been largely ignored from a cultural studies perspective. In contrast, several culturally-informed critiques of news accounts of AIDS in the print and electronic media in western countries have appeared (see, for example, Watney 1987; Austin 1990; Jones 1992; Grover 1992; Treichler 1993; Lupton 1994a). While health promotion advertisements and soap opera may seem to be very different types of television product, they are also quite similar, as we will show. The concept of intertextuality, or the recognition that all AIDS television texts tend to draw on a similar stock of discourses, including medical, scientific and public health expertise and professional assumptions about 'good television' and the needs of the audience, as well as upon each other and other media, is important here.

At the same time as we acknowledge the potentially important role played by television in the construction of meanings around such issues as AIDS, sexuality and injecting drug use, we also emphasise the complex nature of this role. We seek to highlight the importance of acknowledging the part played by everyday life and embodied experience both for those who construct television texts and those in the position of audience members. We examine the three levels of meaning—text and context, production and audience response—for these two different genres of television texts. For the sake of coherence we address each layer of meaning individually while bearing in mind their inevitable interrelationships. In the next chapter we review methods of theorising and analysing television, highlighting the virtues and drawbacks of different theortical paradigms and empirical research methods. Part II (chapters 3 and 4) provides an overview of AIDS health promotion advertisements and mainstream television drama screened in the United States, Britain and Australia from the mid 1980s to the early 1990s. We focus in particular on the Australian AIDS public education advertisements screened between 1987 and 1994 and a series of four episodes of the Australian soap opera *A Country Practice* involving a storyline about a young woman who has HIV/AIDS. In Part III (chapters 5, 6 and 7) we move to the analysis of the production cultures of these texts. In these chapters we examine the imperatives and models of communication and culture inherent in bureaucratic and commercial contexts of television production. Part IV (chapters 8, 9, 10 and 11) incorporates analyses of audience responses to these same texts. The data we used here mainly involved young people in secondary schools as they were the primary group we had been funded to research. The book ends with a brief conclusion bringing together the main arguments and findings.

2

INTERPRETING TELEVISION

Like all research, mass communication research is inevitably theory driven (whether explicitly or implicitly). There are a number of different communication paradigms that have been used to think about and interpret the ways that television is made by professionals and understood by audiences. The kinds of theories and methods chosen for research examining television will vary according to whether a researcher believes that a 'preferred' meaning resides in a text like a public health advertisement, in the audiences that 'read' that text, in the analytical position of the researcher, or in some combination of these.

One major paradigm has emerged primarily from the United States. This paradigm, sometimes called the 'effects' model, is associated with quantitative research methods and is interested in the ways that discrete messages in television texts are conveyed to audiences. The 'effects' model outlines a predominantly linear process of communication, in which a discrete message is 'sent', 'transmitted' and 'received' (or 'not received') by the audience. Some critics have called this approach to communication the 'hypodermic needle' model, as it implies that messages can be 'injected' into audiences. Proponents of this model usually devote their attention to measuring the extent to which the message has reached the target audience and identifying the possible barriers (or 'noise') affecting reception of the message. Another paradigm, coming from a European intellectual tradition, focuses on the cultural meanings of television and the concept of the 'active' audience, or the audience that constantly negotiates, reworks and often subverts these meanings. This approach emphasises the class, gender, ethnic (and occasionally age) dimensions of actual audience readings and tends to favour qualitative (or 'ethnographic') research methods such as interviewing and participant observation. It is this paradigm that largely underpins research on television in contemporary cultural studies.

In this chapter we discuss the different ways available to understand, theorise and empirically research AIDS television. We first review how health communication, as a specialised field of mass communication research, has tended to approach the study of television, commenting on the ways that cultural studies perspectives have tended to be ignored in this field. The chapter then looks at the empirical research methods most commonly employed to analyse television, discussing the pros and cons of quantitative and qualitative methods.

CONCEPTUALISING 'HEALTH COMMUNICATION': TOWARDS A CULTURAL STUDIES PERSPECTIVE

Health communication research, particularly in the United States, has tended to rely upon the 'effects' model of communication, largely ignoring the developments in social and cultural theory that have taken place in other areas of mass communication research. The field of 'health communication' is generally understood as applying communication theory and research to the health care setting to overcome 'communication difficulties' (see, for example, Kreps 1989). The focus of research in health communication has therefore been devoted to increasing the efficacy of messages deemed 'health promoting' and to encouraging behaviours believed to be associated with good health. The intention is to assist health care workers, including doctors, nurses and health promoters, to convey their 'messages' effectively to their target populations, whether they be patients, specific social groups or the general public. 'Culture' is either largely ignored or discussed very narrowly in terms of 'other cultures' or ethnic traditions that differ from the dominant culture: in the case of Anglophone western countries, non-English-speaking and non-white ethnicities. 'Culture', therefore, is represented as something possessed by 'other social groups', particularly those that are marginalised in some way. In much health communication and health promotion literature, 'culture', understood in this very specific way, is viewed as a 'barrier' that creates problems or the failure of health promotion strategies because of clashing norms and assumptions or linguistic problems (ten Brummelhuis & Herdt 1995, p. ix).

In conceiving of health communication ultimately as a pedagogic process, researchers and practitioners have often failed to recognise that individuals' understandings of health, illness and disease are constructed as part of social and cultural practices and milieux and have a historical dimension. Research and scholarship in health communication have largely ignored the rich insights into the socio-cultural construction of health, illness and disease offered by fields such as anthropology, sociology, philosophy and cultural studies. If it is accepted that communication involves the production and exchange of meaning sited within social and cultural practices, the field of health communication could potentially incorporate social and cultural theory in understanding how individuals make sense of and experience medicine, health, illness and disease. Yet in both health promotion and health communication, such theory has received little attention. This is largely a product of the emergence of these fields from and their remaining close links with medicine and behavioural psychology rather than a strong association with the humanities or qualitative social science.

The 'effects' model of communication still tends to influence much research in health promotion and health communication despite its decline in influence in other communication fields. Health communication campaigns are understood as 'inoculating' audience members against the risk of contracting an illness or disease by changing their attitudes, beliefs and behaviours. Communication, therefore, is seen as a therapeutic exercise, treating the 'pathogen' of misunderstanding (Lievrouw 1994, p. 9). Flora and Thoresen (1988) argue, for example, that AIDS educators should develop media messages that teach adolescents to 'inoculate' themselves against 'social pressures' that stop them engaging in safer sex practices. Ling has described 'a new variety of contagious disease' including HIV/AIDS, cancer, heart disease, alcohol and drug abuse and stress disorders which he argues are 'transmitted through the information media' (1989, p. 254). As these comments suggest, commercial television products are typically represented in the health communication literature as 'transmitting' impediments to appropriate health messages (for example, in advertisements for 'unhealthy' products such as alcohol and cigarettes). The media are viewed as a battleground for the struggle over representations: on one side, the 'unhealthy' and 'distorted' messages disseminated in the commercial media; on the other, the 'healthy facts' pushed in government-sponsored campaigns. Alternatively, the commercial media are seen as the conduits for subtle health messages inserted in the storylines of television drama (see, for example, Montgomery 1990).

In the field of health communication, research into the 'effects' of messages conveyed in television products tends to focus upon the individual psychological level. Television is represented as a 'persuasive' medium and research is therefore carried out to determine its ability to persuade. Audience members may be differentiated by such characteristics or 'receiver factors' as age, education level, intelligence, gender, lifestyle and personality type. The process of communication of messages, however, is regarded as a hierarchy of effect in which one step must take place before another can occur (see, for example, McGuire 1989; Atkin & Freimuth 1989; Backer et al. 1992).

Related to the 'process' model of communication is the Knowledge–Attitude–Behaviour (KAB) model that underlies much health communication research and practice. The assumption of this model and its refinements is that knowledge about a health problem is required to change attitudes, which then leads to a change in behaviour. This model represents 'knowledge' as a translation from unproblematic scientific 'facts' (for example, how HIV is transmitted) into popular understandings. 'Unhealthy' behaviours are located in the individual, requiring the replacement of lay 'myths' with hard science to enable the individual to change his or her attitudes and behaviour. 'Information' is represented as a commodity that 'corrects' behaviour (Patton 1990, pp. 70–1). It becomes an objective entity that exists outside human construction and which can be 'transmitted' and 'received' at different levels of 'effectiveness', while individuals are portrayed as 'information deficient' and in a state of 'information need' (Dervin 1992, pp. 64–5).

Models of behaviour informing this research, such as the 'health belief' model, assume that individuals follow 'rational' and linear processes of decision-making after exposure to a health-related message before adopting recommended behaviours. These include awareness of personal vulnerability to a disease or illness, awareness of the protective benefits of taking recommended actions and a perception of barriers to adopting these actions. The concept of knowledge thus forms an integral basis for such models of health-related behaviour, as does the concept of the rational, logical actor who carefully weighs up costs and benefits of behaviours (Lupton 1995, pp. 56–7). The 'social marketing' approach has been recently advocated within the fields of health communication and health promotion. This approach has attempted to construct health messages as if they were commodities, subsequently seeking to market them using commercial strategies such as 'audience segmentation' and 'product placement' and constructing audience members as malleable and open to manipulation and persuasion (Lupton 1995, pp. 111–12).

Such models ignore the symbiotic dimension of knowledge/attitudes/behaviour. Knowledge, beliefs, attitudes and perceptions are conceptualised in these models as discrete things affecting each other in a linear way. Yet knowledge, attitudes and beliefs often overlap, and knowledge and attitudes may be shaped by practice as well as acting on behaviour. To single out each component of this relationship is almost impossible for they are constituted together. For example, 'knowledge' of safer sex practices is inextricably linked to practice: 'there is a tendency to judge practices in which one engages as safe and those not practised as unsafe' (Crawford et al. 1992, p. 12). Rationality is defined and measured in extremely individualistic and narrow terms (those assumed by health promotion workers) in which good health is privileged over all other 'benefits' and pleasures. The KAB model, in taking this individualistic approach, fails to locate behaviour within a social and cultural context.

To speak only about the individual 'effects' of television texts about health issues such as AIDS upon audiences is thus highly problematic for it ignores the continual struggle over the production of meaning, the unintended consequences of televisual representations, the sub-textual discourses and meanings that find expression in such texts and the sometimes unpredictable responses of audiences. As contemporary cultural studies theory argues, the production and reception of the meanings of television are highly contextual, contingent in time and space, as well as intertextual. Thus the producers of television products, both from the commercial and health promotion spheres, have multiple and often competing professional and personal objectives that influence the meanings of their creations. Audience members themselves actively participate in the production of meaning of televisual products:

> questions of identity and identification appear to involve memory, the nervous system, present goals and activities, life experience, familiarity with and pleasure in the conventions of a given narrative genre, demographic and circumstantial characteristics of the human figures (including their physical appearance, political perspective, values, real-life similarities and differences—class, gender, etc.), emotional and political connections

to the text, and psychic commitments. Identification can obviously also be partial, can shift in the course of a performance or text, and can piggyback on formal elements of a dramatic work . . . Finally, the text can draw us in by virtue of its own structure and its relationship to other texts. (Treichler 1993, pp. 186–7)

This approach to mass media representations which emphasises a differentiated, non-homogeneous culture combined with the notion of the 'active audience' leads to research focusing on the meanings of health risks such as HIV/AIDS for specific sub-cultural groups. The cultural studies approach explores these groups' lay beliefs as they mediate messages and meanings about risk according to their own narratives, experiences and social meanings. Part of what this approach is exploring is cultural reproduction or the ways in which social structures and meanings both are passed on and are amenable to change. The reproduction of culture does not involve simple replication or imitation, but active interpretation and reshaping: a generative and fluid rather than fixed process (Jenks 1993, p. 5).

That is not to argue, however, that media texts can simply be interpreted in any way for the producers of such texts clearly structure them in certain ways that prefer some dominant meanings over others. As Morley (1992, p. 21) notes, there are 'directive closures encoded in the message' that will structure, to some extent at least, its interpretation by audiences. Some directive closures will be more obviously directive than others. An AIDS television program will generally clearly signal its topic by its name and subject matter, for example, so that audience members read it as being 'about AIDS' rather than some other illness. There will not be much potential for ambiguous or oppositional readings. Other aspects of its meaning, however, may be far more ambiguous and open. The extent to which a program is sympathetic to people living with HIV/AIDS, for example, may be more open to interpretation on the part of audiences.

ANALYSING TELEVISION: EMPIRICAL RESEARCH APPROACHES

Surveys of social research methodologies generally divide analytical procedures into two categories: quantitative and qualitative. The former approach focuses upon enumeration and statistical analysis, while the latter is more interested in the interpretation of meaning. There are, however, overlaps between these categories. For example, the content of a series of one-to-one interviews or focus groups that explore issues in depth (usually described as a 'qualitative' method) may be quantified through the use of counting, while, on the other hand, self-administered questionnaires may include open-ended questions in which the respondents are asked to expand on their views in their own words. Each method of analysis has its advantages and drawbacks; which method is chosen for researching television depends upon such factors as the purpose of the research, the specific research questions and the available resources (including time) and research expertise.

The usual reason for employing quantitative research to study television is to be able to count or measure phenomena. Quantitative research relies heavily upon numbers and tests of statistical significance to demonstrate the validity of its findings. The samples (texts or audience members) used in this type of research are usually larger than those used in qualitative research studies and are designed to allow generalisability to a wider population. Quantitative media research has predominantly focused on the analysis of media texts or audience response to media (for example, the regular ratings surveys carried out for television channels). Very little research, thus far, has been carried out using quantitative methods in relation to the production of media.

Quantitative content analysis of television texts is primarily directed towards quantifying the recurrence of specific features over a large number of texts: counting the number of times a phenomenon such as HIV/AIDS appears, the types of people shown (heterosexuals compared with gay men, women compared with men) and so on. The standard method of quantification used in audience research is the survey questionnaire. This may either be administered to participants by an interviewer reading out the questions and filling in the questionnaire for the respondent, or may be completed by the respondents themselves (self-administered). Other methods of measuring responses to television texts include providing audience members with electronic devices to indicate the level of their response as the text is screening. The responses are then represented numerically.

Quantitative research can indicate how certain themes or subjects in television change over time or may be compared in different television genres. They can identify what kinds of television programs people watch, how many viewers tune in and whether there are differences based on variables such as gender, social class, ethnicity or age. Several problems, however, associated with this approach have been discussed in the cultural studies literature. Familiar criticisms include:

- the over-reliance on notions of 'science', 'objectivity' and 'neutrality' in quantitative research, where attention to size and randomness of a sample can often be at the expense of understanding the ways in which items on questionnaires (and other aspects of the research) serve to shape the findings themselves;
- the emphasis in quantitative textual analysis on breaking a complex text into bits that can be counted separately, and thus not attending to the ways in which narrative, sub-textual and formal features of texts act together to produce meaning;
- the over-emphasis in audience surveys on 'analytical efficiency at the methodological level for explanatory value at the theoretical level' (Jensen 1991, p. 7);
- the simplification involved in using rigidly structured survey questionnaires to collect information about complex (and often sensitive) behaviours, giving little opportunity for unprompted opinions on the part of respondents;
- the isolation of single behavioural alternatives and consequences for attention and the focus upon the behaviour of large groups rather than that of individuals over time and in different contexts;
- the lack of theorising of the data, with an emphasis on description over socio-cultural analysis. (See Jensen 1991; Morley & Silverstone 1991; and Lewis 1991 for an expanded discussion of these issues.)

A range of qualitative methods has been developed to meet these different problems. Qualitative approaches to the content, production and audience responses to television texts focus more on the interpretation of the communication of meaning as a *process*, seeking to site texts, producers and audiences within their socio-cultural and political contexts. These approaches are often ethnographic in tendency, attempting to provide a dynamic account of everyday life and interaction within a cultural group. Ethnography is centrally concerned with socio-cultural process and with what space and time means in that process. Ethnographic analysis is situational, working outwards, often inductively, from the cultural group in question rather than inwards via sampling procedures and statistical techniques. This is because ethnographers argue that 'variables' cannot readily be isolated until cultural meanings are isolated (hence some of our own quantitative work in this book was first based on an ethnography of production). Quantified (or theoreticised) findings will otherwise make little sense at the local level. Ethnographic analysis does allow us to get some access to the subjective experience of participants in the culture, even if this access is only ever partial.

The most common qualitative methods used in research analysing the production of television texts and audience response are semi-structured or unstructured one-to-one interviews, group discussions and participant observation. Such interviews and group discussions allow the collection of more complex information than structured questionnaires. They provide the interviewer with the opportunity to explain questions and probe ambiguous replies. The respondent has greater scope to enlarge upon his or her opinions and ask for clarification from the interviewer. The open-ended interview allows the researcher to probe the respondents' categories of interpretation, isolate discourses they draw on in making interpretive moves and, equally importantly, to spot the symptomatic 'silences' in the conversation.

Participant observation involves adopting an anthropological stance in watching the practices of people such as television workers as they go about their day-to-day activities and routines in the production of a television text, or observing the ways in which audience members view television. These observations are usually combined with interviews or group discussions in which the researcher may probe for the participants' interpretations of the practices she or he has observed. The analysis of written texts can also be useful in studies of the production of television texts. In our own research, for example, we have used the analysis of the discourses of official documents to explore the logics underlying the production of government AIDS television advertisements (see chapter 5). Scripts and production notes are also useful documents when undertaking analyses of the production of television.

Television texts themselves as they go to air, of course, are not 'written' texts and so analytic approaches to the 'semiotic density' of audio-visual texts need to be employed. A 'processual poetics of production' as applied to the representation of AIDS messages in the media draws on Keir Elam's (1980) sense of emphasising the pragmatic character of performance as works or productions, focusing on production strategies and professional values of practice in transforming and transcoding the written text into the 'semiotically thick' audio-visual text. That is, it focuses attention on how meanings are made and the different agendas involved in the production process from a dynamic perspective. A processual poetics of production assumes that cultural 'reading', interpretation and construction takes place at each point of the communication process in contrast to the earlier, overly-linear American 'sender–receiver' model of communication. Rather than an 'expert' source, 'noise-less' transmitter, 'passive' receiver process, cultural and ideological work takes place at each of these 'expert', 'media' and 'audience' moments in the process. The intention of this type of 'deconstructive' analysis is to go beyond the surface level of meaning to the sub-textual level. In doing so, the analyst looks for the ways in which the text is structured so that some meanings are privileged over others as 'directive closures'. Unlike quantitative content analyses, the meaning of a text is derived from the context including the rest of the text as a whole (Jensen 1991, p. 31).

Despite the many advantages of these qualitative methods, they too have a number of problems that also need to be acknowledged, including the following:

- the tendency of researchers using qualitative methods to downplay or ignore issues of reliability and validity;
- the assumption that researchers are somehow accessing the 'authentic' voices of participants or collecting 'naturally-occurring' data by using qualitative rather than quantitative methods;
- problems with lack of anonymity in the interview or focus group discussion (compared with self-administered questionnaires or telephone surveys, for example);
- the assumption that qualitative research is untainted by power relations, politics and professional concerns;
- issues of generalisability: because random sampling and large sample sizes are generally not used in qualitative research the findings cannot usually be applied beyond the sample used;

- the tendency of some researchers to select data that confirm and support their preconceived conceptions of the phenomenon under study and ignore those findings that appear contradictory. (See Morley & Silverstone 1991 and Silverman 1993 for expansions on many of these issues.)

Media research, like any other type of research, is never a neat process; it is replete with 'messiness', and this 'messiness' may be more or less obvious to the researchers and participants. A multitude of cultural factors inevitably interacts with any research process, including the language and discourses people choose to describe themselves and their worlds to researchers. Furthermore, subjectivity is fragmented, dynamic, continually produced, reproduced, constituted and reconstituted and highly contextual. At some times and places, people present a self that differs from other times and places. People's own understandings of self and the body are only ever partial, given the unconscious and sub-conscious dimensions of subjectivity. Language and discourse mediate individuals' views and experiences of reality and their embodied sensations, both when making sense of these themselves and when explaining them to others, including researchers.

It cannot be simply accepted, therefore, that the use of qualitative strategies is a means of uncovering the 'true identity' of research participants. Some of the questions we ask research participants they will find difficult to answer. They may not be able to remember events, the question may simply be inappropriate for their life situation or it may be ambiguous, open to differing interpretations. There are some things about their lives that people will be more easily able to tell us than others. These problems persist regardless of whether research participants are asked to fill in a questionnaire or engage in a one-to-one interview. Similarly, observations of people's behaviour in ethnographic research or the analysis of pre-existing media texts are never 'uncontaminated' by socio-cultural processes. The position of the observer/analyst as a member of the social world in which such activities take place and such texts are produced inevitably leads him or her to observe or analyse in certain structured ways. These include the aspects of the event or text the researcher considers are important to look for, note down and analyse.

The identification and acknowledgment of these problems does not imply that qualitative (or quantitative) media research should not be undertaken. Nonetheless, an awareness of the constructed nature of research findings is important to inform researchers' attempts to elicit the attitudes, beliefs and lived experiences of research participants via the use of empirical methods, whether they are quantitative or qualitative. Mass communication research, therefore, should be understood as an attempt at description and interpretation of a specific reality that is contingent. Given that this is true of all types of research methods, we argue for the value of using different approaches as appropriate to researching television, AIDS and risk and the importance of accessing different 'voices', including both 'lay' and 'expert/professional' knowledges. In that way, at least, the 'messiness' of media research can be recognised and worked with, rather than simply ignored or discounted.

CONCLUDING COMMENTS

We have pointed out in this chapter that cultural studies theory and qualitative methods have yet to be incorporated into mainstream health communication. Health communication research into media tends to take a quantitative approach based on the 'effects' model of communication, while contemporary research in the field of cultural studies has, by and large, avoided quantification, seeing it as too 'empiricist'. Recently, however, a number of cultural theorists involved in qualitative audience research have criticised the unwarranted generalisations so often found there. These generalisations are the result, as David Morley puts it, of 'the rejection of all forms of quantification (as a kind of methodological–ethical principle)' (1992, p. 30; see also Lewis 1991; Silverman 1993). Such critics have suggested that there is a need to develop research strategies that draw on the strengths of both enumeration and interpretation, a method 'which makes it possible to incorporate and preserve qualitative data through a process of quantification, enabling the researcher to discern the demographic patterning of audience responses' (Schroder, quoted in Morley 1992, p. 30).

We agree that the qualitative methods that tend to be used in cultural studies research might be linked to the quantitative approaches more often found in other communication paradigms to raise issues of how knowledges are constructed through the mass media and how media forms are understood and used by audiences. Reflections on the ways that research may be conceptualised and interpreted, the absences as well as the presences in ways of approaching television analysis, form part of our own experiences over the past few years in undertaking empirical research into television, AIDS and risk. The discussion in this chapter therefore serves as a foreground to the discussions of our own empirical research in Parts III and IV in which we have attempted to take up some of the criticisms of health communication research we have outlined and work through them in planning and conducting analysis of the production and reception of AIDS television texts.

PART II

AIDS ON TELEVISION: TEXT AND CONTEXT

3

ADVERTISING AIDS

The usual approach to analysing health communication campaigns has a predominantly instrumental perspective. As noted in chapter 2, health communication, as it has developed thus far, is dominated by an interest in the one-way, purposeful communication of health messages from public health agencies or health professionals to the general public. In much of the mainstream health communication literature there is the assumption that such campaigns are important instructive or persuasive texts with the objective of achieving a 'therapeutic' goal. Thus, the bulk of research directed at content analyses of health education television advertisements has examined and quantified such features as the number of discrete messages present in the advertisement, the resultant potential for 'information overload', the 'comprehensibility' of the advertisement, features of the actors in the advertisement (for example, male or female, type of ethnicity) and the types of appeals employed. We have pointed out the shortcomings of such approaches and called for a more theoretically informed analysis of such television texts. In this chapter, in line with our intention throughout this book to apply cultural studies perspectives to television texts, we examine AIDS television advertisements from a more critical and interpretive perspective.

CULTURAL ASPECTS OF HEALTH CAMPAIGNS

Public health campaigns are, as Sander Gilman contends, 'the products of a sophisticated advertising culture . . . that has specific assumptions about its audience and that audience's capacity for the quick assimilation of information as well as the best means to communicate this information' (1995, p. 116). The images and words they use are drawn from discourses, meanings and suppositions already circulating in a culture. If we view television health campaigns as cultural products, we see that such campaigns serve several functions. The stylistic and discursive features of such campaigns may be viewed as a specific genre of television. Health promoters have embraced the potential persuasive capacities of advertising, viewing it as an instrument of social change. As 'advertisements', such campaigns are similar in style to the advertisements developed for commercial commodities: they are of a similar length, they are run with commercial advertisements in program breaks, they adopt many of the visual and aural codes of such texts. What these advertisements seek to 'sell', however, is not a tangible commodity that requires monetary payment, but less tangible phenomena such as awareness, beliefs, attitudes and behaviours.

The mode of audience address in public health advertisements also differs quite dramatically from most commercial advertisements. The overt role of such campaigns, which may be sponsored by both government and non-government organisations, is to disseminate a social message. As a result, public health advertisements are often self-consciously didactic and paternalistic in style. Unlike the genre of television drama which might incorporate discussion of a health issue such as AIDS as only one aspect of its intention to entertain audiences, public health advertisements are designed for a specifically pedagogic and reforming function: to raise public awareness of a health risk and in some cases (more ambitiously) to change attitudes and behaviours. As a result they often construct the audience as more infantile and passive than do commercial advertisements. It is for this reason that the public discourse circulating around these advertisements (for instance in parliament, the media, academia or the medical profession) so often focuses on how childishly coy they are or conversely on how uninformatively frightening they are. In either case the assumption of the need to transfer a didactic and surveillant message to a passive audience eschews the notion of an active audience reflexively monitoring both these advertisements and their own bodies. The very notion of a 'campaign' denotes the assertiveness and defined end-point of such texts.

Norman Fairclough (1992, p. 215) argues that the 'technologisation of discourse', or the incorporation of discourse strategies to serve bureaucratic and managerial purposes, is becoming a widespread practice, particularly in public institutions. He gives as examples the practices of interviewing, teaching, counselling and commercial advertising. Other obvious areas in which discourse technologies are employed include public relations, political advocacy and health and other public communication campaigns. Individuals, as specialist discourse technologists or discourse 'experts', are trained to use these strategies and to train others to use them, while researchers are employed to refine them. Discourse technologies, Fairclough argues, are purposively directed towards using the fine details of linguistic and other communicative choices to bring about discursive change. The context of the exertion of discourse technologies is generally that of an individual, agency or institution seeking to exert some kind of influence upon a 'public': 'Those who are targeted for training in discourse technologies tend to be teachers, interviewers, advertisers, and other "gate-keepers", and power-holders, whereas discourse technologies are generally designed to have particular effects upon publics (clients, customers, consumers) who are not trained in them' (Fairclough 1992, p. 216).

It is clear that health communication is a major field in which specialists in discourse technologies exercise their skills. Health communication texts are replete with assertions concerning the importance of adopting appropriate language and discourse strategies to achieve the goals of health promotion. The emphasis, for example, on achieving more 'effective' health communication campaigns by carefully targeting or segmenting the audience, emphasising 'positive' behaviour change and 'current rewards' and avoiding fear appeals and using commercial marketing strategies to attract audiences' attention (as outlined in Backer et al. 1992, pp. 30–2) involves the technologisation of discourse. In health communication and health promotion, television advertisements have been used in the attempt to raise community awareness of the prevalence, symptoms and risk factors associated with illness and disease and the importance of engaging in 'health-protective' behaviours. Advertisements directed at alcohol use, drink-driving, cigarette smoking, diet and physical fitness have appeared on television screens in western countries for decades.

There is no doubt that government public health authorities remain committed to the television advertising campaign as an educational strategy, as the continuing presence of such advertisements on our screens demonstrates. In relation to HIV/AIDS, mass media health education campaigns are still regularly devised in the attempt to achieve risk awareness and behaviour change. The mainstream health communication literature still tends to betray an instrumental intention to persuade an 'ignorant', 'passive', 'apathetic' or 'recalcitrant' public that it should adopt behaviours deemed to be health-protective. While disseminating information about health risks appears a laudable and important objective, the ways in which such information tends to be conveyed betrays a set of moralistic, judgemental and patronising beliefs about the 'lay public' (Lupton 1995, pp. 110–11). Such a conceptualisation is evident in the following statement commenting on the development of health promotion advertisements: 'Messages are designed based on the analysis of the knowledge, ignorance, or misconceptions of the audience about a health issue' (Alcalay & Taplin 1989, p. 110). The acceptance of what is considered to be 'information' and 'knowledge' in the public health field needs also to be critiqued. 'Facts' derived from medical and scientific 'expertise' are generally privileged over lay knowledges which tend to be represented as 'inaccurate'.

Health communication proponents often have little sympathy for those individuals who 'know the facts' about such behaviours as unsafe sex, alcohol and tobacco use but continue to engage in them, and limited insight into the pleasures of such activities, viewing them only as pathological, requiring containment. Health education campaigns, therefore, demonstrate a set of assumptions about the ideal human actor. The 'rational actor' is championed; that is, the individual who is made aware of the alleged health-damaging effects of specific activities through the campaign, who then takes steps to protect him or herself against them by changing personal behaviour, who is therefore able to regulate his or her desires in the interests of good health (Lupton 1995, ch. 4). Such an idealised figure draws upon the notion of the 'civilised' body that has been current in western cultures since the Enlightenment (Elias 1978). The 'civilised' body is subject to conscious restraint on the part of its 'owner', rejecting the 'animality' that lurks beneath the veneer of civility. A potent example of this disdain for 'animalistic' behaviour is an Australian health campaign against the over-consumption of alcohol screened on television in the early 1990s. The advertisement showed people at a dinner table being transformed into animals after they had had too much to drink and who were then treated with contempt by their companions. The intended meaning of the advertisement was clear: excessive alcohol consumption leads to uncontrolled, animalistic behaviour, which leads to personal embarrassment and social opprobrium. The political function of health education campaigns in the mass media also requires acknowledgment. Quite apart from the use of such campaigns to both address and therefore contribute to the constitution of a 'health problem', they are a highly public means to demonstrate that 'something is being done' by the government authorities responsible for dealing with this 'problem'. Television health promotion advertisements have a dual function as advertising texts: they advertise the 'problem' at the same time as they advertise the government agency which is taking charge of the 'problem'. The very 'mass' nature of media such as television provides an opportunity for health departments and associated bodies to self-promote. A glossy, attention-attracting television advertisement, bearing the logo of a department or health authority, is tangible evidence of action, even if it only denotes that money is being spent. Such campaigns also serve to deflect attention away from the social structural reasons for ill-health, for they nearly always address members of the audience as being responsible for their own health status.

The positioning of the health promotion workers who develop such campaigns within state-funded bureaucratic departments or agencies is, of course, a major defining feature of the types of messages and meanings that are produced in such television campaigns. As a result, rarely, if ever, are government-sponsored mass media campaigns used to draw attention to deficiencies of the state's activities in protecting its citizens against ill-health, or to the vested interests associated with illness and disease. Thus, television campaigns warning people not to smoke in the interests of their health are common in most western countries, while there are none addressing the issue of state regulation of the production and marketing of tobacco or drawing audiences' attention to the role played by tobacco companies in encouraging people to smoke. While independent groups or agencies from outside the state bureaucracy may constitute a source of alternative and more critical televisual representations of health issues, they generally lack the resources to produce and screen television advertisements.

We are not arguing here for a 'conspiracy' theory of the state, seeing state-employed health promoters and advertising companies as joining together to deliberately oppress the freedom of individuals and stigmatise minority groups. Such a critique is far too reductive, failing to recognise the contradictions and struggles inherent in the process of producing health education campaigns (as we demonstrate in chapter 5). Health promotion, rather, should be viewed as a normalising institution that seeks to assist individuals to achieve and maintain states of 'good health' in order to achieve personal happiness and fulfilment. Like other institutions, such as the education system, the law, medicine and science, health promotion works to produce 'civilised' and autonomous subjects who recognise the importance of adopting behaviours deemed health-protective for their own sake. Health education mass media campaigns act as regulatory strategies, defining notions of acceptable behaviour according to 'expert' medical and public health knowledges. The methods used are sometimes coercive in their attempts to inspire guilt, shame, anxiety or fear to 'persuade' people to change their attitudes and behaviour. Other campaigns are more subtle, albeit still mainly relying upon appeals to the moralism inherent in judgements about the 'civilised' or self-controlled body versus that of the 'grotesque' or uncontrolled body. Through the use of such appeals, audiences are addressed as citizens who 'care' about themselves and wish to maintain good health and achieve longevity (see Lupton 1995, ch. 4; Petersen & Lupton 1996, ch. 3).

AIDS ADVERTISEMENTS IN THE UNITED STATES AND BRITAIN

Since the emergence of the AIDS epidemic, a plethora of television health promotion advertisements has appeared directed at containing the spread of the epidemic. Most advertisements in western countries appeared from 1986 onwards, in concert with a growing sense of urgency on the part of state health officials and AIDS 'experts' about the threat posed by HIV/AIDS to heterosexuals. Until that time, because the epidemic was largely perceived as being confined to such groups as gay men and injecting drug users, few countries felt the need to fund advertisements about AIDS for educative purposes. Instead, the bulk of educative efforts originated from non-government organisations or community action groups related to the gay community, which tended not to use expensive and diffuse mass media strategies such as television advertisements but preferred more discrete and individualised methods such as the distribution of information pamphlets and booklets and the holding of workshops.

As with campaigns directed at other health problems, the rationale for producing television AIDS advertisements is the assumption that the dissemination of information and arresting images via the medium of television is an effective means of persuading individuals to avoid behaviours deemed to be 'risky'. Examples of AIDS television advertisements in western countries include the 'America Responds to AIDS' series of advertisements sponsored by the United States Department of Health and Human Services in conjunction with the Centers for Disease Control. This campaign was launched in September 1987 with four stated main objectives: 'To have national significance and visibility; To reach both the general population and specific target audiences; To motivate the American public to take action to understand and prevent the transmission of AIDS [sic]; To create a communication testing arena for future campaign strategies' (Dan 1987, p. 1942). The campaign also had a number of related and more abstract aims, positioning the threat of AIDS as a means of fostering national unity and patriotism:

> The campaign hopes to invoke a feeling of pride among Americans in our nation's ability to work together to overcome any obstacle. It suggests that each and every American has a role to play in stopping the spread of this epidemic, either by educating others or by willing to be educated themselves. The campaign recalls both the spirit of patriotism of World War II and the challenge of putting a man on the moon. (Dan 1987, p. 1942)

In addition to the twenty-nine television advertisements shown between 1987 and 1989, radio and print advertising, posters, a national AIDS hotline and information clearing-house were included. It was estimated that 80 per cent of all American households were 'exposed' to the introductory campaign in 1987 (Bush and Boller 1991, pp. 30–1).

A rhetorical content analysis of the three years/phases of the television campaign carried out by Bush and Boller (1991) found that the first phase of the campaign, in 1987, adopted a 'mass appeal' approach emphasising information and personal responsibility, using such terms as 'anybody can acquire AIDS' [sic] and 'Know the facts about AIDS'. Spokespeople used in the campaign included medical experts, AIDS authorities and people with personal experience of the epidemic. The advertisements adopted a 'documentary' style to 'lecture' the audience on AIDS or provide real-life 'testimonials' on the experience of having HIV/AIDS (1991, p. 32). The second phase in 1988 was dramatically different, employing the strategy of fictional characterisation in morality tales; for example, the young, sexually-active single man, the unfaithful husband, the widow of an injecting drug user. The advertisements emphasised the negative outcomes of ignorance and engaging in risk behaviours, including those engaged in by one's trusted partners: 'I was cheating [on my wife] . . . it's not worth it'; 'my man was shooting up drugs and sharing needles' (1991, p. 33). The major thrust of these advertisements was a warning to change one's own behaviour and not to place one's trust in others. The third year of the 'America Responds to AIDS' campaign developed television advertisements that focused on the prevention of HIV/AIDS. Parents and their children were specifically targeted with advertisements showing father and son or mother and daughter discussing sexuality and the risks of AIDS. The intention was to convey to audiences in those target groups that providing information about AIDS in the context of the family was vitally important and that parents should overcome any reluctance or embarrassment they may harbour to do so. One major message was 'We can help you talk about AIDS—call for a guide' (1991, p. 33).

British health authorities released that country's first mass AIDS advertising campaign in 1986. The theme of the campaign was 'Don't Die of Ignorance' and its intention was to raise general awareness of the threat posed to all members of the population by HIV/AIDS. To that end, the television advertisements used apocalyptic, forbidding images of coffins, tombstones, pneumatic drills, icebergs and volcanoes. 'The overall impetus of the campaign is summed up in the slogan, "AIDS: how big does it have to be before you take notice?", where "it" is deliberately left undefined, portentous and ambiguous: the deliberate aim being to arouse curiosity rather than to inform' (Rhodes & Shaughnessy 1990, p. 56). The campaign was widely criticised by gay and medical organisations and some members of the advertising industry itself for its unrelentingly negative stance, its ambiguity and its attempts to arouse fear, anxiety and guilt in the audience (1990, pp. 56–7).

Watney (1989) points out that the level of 'public' address in such advertisements served to reveal who was considered to be important by the government authorities sponsoring the advertisement. The 'population' in this discourse became 'those who are not gay', while gay men and others who stand outside the institution of marriage were absent as members of the 'general public'. Exhorting audiences 'not to die of ignorance' and addressing them as members of the 'general public' presupposes that the audience does not know anything about AIDS. This supposition, of course, does not incorporate those gay men who had become ill from HIV/AIDS or who had watched their friends and lovers die from the syndrome, or other people associated with the gay community. As a result, argues Watney, 'At every level of "public" address and readership, ignorance is sustained on a massively institutionalised scale' (1989, p. 73). The 'general public' is constituted in such discourses as the 'body' which is rendered vulnerable to 'attack' on the part of the contagious Other. In the case of AIDS, this Other is comprised of gay men or injecting drug users, for they had earlier been constructed as the 'victims' of HIV infection in public discourses, particularly news reports.

Rhodes and Shaughnessy (1990) also undertook a critical analysis of two later British television and cinema advertisements developed by the Health Education Authority and launched in early 1988. One advertisement, 'Stay', depicted a young man and woman dining together at her flat, ending with an invitation on the part of the young woman for the man to stay the night. The other, 'Disco', aimed at a younger audience, showed a young man and woman meeting at a nightclub, with the man this time inviting the woman back to his place. The message of both is 'you can't tell by looking who is infected'. A similar television advertisement from the 'America Responds to AIDS' campaign showed a mirror with the voice-over: 'If you want to know what someone with HIV infection might look like, look in the mirror . . . and ask yourself if you're at risk'. These advertisements trade upon the visual convention of the 'before and after' shots of people with HIV/AIDS that is common in news reporting and inverts it, alerting the audience to the invisibility of the disease. It is not until the seropositive person has progressed to the last stages of AIDS that the stigmata of the syndrome, the Kaposi's sarcoma lesions (which do not appear on all people with HIV/AIDS) and the emaciated body, emerge. The face of seropositivity is unmarked, covering over the 'truth' of infection lying within (the microscopic image of HIV): 'It is a murderer that hides within our own bodies, an alien other which becomes a part of ourselves' (McGrath 1992, p. 144). This portrayal is a greater horror for it highlights the point that *anyone* could be infected, and that there is no way of telling simply from visual signs. Caution must extend to all individuals, however 'innocent' and healthy they may look.

Rhodes and Shaughnessy argue that the persuasive advertising strategy used in AIDS television campaigns tends to conflict with its educational objectives for 'if AIDS education is to be instrumental in modifying sexual behaviour—its ostensible aim—it will inevitably need to confront the very stereotypes and pre-conceptions about sexuality and gender that advertising in general upholds, exploits and reproduces' (1990, p. 56). In the dinner advertisement, for example, shots of the woman's body are alternated with the man's approving observing eye. Rhodes and Shaughnessy contend that the advertisements arouse voyeurism on the part of the viewer, serving to incite erotic feelings. At the same time, they work to associate sex with guilt and death, seeking to convey the message that only heterosexual monogamy is 'safe' and a legitimate form of sexual behaviour (1990, pp. 58–9).

Ironically, however, should advertisements attempt to be explicit in their depictions of risk behaviours and means of protecting against HIV, particularly in relation to gay sexual practices, injecting drug use or showing genitalia (particularly penises), their producers become vulnerable to charges of pornography and breach of censorship regulations, or to concerns on the part of television channels about offending audiences and advertisers. One campaign planned in the early 1990s for heterosexual men in New South Wales and developed using focus groups of male builders' labourers, originally intended, on the men's advice, to show images of the symptoms of sexually transmissible diseases (STDs) in pubs. Government agencies refused to allow this plan to go ahead. Even independent AIDS organisations have been wary of mass dissemination of educational materials with explicit depiction of sexuality for fear of charges of 'promoting homosexuality', leading to controversy and possible loss of funding (Watney 1993, p. 16). The word 'condom' or its image has proved problematic for television because of the direct link of condoms with the penis. One content analysis of 317 AIDS advertisements from 33 countries found that less than one in five included the recommendation to use condoms. Even fewer mentioned injecting drug use, with vague warnings such as 'Be careful' appearing in 30 per cent of the advertisements. Most targeted heterosexual or unspecified audiences rather than gay men or injecting drug users (Johnson & Rimal 1994).

In continental European countries there has been less reluctance to depict erect penises and condoms in television advertisements—albeit in cartoon form, using humour rather than eroticism. Depiction of genitals is a particular problem in the United States which is more prurient about the representation of sexuality on television screens and where the producers of health promotion advertisements tend not to pay for air-time, instead relying upon the goodwill of channels to screen the advertisements. American conservative politicians have frequently intervened in the production of AIDS education campaign materials, denouncing them for their promotion of 'sodomy' and 'promiscuity' (Brown et al. 1989, pp. 104–5). As a result, as is the case with other televisual texts, sexuality in AIDS advertisements is commonly suggested through accepted codes of erotic imagery and double entendre. Alternatively, violent or doom-laden imagery, such as that appearing in the British 'Don't Die of Ignorance' campaign, highly sanitised portrayals of risk behaviours or 'experts' dispensing advice step in to fill the gap. Even when condom use is directly referred to, other, more controversial and 'explicit' strategies of safer sex such as mutual masturbation fail to achieve recognition in television advertisements because of their 'unmentionable' nature.

AUSTRALIAN AIDS ADVERTISEMENTS

The Australian Commonwealth Department of Health and Community Services (at the time of writing renamed the Department of Human Services and Health) was responsible for developing a number of television AIDS education campaigns in the late 1980s and early 1990s through its special AIDS body, the National Advisory Council on AIDS (NACAIDS).

The 'Grim Reaper' advertisement

The first Australian AIDS advertisement to be screened, the 'Grim Reaper' advertisement, has become well-known through its controversial use of 'shock tactics' and grotesque images of death and decay to draw attention to heterosexual behaviour in relation to HIV/AIDS risk. The campaign was planned by the NACAIDS over some months and launched in April 1987. It was expected that 80 per cent of the Australian population, over a period of two weeks, would see the 'Grim Reaper' television advertisement at least five times. The same advertisement was also to be shown in cinemas and the campaign included radio and print advertisements and brochures explaining the risk factors for HIV/AIDS and how to use a condom.

The television advertisement for this campaign used the medieval figure of death, the skeletal and scythe-carrying grim reaper, as a symbol to convey the fatal, frightening nature of AIDS, combining this with twentieth-century popular culture—the bowling alley. Such a blatant *memento mori*, in which death is foregrounded rather than hinted at, is rare in AIDS media campaigns (Gilman 1995). The terrifying figure of the grim reaper, swathed in swirls of mist, is shown aiming a bowling ball at collections of people, all dressed to represent white, respectable and healthy 'middle-Australia' (the women in dresses, the men wearing shirts and ties). These figures are set up like bowling pins and then are all knocked over by the giant bowling ball, and finally are shown lying as if dead. Images include a little girl crying in fear as the bowling ball comes rolling towards her and a baby being knocked from its mother's arms as both are bowled over by the giant ball. The grim reaper then raises its arm in a victory gesture and bares its teeth in a grisly smile, celebrating its 'strike'. The closing shots of the advertisement show a collection of grim reapers all busily engaged in their game of knocking over people with bowling balls, suggesting the proliferation and rapid spread of AIDS. The accompanying voice-over, a deep and sonorous male voice, warned the audience that 'if not stopped, [AIDS] could kill more Australians than World War II. But AIDS can be stopped, and you can help stop it'. Audiences were then exhorted, 'If you have sex, have just one safe partner, or always use condoms—-always'. The final written message on the screen was 'AIDS. Prevention is the only cure we've got'.

At the level of *denotation* (the first level of meaning), the visual signifiers of the 'Grim Reaper' campaign were a combination of figures, movement and colour: people being lowered in rows, one line after another, and being knocked over in a featureless, misty environment by the bowling balls of the black hooded figure with a skull-like face. What these images *connote* (the second level of meaning) is death: they signify that everyone is at risk of this death, and that against this disease people are as helpless as pins in a bowling alley. While the participants in the advertisements may look young, healthy and 'normal', death is waiting to claim them. The iconography of the 'Grim Reaper' advertisement made reference to medieval plagues in its use of the skeletal figure of death. As was common in medieval imagery representing the 'Dance of Death', the use of this figure was intended to incite anxiety about the apparently meaningless and arbitrary nature of epidemic illness: death can descend from anywhere. It has particular resonance with the fear and panic engendered by the Black Death, the plague that caused mass deaths in Europe periodically from the Middle Ages up until the late seventeenth century. The centuries-old icon of the grim reaper was combined with more current horror-movie imagery in depicting the decaying/diseased body posing a threat to 'ordinary' people. The 'Grim Reaper' advertisement is therefore typical of the gothic genre (monkish skeletal figures, swirling mist, the use of 'death tolls' in the sound effects and so on), in its attempts to incite frissons of fear and horror, its use of the lurking villain and vulnerable victims and its deployment of threat combined with innocence (Williamson 1989).

The mythical power of the 'Grim Reaper' advertisement depended on its positioning of 'the family' and 'innocents' (particularly the mother, little girl and babe-in-arms) as 'at risk'. It drew powerfully on the closure, entrapment and human passivity of the gothic horror genre: there is nowhere for the victims to run. Its particular power within the genre of television advertisement was in its rejection of the notion of science as saviour. Most commercial advertisements suggest a problem (ingrained dirt in clothes, body odour, bad breath) and then present the product, often the result of 'science', to deal with it. In this advertisement, death is the problem and 'prevention is the only cure we've got': science cannot come to the rescue this time. The voice-over of the 'Grim Reaper' advertisement also emphasised that members of the audience, (hailed as 'you'), can 'help stop [AIDS]' by having 'one safe partner' or using a condom in every sexual encounter. However, this message of personal responsibility and agency jars with the images of the advertisement which depict the random nature of death from AIDS and the passivity of the victims.

Like the British 'Don't Die of Ignorance' television advertisements appearing a year previously, the 'Grim Reaper' appealed at the emotional and visceral level rather than at the level of 'rational' response. It positioned AIDS as the spectral, unknowable Other, outside 'normal' society seeking entrance through violent, horrifying means. There was also the implication that the skeletal figure of the grim reaper represented the gaunt, decaying body of the gay man dying of HIV/AIDS, seeking to spread contamination to members of the 'general public' and the previously protected circle of 'the family'.

The 'Russian Roulette' advertisement

Later in 1987, a second television advertisement, entitled 'Russian Roulette', was produced jointly by the NACAIDS and the National Campaign Against Drug Abuse. This advertisement, while directed at young injecting drug users, never directly showed syringes or injecting behaviour. Instead, it employed an analogy of the gun with the syringe, depicting a young man and woman playing 'Russian roulette'. The man is shown offering the gun to the woman. As she considers taking it, suddenly the door creaks open and a shadow falls across the couple who look up in trepidation. The figure at the doorway is never glimpsed by the audience: all that is shown is a hand encased in a black leather glove which reaches out to seize the gun from the man's hand, inserts a red bullet, hands the gun back to the man and then withdraws. The shadow and the hand, we assume, is an intertextual reference to the 'Grim Reaper' as icon of death/AIDS. The youth again offers the gun to his companion, but the frightened woman now shakes her head, saying, 'I'm not playing'. The voice-over warns:

> Shooting up drugs is like playing Russian roulette. You could OD [overdose], die from blood poisoning or get brain damage. If that's not risky enough there's now a new player in the game—AIDS. Use a shared needle and you run a very real risk of catching AIDS. One shot from a conventional needle is enough to kill you.

Again, the threatening emphasis of this advertisement is via the *chiaroscuro* lighting, drawn from the gothic and *film noir* genres. Again the public is positioned as passive—against the arbitrary 'AIDS bullet' of Russian roulette.

The 'Beds' and 'Feet' advertisements

The next phase of Australian AIDS television advertisements, launched in the summer of 1988, sought to target young, sexually active heterosexuals. Two television advertisements featured in this phase. 'Beds' depicted a young, naked male–female couple passionately embracing and kissing in a double bed and then panned out to show more and more (also heterosexual) young couples doing the same in beds in a vast space around them. The advertisement was designed to highlight the chain of infection that could spread beyond one's current sexual partner to those others with whom he or she may have had sexual contact in the past. The narration said:

> Next time you go to bed with someone, ask yourself, 'Do you know how many people they've been to bed with?' Because it's quite possible that they've had several partners and it's just as likely that these partners had several partners too. And they've had partners and so on and any one of them could have been infected with the AIDS virus and passed it on. But you don't know. That's why you should always use a condom. Because you can never be sure just how many people you're really going to bed with. Cover yourself against AIDS.

Here the domestic site of the bed is given a non-domestic connotation. Rather than sexual activity taking place in the privacy of the bedroom, it takes place in the open, subject to the gaze of others. There is, therefore, a dimension of voyeurism in the advertisement in terms of the positioning of the audience. The major message conveyed by the imagery of the multiple beds containing love-making couples is that the apparently individual act of having sex with one's partner is never as private as it seems to those involved: there are implications that spread well beyond the privacy of that act.

The 'Feet' advertisement attempted to provide a model for negotiations over the use of condoms so as to avoid feelings of embarrassment or rejection. It showed the naked legs and feet of a man and a woman in bed. From the voice-over and the intertwining movements of the legs and feet, we learn that the couple is engaging in foreplay and is about to have sex. The woman raises the issue of condom use: 'You've got the condoms, haven't you?' The man replies that he forgot. His partner responds, 'But we agreed we'd use one'. He says, 'I know, but I haven't got AIDS, have I?' She says, 'I don't know. That's the problem. You could have it. I could have it. Just because we've known each other a while doesn't mean anything'. The advertisement ends with the woman insisting, 'No condom. No sex,' and suggesting that her partner visit the late-night chemist around the corner to purchase some. This advertisement avoids fear tactics in its attempt to demonstrate 'realistically' the process by which men and women may negotiate condom use. It is worth noting, however, that in the 'Feet' advertisement it is the woman who insists on condom use while the man is reluctant. Such portrayals in relation to the negotiation of condom use, representing women as the 'responsible' partners who need to insist on condom use because their partners will be negligent are common in AIDS education campaigns. This portrayal, while recognising the importance of women being 'active' rather than 'passive' in their sexual negotiations, also constructs women as the 'gate-keepers' and regulators of men's 'insatiable' sexual desire (Waldby et al. 1993, p. 38). Furthermore, it privileges condom use as the only 'safe' alternative to unprotected penetrative sex, failing to raise the possibility of other sources of safe sexual pleasure for both partners in the absence of a condom. In this construction of heterosexual sexuality, 'sex' equals vaginal penetration. In contrast, much of the AIDS advertising directed at gay men has championed non-penetrative sexual activities as forms of 'safer sex', with the implication that penetrative sex is not acceptable for gay men (Hart 1993).

The 'Needle Bed', 'Testimonials' and 'Vox Pop Condom' advertisements

The 1990 phase of AIDS advertising used three types of television advertisements to address young people under the age of 24 who were sexually active heterosexuals or injecting drug users or both. One was the 'Needle Bed' advertisement, designed in an attempt to demonstrate to viewers the risks of having unprotected sex with people who may have had previous partners who shared needles. This advertisement, like the 'Grim Reaper', employed emotive fear appeals. It portrays a young man and woman in a darkened room, kissing and hugging in soft, romantic light. A 'flashback' of the man embracing in a similar manner a previous female partner appears, signalling his sexual past. The voice-over warns:

Before you go to bed with someone, ask yourself, who have they been to bed with? They could have slept with someone who's been doing drugs, and shared a needle with someone who shared a needle with someone who had the AIDS virus. And that means any of these people could have passed on the AIDS virus to your partner. Because when you sleep with someone, you're also sleeping with their past.

As these words are enunciated, the visuals show a double-bed mattress with male and female hands placing syringes on the mattress, one by one, so that their sharp tips point upwards. These images are focused in stark *chiaroscuro* that contrasts with the romantic lighting at the beginning of the advertisement. The couple, still locked in their embrace, are then shown falling towards the bed in slow motion. The suggestion is that the couple will be impaled upon the needles as they continue their clinch and fall onto the bed.

While the needle imagery was employed in an attempt to denote the link between sexual activity and the injecting drug use of previous partners, the punitive, almost sadistic connotations of this imagery are clear. Sexual excitement and heterosexual romance are linked in a quite bizarre juxtaposition of erotic images with fear, horror and physical pain. There is also a strong link with the previous 'Beds' advertisement in terms of the representation of the 'chain of infection' leading from one's sexual partner to a whole range of other 'unknowns'. The different inflection of the 'Needle Bed' advertisement is the implication that everyone is potentially linked to HIV infection via drug use (not just sexual activity), even if they themselves or their sexual partners have never used injecting drugs.

The second series of advertisements used in the 1990 campaign comprised testimonials of six 'real' heterosexual people living with HIV/AIDS ('Sarah', 'Chris', 'Debby', 'Laura', 'Emma' and 'Tracy') talking to camera about their situation. Like the 'Needle Bed' advertisement, the mood of the 'Testimonials' was sombre, conveyed by stark *film noir* lighting and the tense and serious tone of voice used by the participants to tell their stories of infection. All participants in the advertisements were heterosexual: three had contracted HIV through sexual activity while the other three were HIV positive after sharing needles to inject drugs. Sarah had contracted HIV by having a sexual relationship with a man who was infected. Chris had become positive after sharing infected needles once too often. Debby had shared a needle only once, yet had contracted the virus, while the male partners of Laura and Tracy, who unknown to them used injecting drugs, had passed the virus to them through sexual activity. Emma was a casual injecting drug user who had contracted HIV through sharing needles.

The 'personal testimony' style of the advertisements supported the message of a cataclysmic world 'where AIDS was still around', where 'once is enough' to contract HIV, and where casual acts and invisible assailants combined to create a brooding, threatening environment in which the realisation of personal responsibility was essential for people to protect their own health. The emphasis is upon the individuals' lack of care in contracting HIV. For example, Debby and her partner had shared a needle 'one time away from home', which was enough for her to become infected. Chris said that he occasionally shared needles and had thought that he was careful, but notes that, 'I obviously wasn't careful enough. I contracted the AIDS virus'. He also admits his responsibility in passing on the virus (albeit unknowingly) to his girlfriend: 'I was living with a girl—we were sleeping together and, I hate to say this, I'm pretty sure I passed the virus on to her'.

It is notable that of these six people living with HIV/AIDS, only Chris was male. As in other media representations of people living with HIV/AIDS (as we will elaborate in chapter 4), the infected heterosexual man is in the minority. The man is also the only person who is responsible for passing on the virus to another rather than being the passive, trusting recipient. In contrast, three of the five women had contracted HIV as 'passive victims', relying upon their trust and faith in their male partners rather than adopting safer sex practices.

A television news convention for the portrayal of people with HIV/AIDS is to use heavy backlighting, obscuring the faces and therefore the identities of the individuals. This strategy is often used with stigmatised individuals such as criminals, rapists, child abusers and illicit drug users. It was adopted in the 'Testimonial' advertisements: we never see the individuals' faces for they are silhouetted. This convention of representation, while overtly used to protect people's identity, also potentially serves to make people with HIV/AIDS 'look as they have something to hide . . . Even when the coverage is intentionally "sympathetic", the visual tropes of isolation used in journalistic coverage emphasise the [person with HIV/AIDS']

status as radically different, as cut off from life' (Grover 1992, p. 32).
As a result, although the intention of the advertisements was to
'personalise' the risk of AIDS for the young target audience, the
lighting strategy potentially conveyed another meaning: that it is
important to hide oneself, to protect one's identity, if one has
HIV/AIDS.

The third set of advertisements appearing in the 1990 campaign,
'Vox Pop Condom', took a completely different tack in employing
humour. 'Vox Pop Condom' used excerpts from 'in the street interviews' conducted by the well-known Australian comedian Andrew
Denton to portray people's attitudes to condoms in the attempt to
'socialise' condom use in a non-confronting way. There were two
versions of this advertisement: 'Vox Pop Condom (Punk)', which had
a slightly greater emphasis on 'eroticising the condom' (focusing
humorously on people talking about the 'different shapes and colours')
and 'Vox Pop Condom (Granny)', which focused on the responses of
different age groups, including 'mums' and older women. The *mise
en scène* of both advertisements was 'everywhere in daily life' (the
beach, the street, shopping malls, parties, the pub), the narrative was
repetitive rather than sequentially driven ('condoms are fun', 'many
people use them') and the body language was humorous (the embarrassed girl whose 'mum might be watching', the youth who thrusts
his hips to demonstrate when he uses condoms and pulls out his
wallet to show where he keeps them). The lighting was 'natural'
(rather than oppressively dark), the sound was also 'natural'
(unscripted conversations without music overlay), and the voice-over
(where it occurred) was that of a conventional 'vox pop' interviewer
with the added 'humorous' inflection of the comedian. These strategies constructed a casually organised and relaxed yet coherent world
where the young are comfortably and light-heartedly in control of
their fate, enjoying using condoms as part of their sex lives, where
mums are 'glad' to find their sons' condoms, and even grandmothers
once used them for pleasure.

The 'Anti-discrimination' advertisements

The final set of Australian AIDS advertisements appearing to date,
screened in 1994, moved completely away from the prevention of
AIDS to addressing the issue of discrimination against people living
with HIV/AIDS. As we elaborate in chapter 4, the overwhelming

impression conveyed by most televisual images of people with HIV/AIDS is their position as marginalised deviants (with the notable exception of infants or children with HIV/AIDS). This series of three advertisements, again featuring 'real' people, eschewed the 'silhouette' visual strategy used in the 'Testimonials' advertisements in the attempt to engender empathy for people living with HIV/AIDS and to challenge the 'deviant' meanings around such individuals. The advertisements also moved away from the 'innocent/guilty' dichotomy by not revealing *how* the featured individuals had contracted the virus, or providing any identifiers about their sexual orientation or drug-using history. The only sound used in the advertisements was music, a male voice singing a plaintive song. With each image—shots of a 'real' person living with HIV/AIDS in an everyday setting, always interacting with others—a caption appeared: 'Someone's friend. Someone's boss. Someone's husband. Someone's partner'. The advertisements end with stark white writing against a black screen: 'Ordinary people with something in common. They are all HIV positive. HIV is a virus. It doesn't discriminate . . . people do'.

The dominant message was simply that here are people, shown with their family and friends, or at work, who are members of the 'general population', who are appreciated as a friend, relative or workmate, and should not be singled out for discrimination because of their seropositive status. A further nod towards 'realism' was provided by the black-and-white format, signalling the documentary nature of the representations. These advertisements, therefore, were an attempt at social reform, changing attitudes towards people living with HIV/AIDS rather than seeking to persuade audiences to act to protect themselves against contracting the virus. They represent the culmination of the evolution in government concerns about the AIDS epidemic from the mid 1980s to the mid 1990s: from raising general awareness of the threat of HIV/AIDS, to more specific warnings about the risks of heterosexual sex and injecting drug use, to 'socialising' condom use and then to addressing social attitudes to people living with HIV/AIDS.

CONCLUDING COMMENTS

Government-sponsored AIDS television advertisements in western countries have had a clear normalising role to play in regulating the expression of sexuality and reproducing archetypes of masculinity and femininity. The pastoral and regulatory functions of these advertisements are also evident: they are constructed to warn citizens of a 'danger' that threatens their health. In doing so, some advertisements have been overt in their attempts at coercion, in threatening audiences through shocking images redolent of the horror film genre, warning 'change your behaviour or die'. Others, especially those emerging from North America, have adopted a highly conservative approach, appealing to audiences to remain faithful to their partners and protect the institution of the family. Very few Anglophone television advertisements have been humorous or light-hearted in their approach; most have taken a punitive response to those individuals who fail to engage in appropriate bodily regulation.

Such representations as the 'Grim Reaper' and 'Needle Bed' AIDS advertisements, as we have argued, tend to position the 'general public' as being at risk of contagion from marginalised groups such as injecting drug users and gay men. Many AIDS advertisements have attempted to challenge the trust that individuals may harbour in their sexual partners, forcing audiences to challenge the integrity of their romantic/sexual relationships, for, in the words of the 'Beds' advertisement, 'you can never be sure just how many people you're really going to bed with'. These meanings work to position the romantic dyad as a link in a web of contagion in which one can never be 'sure' that one is safe from infection. The dominant messages conveyed by such advertisements are 'protect yourself', 'take responsibility for your own health', 'trust no-one', 'risk is everywhere'. To what extent do commercial television texts share this type of portrayal of AIDS risk, the 'civilised' body and individuals deemed to be 'at risk' or infected with HIV? In the next chapter we turn to an analysis of the representation of the 'AIDS body' in popular television drama, with a particular focus on the genre of soap opera.

THE 'AIDS BODY' IN TELEVISION DRAMA

This chapter discusses the representation of AIDS issues in popular television drama in the United States, Britain and Australia. We adopt a historical approach in tracing the shifting meanings, narratives, images and discourses in these AIDS representations, with a particular focus on the portrayal of the 'AIDS body', or the person living with HIV/AIDS. The chapter ends with a detailed textual analysis of one particular soap opera text: a self-contained series of four episodes of the Australian drama *A Country Practice* which tells the narrative of a young woman who has HIV/AIDS.

AIDS DRAMA IN THE UNITED STATES AND BRITAIN

Television drama, particularly the genre of soap opera, provides an ideal forum for the discussion of AIDS issues in the context of everyday life. Soap opera tends to revolve around the effect of personal and social issues upon the lives of its characters; topics such as rape, marital problems and divorce, illicit sexual encounters, pregnancy, abortion and drug use are the stuff of soap opera plots. Despite the obvious potential of AIDS topics for television drama, however, for some time there was an avoidance of dealing with the subject on prime-time commercial television. The reasons for this neglect include the associated need to discuss the hitherto mostly ignored topic of homosexuality and other transgressive practices associated with HIV transmission such as injecting drug use, as well as debates around the validity of medical information related to the risk practices for HIV. American network heads, for example, were highly concerned about audiences and advertisers' disapproval (Treichler 1993, pp. 163–4). By the late 1980s, however, many producers of television drama had overcome their reluctance to approach the topic of AIDS, and several popular programs featured at least one episode with a character who had HIV/AIDS. The emergence of the AIDS epidemic had the effect of bringing the gay male body into the spotlight. In the mid to late 1980s, the gay male was the dominant 'AIDS body' to be portrayed in television drama as in other mass media. Indeed, in the early 1980s the previous invisibility of the gay man on mainstream American television had been overcome, but usually only in the context of AIDS-related stories and only in representing the gay man as either 'victim' or 'villain'. As a result, 'the public image of gay men has been inescapably linked with the spectre of plague' (Gross 1989, p. 138). The common representation of the gay 'AIDS body' in the mass media is either that of the 'AIDS carrier' posing a threat to others or the 'AIDS victim' whose ravaged body demonstrates the wages of sin. This narrative is drawn from a pre-established stock of discourses in the popular media about mysterious killer-diseases, deviant sexuality and dangerous strangers (Watney 1992, p. 153).

In a culture in which death, at least for the young, has become almost unimaginable, there is somewhat of a taboo on directly representing death and dying in media representations of HIV/AIDS; 'The dynamic reality of dying as part of the life-cycle and its real, concrete, frightening presence for those stricken with AIDS is denied and repressed' (Gilman 1995, pp. 162–3). One exception is the archetypal 'AIDS body' in television news and documentaries, which, in the tradition of the quest for verisimilitude and visuality in news, is frequently represented as horrific: decaying from within, gaunt and covered with the disfiguring lesions of Kaposi's sarcoma. 'Much television coverage of AIDS has been preoccupied with morbidity and with transforming the complex symptoms of AIDS into a recognisable image' (Alcorn 1989, p. 207). A *cinéma-vérité* approach has often been adopted in television documentaries on people living with HIV/AIDS, detailing the encroaching illness and death of a 'real person'. This approach to the portrayal of people living with HIV/AIDS is emotionally absorbing, allowing viewers to participate vicariously in the travails of the HIV/AIDS experience. There is the potential for such programs to 'humanise' the person living with HIV/AIDS. However, such programs often also work to further entrench stereotypes about such individuals, constructing 'heavily moralised *tableaux* that tell us much about the complex moral management of modern sexuality but little or nothing about the complex, shifting realities of the epidemic as it is lived all around the world' (Watney 1992, p. 154).

While fictionalised representations of the 'AIDS body' in popular television drama have also employed these stock narratives, the visual representation of people living with HIV/AIDS has differed somewhat from television news and documentaries. The emphasis has been not so much on the decaying or diseased AIDS body, but on the 'normal' or 'healthy'-appearing body that harbours the infection silently within. One obvious reason for this is that most of the actors who have played the part of people living with HIV/AIDS do not themselves have the syndrome, and cannot, therefore, realistically depict the end stages of AIDS, particularly the extreme thinness associated with the syndrome. Another reason is the influence of AIDS activists and experts on the construction of AIDS in television drama. A dominant concern has been to 'destigmatise' people living with HIV/AIDS; in effect, to show that they are 'just like you and me' and are not necessarily living within bodies that are overtly ill or wasting away (as in the Australian anti-discrimination advertisements described in chapter 3). As Patton (1990, pp. 117–18) notes, from the mid 1980s on 'there was a concerted effort to "degay" AIDS' in the popular media in the attempt to stem anti-gay discrimination.

The first feature-length drama about AIDS on American network television, *An Early Frost*, was screened in the United States in late 1985, achieving high ratings. The drama, shown on the NBC network, had a deliberate pedagogic function: it was promoted by the network as featuring a vital public health issue and a special AIDS information program was aired afterwards (Treichler 1993, p. 163). *An Early Frost* featured a young, white gay male lawyer who discovers he has HIV/AIDS and leaves his lover to return to his family to die. Much of the narrative centres around the conflict between the man's father, who is vehemently opposed to homosexuality, and the protagonist. This portrayal of the 'AIDS body' was overtly largely sympathetic, seeking to 'personalise' the experience of having and dying of the syndrome. *An Early Frost* was criticised, however, by some for spending more time focusing on the effects of the man's illness on his family than on his own dilemma in having HIV/AIDS. Watney, for example, argues that the extreme negativity displayed by the man's family to news of his homosexuality is portrayed by the film as 'quite natural and inevitable, if ultimately susceptible to reason and "love"' (1992, p. 156; see also Goldstein 1990, p. 307). Other American television drama portrayals of the gay 'AIDS body' have been overtly negative towards gay men. For example, a 1988 episode of the prime-time series *Midnight Caller* featured a gay male character with HIV/AIDS who was deliberately spreading the virus, thus presenting him as a dangerous and sadistic 'AIDS carrier' (Treichler 1992, p. 144).

For some years in mass media coverage of AIDS in countries such as Britain, the United States and Australia, images of women were absent from the archetypal representation of people with HIV/AIDS. This slowly changed in the mid to late 1980s as a growing fear about the potential 'heterosexual epidemic' of HIV/AIDS began to emerge in these countries. From 1986, the 'gay plague' representation of AIDS changed in Anglophone media, incorporating the apocalyptic visions of AIDS as a threat to everyone. When the circle of infection was widened, however, discrimination was evident against minority groups other than gay men. Juhasz (1990), for example, describes a series of four television documentaries on the risk of HIV/AIDS to heterosexuals that was broadcast in the United States in 1986 and 1987, including a special news report produced by NBC, a CBS special, a special program of the talk-show *Donahue* shown on NBC and an independently produced documentary aired on PBS. Each had a focus on the role played by women in the epidemic. Juhasz observes that in these documentaries women were depicted as 'contained threats'; that is, as both a source of danger/infection and as easily controlled subjects. Certain categories of women—black or hispanic, working class, prostitutes—were portrayed far more negatively as objects of contagion in the documentaries than were 'respectable', white and especially married women.

At the same time as the news media were beginning to focus on the threat posed by HIV/AIDS to heterosexuals, North American television drama began to incorporate images of women infected with HIV/AIDS who had contracted the virus via sexual intercourse. By mid 1988, three major American soap operas—*The Young and the Restless*, *All My Children* and *Another World*—had featured storylines about women with HIV/AIDS who had contracted the illness heterosexually (Watney 1992, p. 156). Like the documentaries described above, television drama has tended to represent the sympathetic female 'AIDS body' as white and 'respectable', 'a young, virtuous, and vulnerable woman: the traditional emblem of innocence' (Goldstein 1990, p. 305). This has been the case in American daytime soap opera, a genre that even by the mid 1990s had failed to address AIDS in the context of homosexuality (Fuqua 1995, p. 202). The soap opera *As the World Turns*, for example, featured in 1992 the story of Margo, a white, heterosexual police detective who is raped by a man with HIV/AIDS (Fuqua 1995, p. 203). Fuqua (1995: 202) argues that this pattern of representation in American daytime soap opera reflects a general avoidance of homosexuality by the programs' producers and an attempt to portray the 'innocent' and passive 'victim' of HIV/AIDS in a somewhat 'sanitised' fashion.

In the late 1980s there were reports in the news media that AIDS was producing a 'new moral climate', in which it was no longer acceptable for characters in television or film drama to engage in casual sex without fear of the consequences. The producer of the American television series focusing on female police officers in New York, *Cagney and Lacey*, was quoted in one newspaper report as asserting, 'it is starting to seem a little distasteful and irresponsible for Cagney to hop in and out of bed with different men all the time. She's a New York cop, and in 1987 she should be seen to be showing concern about AIDS' (*Weekend Australian*, 28–29 March 1987). Television dramas directed at young people made particular attempts to convey a 'safer sex' message to their audiences. The Canadian youth drama *21 Jump St* featured characters with HIV in both 1988 and 1990, the first a gay male adolescent, the second a young woman who had contracted HIV from her boyfriend. This latter episode was followed by a speech to camera by one of the program's regular actors, Michael Bendetti, warning his audience to 'please, practise safe sex'. The popular American series *Beverly Hills 90210* devoted at least two episodes to AIDS issues in 1990 and 1992. The first featured a young woman who visits Beverly Hills High as a peer-educator to tell students about how she had contracted HIV after her first sexual encounter, and the second concerned the students' attempts to introduce AIDS education programs and promote condom availability in their school.

The producers of the British soap operas *EastEnders* and *Brookside* made a deliberate attempt to cover HIV/AIDS issues in the 1980s by avoiding the 'gay plague' association. *Brookside* included a self-contained storyline about a heterosexual man with HIV who was ostracised by his workmates, while *EastEnders* included for a short time a peripheral character who was a male prisoner with HIV and had to cope both with his own fears about AIDS and those of his wife (Geraghty 1995, pp. 74–5). These serials also included regular gay male characters who had occasional fears about having HIV when suffering from an illness, but who always tested negative (1995, p. 74). It was not until the 1990s that *EastEnders* included a regular character with HIV/AIDS (Mark Fowler, a heterosexual man who discovered he was HIV positive and whose wife dies of AIDS), thus dealing with the issue on a long-term basis (1995, p. 77). This character is one of the few heterosexual men living with HIV/AIDS to have appeared in television drama. One notable exception is *Intimate Contact*, a four-part mini-series that was screened on British television in 1987. The series told the story of a middle-class British man who contracts HIV from a prostitute while on a business trip to New York and must deal with the reactions of his wife and family when he discovers his seropositivity. While this character was also a heterosexual man, he died early in the series, and the main focus of the drama was on his wife's experiences of coping with the cause of his death (Watney 1992, p. 156). While there may have been some portrayals of heterosexual men with HIV/AIDS in television drama, we rarely view images of such men becoming ill. The standard documentary representation of the wasted, ravaged body rarely uses a heterosexual male body. Even when a well-known heterosexual man such as the American basketball player 'Magic' Johnson reveals that he is HIV positive, the emphasis is on his will to conquer the syndrome, to continue engaging in physical activities and defeat death (King 1993).

The gay male with HIV/AIDS is still a feature of television representations in the mid 1990s. The emphasis in soap opera, however, has turned to the long-term implications of having HIV, in concert with medical awareness that people living with HIV/AIDS may live for decades without exhibiting the symptoms of AIDS. For example, in the 1994 season of the American soap opera *Melrose Place*, Jeffrey, an ex-partner of the regular gay character, Matt, revealed that he was HIV positive. Subsequent scenes between Matt and Jeffrey centred around Matt's uncertainty about making an emotional commitment to a person diagnosed with HIV. Rather than set speeches being made about the impossibility of contracting HIV via such contact as hugging or touching an infected person, or emphasising the importance of safer sex, as were common in the mid to late 1980s, the dialogue focused on the emotional relationship between the two and the possibility of 'heartbreak' should Matt decide to commit himself. In response to Matt's fears, Jeffrey countered that he felt perfectly healthy and could have the virus for twenty years without being ill, by which time effective treatments could well be available. As this suggests, HIV/AIDS as a chronic condition rather than an inevitable death sentence is beginning to receive acknowledgment in television drama.

AIDS IN AUSTRALIAN TELEVISION DRAMA

As in other countries, the Australian media tended to portray the archetypal 'AIDS body' as a gay male until well into the late 1980s. The first Australian television drama to feature a person living with HIV/AIDS was *The Flying Doctors*, a series about doctors working in an outback Australian town, Cooper's Crossing. In 1986, one episode, 'Return of the Hero', portrayed the story of Les Foster, a middle-aged Vietnam war veteran who finds that he has HIV/AIDS. Les decides to move back to Cooper's Crossing, where he grew up, to die, bringing with him his lover, Johnny. Once the closely guarded secret of his homosexuality and illness is out, Les is subject to the hostility and shock of his brother and rejection and suspicion on the part of his male friends. Johnny is threatened with violence by local men while walking in the street. Even a nurse at the local hospital demonstrates fear of contagion when Les is brought in after collapsing, refusing to admit him. The episode ends with Les' death and funeral, the townsfolk shamed by their prejudice.

It was not until the 1987 'Grim Reaper' campaign, with its emphasis on heterosexual sexual activity as a risk behaviour for HIV infection (described in chapter 3), that the figure of the woman with HIV/AIDS became overt in Australian televisual portrayals of AIDS. Around this time, news media reporting of AIDS began to feature images of women. The personalised account of the young woman with HIV/AIDS was a frequent strategy used in press reports to convey the anxieties around the heterosexual transmission of HIV (Lupton 1994a, pp. 78–80). Australian television portrayals of women with HIV/AIDS have been relatively few. One major television documentary, however, entitled *Suzi's Story*, received much attention in the news media upon release. This documentary, first shown in 1987, told the story of a young heterosexual woman, the eponymous Suzi Lovegrove, who had contracted HIV from a man with whom she had had a casual affair while living in New York before her marriage. Suzi later discovered that this man was bisexual and HIV positive, but not until she herself had found that she had contracted the virus. By this time, Suzi had married an Australian, moved to Sydney, and had given birth to a son who was also found to be infected with HIV. Suzi Lovegrove represented the archetype of the feminine, passive victim of casual sex. The documentary movingly showed the last days of Suzi's life, surrounded by her family—her loving husband, her toddler son and young step-daughter. It graphically revealed the stages by which a once vital and attractive young woman, a professional dancer, had succumbed to AIDS; her body at the end debilitated and uncoordinated, her speech slurred. The moral of her story was clear: heterosexual women should be wary of the risk of contracting HIV from a bisexual male partner.

Unlike many American television dramas, Australian dramas have been willing to examine the political implications of the HIV/AIDS epidemic. In its 1994 season, for example, the long-running medical drama *GP* devoted an episode to the story of a young woman teacher who is HIV positive. The usual issues of discrimination, vilification and loneliness faced by people living with HIV/AIDS were canvassed in this episode (see Lupton 1996). A more innovative major theme was a focus on the lack of research given to the topic of women with HIV/AIDS, including the effects of drugs such as AZT on women. A further interesting feature of the *GP* episode was that no mention was made of *how* the young woman had contracted HIV. A further two episodes in the 1995 season of *GP* went on to explore the controversial issues around euthanasia for people living with HIV/AIDS. They featured the story of a young gay man who has experienced a number of AIDS-related illnesses and is eventually diagnosed with a cerebral lymphoma. He decides that he would rather die than go through the drawn-out suffering he has seen in his fellow AIDS patients. One of the doctors, Martin Dempsey, who is himself gay, agrees to help the man to die and ends up facing criminal charges.

Despite the high-risk nature of sharing needles to inject recreational drugs, very few television dramas in Australia, the United States or Britain have explored issues relating to injecting drug use and HIV/AIDS risk. A suggested reason for this neglect is the difficulty of rendering such individuals 'sympathetic' to a mass audience, given the 'deviance' of such behaviour (Goldstein 1990, p. 305). One exception is the Australian medical drama *A Country Practice*, which included a set of four episodes about a young woman with HIV/AIDS in its 1988 season. One of us conducted an ethnographic study of the production of these episodes (details of which are included in chapters 6 and 7), and also conducted research into audience responses to the episodes (chapter 10). We will therefore conclude our analysis of the representation of the 'AIDS body' in television drama by providing a detailed discussion of these episodes, to provide a context for the ensuing production and audience response chapters.

THE 'SOPHIE' EPISODES

A Country Practice (*ACP*) is an Australian rural medical soap opera which ran for twelve years from 1981 to 1993 on the commercial station Channel 7. Two one-hour episodes screened each week in prime time. For much of this time *ACP* rated very highly as the most popular drama serial on Australian television, and its production house JNP received over a thousand fan letters a week. *ACP* succeeded in 1989 in becoming Australia's longest-running television serial, due to its successful audience aggregation, picking up a strong audience following in most age groups from adolescents to over 65-year-olds. Like other Australian soap operas, *ACP* was shown on European television for some years (Britain is a particularly strong market for Australian soap operas) and was also screened in the United States, India, Zimbabwe, Zambia and Hong Kong. After being cancelled by Channel 7 in 1993, the series was briefly revived by the rival Channel 10, retaining some of the original characters and the actors who played them. *ACP* failed to succeed in this incarnation, however, and finally ceased production in 1994.

Like the British television serials *Brookside* and *EastEnders*, and its fellow Australian medical drama *GP*, *ACP* was devised as a 'realist' soap opera, attempting to canvass a wide range of contemporary medical and social issues from a 'responsible' and 'realistic' position (as compared with 'fantasy' soap operas such as *Dallas* and *Melrose Place*). The producers and writers of *ACP* saw the program as having a strong pedagogic function. As one writer for the series commented, 'The show goes as far as it can as a popular piece of commercial dramatic fiction—much further than a lot of others in at least acknowledging that social problems exist' (David Allen, quoted in Tulloch & Moran 1986, p. 38). They therefore attempted to achieve topicality and accuracy, but at the same time to appeal to a broad audience, striking the right balance between entertainment and social relevance, between melodrama and naturalism, between 'up' and 'down' moments. An emphasis was placed on developing attractive characters who were endearing to viewers so as to maximise ratings and viewer loyalty (Tulloch & Moran 1986).

When *ACP* was first devised, the decision was made to set it in the country because of a belief on the part of the executive producer, James Davern, that 'in the subconscious of every Australian there's a yearning for the country'. The emphasis in the series was upon the close-knit nature of country life and the central role played by the local doctors and vets in the lives of the residents of Wandin Valley, a mythical area set in New South Wales some distance from Sydney. Unlike some soap operas, which are largely open-ended, the narrative format of *ACP* usually had a self-contained beginning, middle and an end to its main stories inside the weekly block of two episodes. The dramatic events of the series tended to revolve around characters from the 'outside' world (often 'the city') entering the community's 'inside' and causing conflict. The 'inside' of the Wandin Valley community consisted of the professionals (doctors, nurses, vets, police officers) and the comic characters (the cook at the local club, the plumber, the town gossip). The formula for *ACP* in attempting to reach a broad audience was that of a combination of 'heavy and light' and 'laughter and tears'. The characters in the town of Wandin Valley acted together as a team when there was a crisis. This rural sense of community and 'togetherness' provided a place of relief for the audience, since the 'heavy story' narrative of each episode, often revolving around 'guest' characters (embodying the illness or social problem featured that week) constantly alternated with a lighter-hearted narrative, usually featuring the regular characters finding themselves in scrapes or developing romantic entanglements with each other.

The style of *ACP* relied heavily upon the pastoral 'dream of nature': the simplicity and safety of the country with its open spaces, fresh air and sunshine. The episodes began with opening credits showing bucolic *mises en scènes* of rural Australia: green hills, sun-drenched bushland, flowery gardens, quaint old cottages and the large old homestead in which the medical practice itself was sited. The scenes in each episode combined such outdoor shots with indoor locations, including the doctor's surgery, the local club, characters' homes and the local police station. Dr Terence Elliot, the local GP, was the major character in the series from its inception to its final episode screened on Channel 10. He had arrived in the community after having 'escaped' the city (Sydney) following a series of personal crises including the death of his eight-year-old son David from appendicitis after Terence had misdiagnosed his illness, Terence's guilt and subsequent slide into alcoholism and the eventual breakdown of his marriage. After a series of romantic relationships, Terence eventually married for a second time in the 1988 season to another doctor, Alex Fraser, but this relationship also eventually failed.

Plot synopsis

The four episodes constituting 'Sophie', screened in 1988, were written around the character of Sophie, the 23-year-old daughter of Terence Elliot, who becomes ill with HIV/AIDS. A convention of the soap opera genre is that characters come together and leave (both each other and the world of the serial). The symbolically most powerful comings together (marriage) and partings (death) are reserved for the 'highlights' or climactic moments of the year and usually attract the highest ratings. Given that the 'world' of the regular characters in soap opera is typically conventional, with conservative moral values usually espoused, one dramatic strategy in soap opera is to introduce particularly controversial issues (such as homosexuality, incest or child abuse) via a new and often marginal or peripheral character, allowing the character to be either tested until proved popular at the margins of the text or to be 'written out' to achieve resolution of the issue (Fuqua 1995, p. 200). For these purposes, Sophie Elliot had been introduced into the series some months earlier as a journalist addicted to heroin, previously estranged from her father. In those earlier episodes Sophie was shown attempting to wean herself off heroin and had returned to the city, only to use the drug again and overdose. The 'Sophie' episodes reintroduced her character into the *ACP* narrative, this time centring around the revelation that she had HIV, and ending with her death from another heroin overdose.

Much of the action of the first two episodes of 'Sophie' occurs in Kings Cross, the real-life 'red-light' district in Sydney which is well known nationwide for its population of male and female sex workers and their clients, 'street kids' and drug users and dealers. In the first episode, a worried Terence travels to Sydney after being informed that Sophie has overdosed on heroin and has been admitted to hospital. He arrives to find that she has checked herself out and, not knowing her address, seeks help in finding her from youth workers at the Wayside Chapel (an actual youth refuge in Kings Cross). Meanwhile, his new wife Alex is tearfully complaining to her colleague, the matron of the hospital, Maggie Sloan, about the effect Sophie's heroin addiction is having on Terence's state of mind and their relationship. Back in Sydney, Terence is taken around the streets of Kings Cross by one of the youth workers from the Wayside Chapel, looking for Sophie. They come across Paul, a heroin addict and male sex worker in his late adolescence. Paul is in a sexual relationship with Sophie and shares a flat with her, but he refuses to tell Terence where she is. Later scenes show Paul and Sophie in their sordid, tiny flat, strewn with clothes and empty bottles, with little furniture, a mattress on the floor instead of a bed, graffiti on the walls. Both are desperate for a 'hit' of heroin but lack the money to pay for it. Paul tells Sophie that her father is looking for her. She panics at the news, saying, 'I don't want him to see me like this—never!' However, after much dogged searching, Terence eventually finds Sophie in the flat. She refuses to talk to him and runs away. Continuing to wander the streets of Kings Cross, Terence sees Sophie again, attempting to prostitute herself in the attempt to earn money to buy drugs. She runs away from Terence again, into the night.

In the second episode of the 'Sophie' quartet, Terence is still in Sydney and still trying to talk to Sophie. He visits the flat again and is able to persuade Sophie to discuss her heroin use with him. They talk about their family life when Sophie was a child and the happy times that ended after the death of David, Sophie's younger brother. Terence can't understand why Sophie, a young woman from a privileged background, has allowed herself to fall prey to heroin addiction:

Terence: I can't begin to understand how a girl like you—
Sophie: A *woman*!
Terence: —a woman, a *young* woman like you, could do this to yourself!
It's not pretty, is it Sophie? You've got to admit, it's not pretty. You had
a career, you had prospects.
Sophie: And I grew up, and I had a choice. And I chose to be a junkie.

They leave the flat and start walking in a nearby park, where Sophie
explains why she left her profession as a journalist and turned to
using heroin as the major force in her life:

I saw this kid, over there, a kid sitting on a bench and shooting up.
And I realised that he'd come to terms with it—he'd got his priorities
right—first things first. I just stood there watching him. It was like
some sort of a revelation—a life-changing experience. I mean, here's some
boy who knows what's important, and goes for it . . . He wasn't fooling
himself—the honesty was breathtaking, Dad. After all this hypocrisy,
this kid's honesty just blew me away!

It turns out that this boy was Paul who had been living on the streets
since his early adolescence. Terence and Sophie return to her flat and
talk again about how it all went wrong. Sophie describes how close
she was to her younger brother David, and how devastated she was
when he died. David's death was followed by Terence leaving the
family: first by withdrawing into himself by drinking too much, and
then, after a year, by physically leaving. Sophie recounts to Terence
a memory of seeing him drunk when she was eleven years old, soon
after the death of David and just before Terence left:

I woke up in the night . . . I came down and there was a light on in
your study and I went in to talk to you. You'd gone to sleep in your
chair . . . The bottle on the table was empty, but there was still some
in the glass and I could smell it. You were asleep and your face was—sort
of collapsed. And I knew you'd gone away. And later, the rest of you
left.

Sophie explains that her brother's death and her father's desertion
made her feel as if the happy child that she once was had also 'left'.
Terence eventually persuades Sophie to return to Wandin Valley
to try to overcome her addiction. As soon as Sophie is safely back at
'Camelot', Terence and Alex's house in Wandin Valley, there is some
friction between herself and Alex, her new stepmother. Alex resents

the way that Sophie is demanding Terence's attention and behaving rudely to her in her own house. She and Terence argue about Sophie's behaviour and presence. The next morning, Sophie receives a phone call from the doctor who treated her in Sydney, informing her that she is HIV positive, a fact that she already knew after a test a year before, but had chosen to conceal. Sophie recounts the news to Terence, who is devastated.

Episode three deals with the response of Terence and Alex to Sophie's revelation. Terence is having difficulty coping with the news and wants to know how Sophie contracted HIV. Sophie tells him that she is not sure, but thinks it may have been from sharing needles in her days of recreational use with Brian, her photojournalist lover, with whom she travelled overseas to work. Sophie explains that she and Brian started to use heroin when working in 'trouble-spots' as a means of dealing with fears and uncertainties: 'We were living on the edge, we hit up a lot, that's how we got by'. She does not know whether Brian ever tested positive for HIV; he is now dead, killed in South America during a dangerous assignment. Sophie tells Terence that she had known about her seropositivity for a year, and has gone through all the anguish and has now come to terms with it: 'I've done all that anger thing, all the fear, but I had to handle it, I had to cope'. She tries to console Terence with the hope that she will be one of the people with HIV who never progresses to 'full-blown' AIDS. Alex is less sympathetic, still regarding Sophie as a divisive force. She confesses to her confidante Maggie Sloan: 'Sophie doesn't like me— she's trying to drive a wedge between me and Terence. It's the ultimate emotional blackmail: she's got AIDS'. Sophie, however, soon begins to feel ill, with swollen lymph glands, night sweats and fatigue, and Alex takes on her doctor persona, admitting Sophie to hospital for tests. This angers Terence who thinks that Alex is just trying to get Sophie out of their house by hospitalising her. He warns Alex that she should not force him to choose between herself and his daughter.

At first Alex is not sure if Sophie's symptoms might be due to her withdrawal from heroin, but takes some blood for tests and discovers that Sophie's immune system is failing. It is clear that Sophie is no longer just HIV positive: she has the symptoms of AIDS-related complex. Sophie is extremely upset at this news. She tells Alex that she wants to fight the illness. Alex warns her that to do so she will have to 'clean up' her life: 'Where you go from here depends very much on how you live. No drink, no cigarettes, no drugs. For once in your life you have to live a healthy lifestyle if you want to fight this'. She tells Sophie that it would appear that she is well on the way to developing AIDS. The episode ends with Sophie in tears in her hospital bed at this news, comforted by Alex.

In episode four, the final part of the 'Sophie' episodes, Sophie undergoes something of a transformation. She decides to reform her life, to stay off heroin and to take up writing again. She begins work on a journalistic piece about heroin use and relations between Sophie and Alex appear to improve. However, without warning, Paul arrives at the house from Sydney, looking for Sophie. He and Sophie drive to an abandoned house, used as a squat by unemployed young people. Once there, Paul tells Sophie that he is HIV positive, having used one of Sophie's needles without her knowledge to inject heroin, despite knowing that she had HIV. He offers Sophie some heroin and she succumbs to temptation. It is here that Sophie dies, not from AIDS but from a drug overdose. Terence, alerted by Alex that Sophie has left with Paul, arrives at the scene too late, finding his daughter dead. The closing scenes feature Terence standing alone at Sophie's graveside in a scenic country graveyard, reading Sophie's last piece of writing—a description of her own descent into drug addiction (read in his voice-over):

> I am a junkie. I, Sophie Elliott, 23 years old, brought up with most of the conventional blessings. A not-so-bad journalist, a traveller about the world. I have known men die for many gods and kill for many causes, I have wept for starving children, and mourned for the innocent men mown down in the street. And I have seen, now and then, amidst the pain, acts of great courage and moments of surpassing joy. But in myself, I found neither courage nor joy. I chose instead to increase the sum of suffering, to add my own parents to the list of the bereaved. I am dying now, like all the others, but I cannot blame a god or a cause or a famine. I cannot rail at corrupt politicians or sadists in colonels' uniform, or fanatics who claim to have a hotline to heaven. I can only blame myself.

The subtexts of 'Sophie'

As noted above, *ACP* deliberately drew heavily on the 'pastoral myth', the nostalgic longing for the simplicity and 'cleanliness' of the countryside. The pastoral myth has traditionally been marked by withdrawal from an urban world of strife to a purer, more natural world, where the imperfections of the city can be pondered upon and cured. The 'Sophie' episodes conformed to the classic pastoral mythology; the country as source of strength, life, purity, renewal and enlightenment; the city as the source of contagion and death. More so than most other episodes of *ACP*, which rarely featured city locations, a major theme of the 'Sophie' episodes was the visual opposition between the country, as site of nature, health, hygiene and normality, and the city, as a space of deviance, crime, noise and dirt. 'Sophie' marked a return of the series to the city, as if to remind viewers what the significant absence of all *ACP* narratives—the city—is really like. The city scenes featured many shots of dark alleyways covered with graffiti and littered with rubbish and used syringes. The disorder and danger of Kings Cross, its garish neon signs, its police sirens and car noises, its range of human life, prostitutes in sleazy outfits and junkies desperate for a 'hit', were juxtaposed with the clean and safe environs of the Wandin Valley Hospital and the interior of comfortable, well-appointed family homes in the town and surrounding countryside.

The character of Terence himself stood out as 'different' in the Kings Cross environment, with his neat suit and tie, his air of disorientation, his obvious lack of ease. It is the city that he originally 'escaped from' to find peace from his personal problems. In the city, both Sophie and her partner Paul were portrayed as irrational, lacking self-control. There were scenes in which they quarrelled and screamed at each other, or huddled together in their desperation for a 'hit' of heroin. They were dishevelled, obviously unwell, their faces pale and spotted with sores. In this harsh environment, even Terence, uncharacteristically, began to lose his self-control. He was frustrated and enraged both by Paul's unwillingness to tell him where Sophie is and later by Sophie's insistence that she wanted to stay in the city with Paul, rejecting Terence's appeals that she come home with him. At one stage, in his frustration, Terence was moved to physically threaten Paul, shoving him against the wall of the flat, an action which was very out of character.

Once she returned to Wandin Valley, however, Sophie began to change into the 'respectable', well-dressed, middle-class journalist she once was. It was in that world apart, in the bright, clear light and tranquillity of the country, that Sophie began to take stock and to reform herself to fulfil her lost potential. She rejected the 'irrationality' of heroin dependence for a responsible image as journalist and well-behaved daughter. That is, until Paul arrived, bringing with him the imported vices and corruption of the city. Sophie and Paul left the safety and security of 'Camelot', driving to the abandoned, vandalised house nearby, itself a metonym of the squalor of their city flat with its dark interiors, dirt, graffiti and junk furniture. This house was the squalid site of Sophie's overdose and death.

As we noted earlier in this chapter, the theme of the ordeal faced by families in dealing with a member with HIV/AIDS has been central to dramatic presentations of AIDS in television. Indeed, fluxes in family relationships, with conflicts between strengthening and undermining forces, is a central feature of the genre of soap opera as a whole, propelling the narrative forward (Ang 1985, p. 70). This source of narrative was integral to the 'Sophie' episodes, particularly as it affected the major character in the series, Terence Elliot, and his new wife, Alex. Alex was concerned that she would have to deal with a 'junkie' stepdaughter for the rest of her life, and resented Terence's devotion to Sophie. Terence, for his part, was angered that Alex seemed so unsympathetic to Sophie's plight and did not want her around. Their heightened feelings about Sophie threatened to destroy their new marriage. Sophie also threatened to disrupt the equilibrium of Terence and Alex's relationships with other people in the small town. For example, she was overtly hostile to the town's 'gossip', Esmé Watson, by blatantly flaunting her seropositivity, in one scene asking her, 'How's your friendly little town going to cope with having an AIDS victim running around?'

Sophie was a highly ambiguous and contradictory character, moving from 'junkie' to middle-class journalist and back again. The character of Sophie was portrayed as headstrong and rebellious, refusing at first to reconcile with her concerned and loving father. Alex described her as 'selfish, self-indulgent and self-destructive—she has screwed up her life and now she is going to ruin mine'. Indeed Sophie constructed herself as a disruptive, contagious presence: as she says to Terence, 'I'm a carrier, Typhoid Mary, a public menace . . . I've got it, AIDS, A–I–D–S!' She shocked Terence and Alex by describing how she stole and prostituted herself to obtain the money for heroin. Alex, who was only a few years older than Sophie, stood as an exemplar of a young woman with the hard-working, serious approach to life that Sophie had rejected by choosing her life of heroin use. Yet Sophie had also been a top-ranking and ambitious journalist, travelling the world. By the final part of the 'Sophie' series of episodes, Sophie displayed strength of character, bravery and determination in dealing with her illness, deciding to live a new, 'clean' life and take up journalism again and to 'cope'. As she remarked to Matron Maggie Sloan, 'I may have AIDS, Matron, but I ain't dead yet'. Despite this resolution she easily fell victim to Paul's persuasion to shoot up some heroin one more time.

The multiple subjectivities of Sophie were partly due to her role both as 'outside' disruptive influence and also as the beloved daughter of the series' main character, Dr Terence Elliot. The problems faced by naturalistic soap operas in dealing with potentially disruptive phenomena such as AIDS and illicit drug use are in maintaining a normative moral order while conforming to the demands of 'realism'. The 'issues-based' formula of *ACP*, in which specific problems were raised and then dealt with by the community, moving on to another set of issues the next week, usually served to contain such moral problems. As noted above, these problems usually come from 'outside' the community and do not pose a fundamental threat to its stability. The characters associated with the problems are 'guest' characters who move on or die rather than becoming regular members of the community, thus resolving the issue by their absence. However, the introduction of a person with HIV/AIDS who used injecting drugs, and who was, moreover, a member of the family of a major character, constituted a potential threat to the integrity of the Wandin Valley community and particularly that major character. How could such a character as Dr Terence Elliot, as the senior doctor the most respected and trusted member of the Wandin Valley community, have a daughter who injects drugs, has a 'junkie' boyfriend, prostitutes herself at Kings Cross and lives in conditions of squalor? While this disruption had enormous dramatic potential, the dilemma was to provide a narrative that retained the integrity of Terence Elliot and dealt with the character of Sophie as an 'outside' disruption.

One explanation for Sophie's turn to drugs to 'cope' with her life was provided in episode two of the Sophie series, when Sophie and Terence talked about their family breakdown, the death of David and Terence's departure from the family. The narrative emphasised that Sophie was *not* the 'innocent victim type', since she 'chose' her fate. On the other hand there was the 'alcoholic–deserting father' subtheme to provide an explanation for her actions. Soap opera conventionally circulates its narratives around guilty secrets: incest, forbidden sex, alcoholism and other secret and 'deviant' human practices. One of Terence Elliot's major secrets from his past was his drinking problem which had led to his eventual move to Wandin Valley to 'hide' and recover. Another was his misdiagnosis of his son David's illness, which led to the boy's death. These already established problems provided a context in which to site the 'Sophie' episodes.

In the scene with Terence in her city flat, Sophie recounted how she felt abandoned by her father and how, at a young age she was aware of her father's use of drugs (in his case, alcohol) as a crutch. These scenes took on the 'confessional' format that is familiar in television genres such as talk shows and soap opera. Terence, for his part, confessed his failure as a father, his withdrawal from his family in his grief over the death of his son, and his strong feelings of love and concern for Sophie. Such confessions in television texts (and other sites, such as the counselling encounter) are routinely constructed as therapeutic through the power of 'communication' (Lupton 1994b). Each character reveals to the other their innermost emotions and hurts in order to become closer. Indeed, in 'Sophie' this strategy was shown to work: Sophie and Terence are reconciled following these confessions, and Sophie is persuaded to return to Terence's home to overcome her problem, safe in the bosom of her family. The confessional scenes between Terence and Sophie continued in part three, following her disclosure of HIV positivity: he revealed his desperation and fear at the news, she her initial reactions and eventual stoicism. This time the confessions served to give 'depth' and complexity to the characterisation, uncovering the dependable and authoritative Terence's capacity for emotional vulnerability in his love for his daughter and his desire to protect her, and Sophie's core of courage underneath her wilful and irresponsible exterior.

The final confession, of course, was Sophie's parting piece of writing, in which she melodramatically positioned herself as a 'junkie' despite her privileged upbringing, and went on to expound upon the meaninglessness of her heroin addiction, HIV positivity and inevitable death in the context of world events. Sophie insisted throughout the episodes that her addiction to heroin was a matter of 'choice', the actions of a fully-aware adult. She constructed her heroin use as a means of dealing with the 'hypocrisy', uncertainties and stresses of the world. In her closing statement, 'I can only blame myself', the moral of 'Sophie' was overt. This statement repositioned Sophie ultimately as responsible for her addiction and death, deflecting Terence's role in her addiction (as absent and alcoholic father in her youth), and therefore re-establishing his integrity as the respected character Dr Terence Elliot, mourning for his beloved daughter.

At a deeper level of meaning, the emotions and meanings invested in the 'Sophie' soap opera texts suggest the fantasies that inhere in the father–daughter relationship in the context of disease and death as well as the construction of the drug-using body (among many other things). As discussed above, a range of textual conventions established the country as 'us' and the city as Other, with the character of Paul, the young drug addict, coming to stand as the link between the two, bringing the evil of the city into the country. Terence, the father, saw himself as Sophie's protector, seeking continually to position her as a child, even though she repeatedly sought to evade him and insisted that she was now a woman, an adult, able to choose her own life. Terence's devotion to Sophie, his almost suffocating insistence on acting as her protector, was such that it threatened his marriage. For Terence, Paul embodied the sordidness of the city's red-light district, the evils of addiction. Paul was portrayed in the episodes as desperate, deadened and sluggish, his face pale and marked by sores, often curling into a foetal position on the mattress lying on the floor of his flat. Paul was also the figure who was attempting to replace Terence as his daughter Sophie's protector, inciting Terence's rage and frustration to the point of physically assaulting Paul when he refused to tell Terence where Sophie was. Paul was the source of Sophie's corruption and eventual death by continuing to tempt her with heroin, eventually luring her away from the security of her father's home to the place of her death, while Terence searched frantically for her.

The rivalry between Terence and Paul, as well as the *mise en scène* features of lighting and sound, established Paul as the villainous Other. As Edelman (1993, p. 36) argues, the 'addicted' drug-using body and gay male sexuality are united in popular discourses on AIDS, 'not only as practices through which the body suffers "improper" penetration, but also, and more significantly, as practices that signify the renunciation of active self-mastery and control'. Both Paul and Sophie, but Paul most of all, represented departures from the ideal of the 'civilised' body, the body that can contain 'irrational' urges and seeks to establish good health and longevity. Rather, they were representatives of the body that cannot control its boundaries, and which therefore poses a threat to others.

CONCLUDING COMMENTS

As we have demonstrated in this chapter, representations of people living with HIV/AIDS—or, as we have termed it, of the 'AIDS body'—in popular television drama have changed over time; from the 'guilty' gay male figure that predominated in the mid to late 1980s to the 'innocent' heterosexual woman which began to dominate television drama in the late 1980s and into the 1990s. We have observed that the heterosexual male figure as 'victim' of HIV/AIDS has been rare in television drama. These characterisations have echoed news media coverage of AIDS which has also tended to give most attention to gay men and heterosexual women as the archetypal 'AIDS bodies' (Lupton 1994a). In popular television drama and other media representations, men are generally portrayed as vulnerable to HIV risk only if they are gay or bisexual (and therefore, feminised), illicit drug users or under the dangerous sway of the siren/prostitute. The white, middle-class heterosexual man is positioned as the archetypal healthy, controlled body who is threatened by other, 'risky bodies' (Waldby 1993; Lupton 1996).

Dramatic representations have highlighted that HIV infection is largely an outcome of a lapse of judgement or self-control, whether it be indulging in 'deviant' sexual desire (gay men), investing misguided trust in one's sexual partner (heterosexual women) or giving into one's desire for drugs (injecting drug users). Central to the portrayal of people living with HIV/AIDS in television drama since the early 1980s has been their position as marginalised individuals, inevitably subject to discrimination and loneliness as well as illness and death, particularly if they are doubly stigmatised by also being gay or an injecting drug user. Such portrayals were particularly evident in the late 1980s when government advertising campaigns were also stressing the importance of personal responsibility and self-control. More recent television drama has moved onto issues around living with HIV/AIDS as a chronic condition and the failure of effective treatments for AIDS.

Thus, while these texts were not constructed expressly to convey public health messages, they serve a similar function to AIDS campaigns in reproducing key discourses and portraying 'lessons' or 'morals' about HIV/AIDS. In much television drama there has been an obvious intention to convey a series of messages about HIV/AIDS: that people living with HIV/AIDS should not be subject to discrimination; that HIV cannot be passed on by casual contact with people living with HIV/AIDS; and, from the late 1980s, that all sexually active people—gay, bisexual *and* heterosexual—should realise that they are at risk from HIV and be vigilant in protecting themselves from infection. Like government-sponsored AIDS education advertisements, the fictionalised portrayal of the 'AIDS body' has emphasised that 'you can't tell by looking' if someone has HIV/AIDS. As such, many of these AIDS television texts, particularly from the 'realist' soap opera genre, have a hybrid function as both pedagogical text and commercial commodity. Just as health education campaigns act as regulatory sites, suggesting how individuals should conduct themselves in order to live their lives well, so too do popular television drama texts warn individuals of the dangers of injudicious sexual activity or drug use, commonly employing melodrama to demonstrate the anguish felt by people living with HIV/AIDS and their friends and family.

PART III

MAKING AIDS TELEVISION: EXPERT CULTURES/PRODUCTION CULTURES

5

AIDS ADVERTISEMENTS: THE STATE/MARKETING INTERFACE

In chapter 1 we drew attention to the problem of constructing, translating and communicating notions of health risk in 'expert'/professional cultures. An important area where this occurs is in AIDS television advertisements which are the result of continuous interaction between professionals in different fields, including public health bureaucrats, medically-trained professionals, epidemiologists, advertising workers, market researchers and television production companies. In this chapter we will examine a case study of the state agency/commercial media interface in producing AIDS television advertising campaigns.

THE STATE/MARKETING INTERFACE

As we noted in chapter 3, the construction of public health advertisements involves the participation of a series of 'experts' in discourse technologies. The actual stages of production of such television education campaigns take place within a complex organisational framework which brings together government agencies like the Australian Department of Community Services and Health or the British Health Education Authority with commercial advertising and market research companies. General directives flowing from the government and its agencies are researched, tested and implemented by these companies in a process which has two distinct phases in the case of television texts: *transformation*, or the process of turning the discourses such as those emanating from medical and public health 'experts' into the dramatic 'pre-text' (that is, the plot, script and written plans for filming); and *transcodification*, the process of turning the written or spoken 'pre-text' into the multiple-coded audio-visual texts that appear on television.

This complex organisational relationship between state agencies and commercial companies is strongly influenced by international academic research in public health and related fields such as psychology and communication. Health promotion workers are often trained in programs such as Master of Public Health degrees in the currently accepted research paradigms of health education and health promotion, or employ academics in those fields as consultants. Not only academic research paradigms such as the Knowledge–Attitudes–Behaviour (KAB) model (which we critiqued in chapter 2), but also assumptions about content (oriented to this or that 'target' audience) and style (raising awareness by using fear tactics or humour) are dominant in health promotion in Australia, the United States, Britain and other western countries. These common theories and assumptions establish a climate of opinion and help determine the agenda evident in the policy and research and development documents that underpin television health education campaigns. They provide an important part of the 'culture of production' of such AIDS television texts.

Government-employed health promotion workers and the commercial media workers with whom they develop and construct media campaigns, as members of the wider society, also draw upon and reproduce dominant cultural assumptions and discourses around 'health' and human behaviour that are shared by many of their target audiences. These workers do so, of course, within a socio-political climate that is shaped by certain constraints including the need to not antagonise influential commercial interests (for example, tobacco companies), the electorate or the high-ranking bureaucrats for whom they work, budget limitations and the sheer complexity of most health problems. There are, therefore, also 'cultures' of health promotion work in which some strategies and approaches are deemed acceptable and others are rejected as too difficult, ineffective, costly or controversial.

It is clearly important in understanding the cultures of AIDS television to trace the processes by which these complex sets of relationships and epistemologies interact. Organisational processes of this kind, however, are always difficult to get access to from the 'outside'. Much greater field-work access to the cultures of production is needed to examine the way in which government messages concerning the 'intended' meaning of a health education campaign become production meanings as they are filtered through the daily routines of professional health promotion, advertising and television workers. Such access is very rare, both to health bureaucracies and to television, marketing and advertising companies. This is partly because in these professions the concept of 'research' is far more focused on measuring and evaluating *output* (for example, by audience ratings, or by other measures of consumer awareness of a text) rather than about *processes* (the process, for example, of how the Australian 'Grim Reaper' campaign came into being in the interaction between government, bureaucrats and advertising agencies).

Both state bureaucracies and commercial media companies are often very wary about giving the kind of open research access that ethnographic researchers need, especially given the fact that these researchers are notoriously vague as to what actually are their research intentions and hypotheses. There are also political sensitivities involved in that health bureaucracies are highly aware of the possibility of public critique of their activities, particularly in the news media. Academics who work as consultants for health bureaucracies in undertaking evaluations of their health promotion programs often find that there are indirect and sometimes more overt pressures to present their findings in the most favourable light in any report that will have public dissemination.

In 1990 one of us was a member of a research team which successfully tendered to the Australian Department of Community Services and Health (DCSH) to evaluate the government's AIDS media education campaigns produced between 1987 and 1990. As a review, this was necessarily post-hoc research which could only deal with the documentary traces of many meetings and negotiations which had taken place between the health department and commercial media professionals. The study did, however, give us access to a large body of confidential documentation outlining the aims, intentions and research evaluation of the various government education campaigns during this period. Our brief from the department was to 'examine and review the range of current literature and research material pertaining to the development, implementation and evaluation of AIDS-related public education campaigns in Australia'. As a result we had unusually complete access to the articulated intentions, goals and assumptions underlying these campaigns—to the extent at least that these were incorporated in written documents (we had no access to meetings or other word-of-mouth interaction). Our analysis of 'production intentions' in this chapter is based on these documents, including various reports written for the department by marketing and advertising companies and the department's own reports on the policy and strategies of the television campaigns. While direct involvement in the daily routines of the department and its marketing companies would certainly have given us access to nuances of negotiation that were invisible in the written texts, it is the case that these documents were the visible 'output' of significant government process and funding. As such, these texts are an important source of access to the discursive consciousness (Giddens 1986) of professionals in these institutions. In other words, they represent the articulated consciousness of the discourse technologies circulating among state and commercial agency experts underlying their 'official' policy decisions and their media practice.

It should also be noted that there is a high degree of intertextuality between the texts produced by marketing, advertising and evaluation 'experts' as consultants and those produced by the health bureaucracies for which they work. Each often draws on the other's texts when constructing a 'new' document: health bureaucrats, for example, will 'cut and paste' the words in reports produced by consultants when writing their own reports. Such documents, of course, often inevitably 'gloss over' cracks, disputes, contradictions and inadequacies, and tend not to reveal traces of 'behind closed doors' discussions. Like health campaign texts themselves, they function to some extent as promotional texts, designed to present a certain version of reality and events to represent the department as a rational, effective and efficient bureaucracy concerned for the wellbeing of the citizens for whose health it is responsible. This is particularly the case if the documents were written for public dissemination and consumption. Nonetheless, many of the documents to which we had access were for internal uses only, not written for the public, and thus are distinct from the promotional documents that are constructed for a wider audience.

In this chapter we summarise the final report of the research team (see Crawford et al. 1992 for the complete report). This summary has a specific focus on the documentation held by the department relating to the development, implementation and evaluation of two of its major AIDS public education campaigns: the 1987 'Grim Reaper' campaign and the 1990 campaign using the 'Needle Bed', 'Testimonials' and 'Vox Pop Condom' advertisements, all of which were described in detail in chapter 3. The original report was based on a reading of all the relevant research, development and evaluation documents and an analysis of the assumptions expressed within, overt and sub-textual, about both the process of health communication generally and the understanding of AIDS public education in particular (for reasons of confidentiality we will not give reference details for the documents). Our summary here examines what textual theorists call the 'problematic' of these television campaigns as expressed in the documentation; that is, the organisation of the campaigns in terms of a set of assumptions based on psychological theories of human behaviour and limited notions of 'culture'.

CONSTRUCTING THE MESSAGE AND AUDIENCE

> The media strategy adopted in Australia since 1986 has been to develop well-researched and imaginative campaigns that not only create awareness but deliver memorable messages that contribute to behavioural change. (from a pamphlet produced by the DCSH and distributed at the Fourth National AIDS Conference, 1990)

The Australian research and development documentation on AIDS education campaigns revealed an unresolved blend between American 'effects' (KAB) models of communication flow and 'cultural/ethnographic' models. Primarily, government documents between 1986 and 1990 were dominated by the health communication 'effects' notion of the need to avoid semantic 'noise'. This is not surprising since the major objectives of the campaigns were to find the most efficient way of creating very particular effects (increased knowledge about AIDS, attitude and behavioural change). Furthermore, most communication researchers in the advertising, marketing and commercial fields, as well as those in health promotion, are likely to have received formal training (if they received any at all) in some variant of the American communication tradition rather than the British cultural studies tradition, as the latter has only relatively recently become evident in Australian university curricula and is still largely absent in public health training.

The concept of 'noise' in the American 'effects' communication paradigm betrays its origins in engineering paradigms. 'Noise' includes the static that interrupts radio transmission and the 'snow' that obscures television pictures. Fundamentally, 'noise' derives from a transmission (rather than constructionist) notion of communication. Brenda Dervin has distinguished these two concepts of information use clearly:

> If one assumes that information has an existence apart from human construction, one focuses exclusively on transmission questions (e.g. How much information did someone get? Was the information they got accurate? What can we do to be sure people get more accurate information?) rather than on construction questions (e.g. What strategy did that individual apply that led him or her to call that information accurate? What strategy did he or she apply that led to rejecting information another might call accurate? How can we design systems that allow people to apply the criteria they want to their information searches?) (1992, p. 64).

Technologies of discourse tend to a transmission approach to communication; often, as we have observed, reducing 'receivers' to somewhat static individual and psychological dispositions which are to be mobilised by 'hard-edged' messages. In contrast, as Dervin argues, constructionist approaches to communication seek to situate self-constructing, agentive individuals in the context of the 'culture, history, and institutions [that] define much of the world within which the individual lives' (1992, p. 67).

While the concept of 'noise' was originally discussed in relation to the most 'engineered' moment of transmission (at the level of the technological 'transmitters' of communication such as the static on radio), in principle it can appear anywhere in the 'effects' linear flow of communication. In the DCSH documents we noticed that 'noise' appeared at all points in the 'source'/'transmitter'/'receiver' chain. Indeed, the very terms used in these documents—emphasising the 'noise' and contradictory inputs from all types of 'sources'—indicated the continuing influence in the advertising agencies of the American 'effects' tradition. One document, for example, produced by a consultant marketing company in 1988 for the DCSH pointed to 'noise' at the authoritative expert or 'credible source' end of the communication process, noting that:

> NACAIDS [National Advisory Committee on AIDS] is not the only source of information about AIDS. One of the key features of our society's

response to AIDS has been the diversity of highly visible comment . . . No one organisation is positioned in the public's mind as being the credible information source on AIDS. The sea of competing and conflicting AIDS stories, jokes, innuendos, fears, media snippets etc. only makes effective communication and education in this area even more difficult than it would otherwise have been. If the educational attack on AIDS is to be effective, then it is absolutely imperative that one body be positioned as the recognised authority on the subject.

The marketing consultants advised, as a result, that campaign strategies should be directed at positioning the NACAIDS as this single 'recognised authority' on AIDS. The assumptions evident in these statements are that other sources of information are misleading and inaccurate, serving to 'block' 'effective transmission' of official AIDS information. This discourse also positions and privileges the NACAIDS as the most appropriate source (rather than, for example, AIDS community groups and organisations or people living with HIV/AIDS). This emphasis on single recognised authority 'sources' precludes consideration of expert authority *cultures* as themselves worthy of analysis, in particular such experts' definition of the *meaning* of AIDS. It relies upon the notion that experts 'possess' knowledge that must be 'transmitted' to audiences, and that there is a single, coherent view that may be so 'transmitted' via a series of discrete messages.

Second, the report also pointed to 'noise' (as against 'efficiency' of knowledge flow) as an issue of 'transmitter' style, arguing that health promotion advertisements were often too diffuse and general:

As communication researchers [we] advise that there is a need to be as specific, simple and consistent in our educational thrust as is possible . . . All we can objectively say is that the more general we make our communications, the more we run the risk that people will slip through the educational net and expose themselves to the risks of catching AIDS [sic].

The marketing documents in general supported the use of 'hard-hitting' rather than 'soft' strategies of 'packaging' messages about AIDS at the 'transmitter' point of communication. There was also a general acceptance of the need for the continued use of emotional appeals, particularly the use of fear, at least as far as the national television campaigns were concerned. As we note below, this belief was evident in discourses originating from both DCSH and NACAIDS officials and the advertising workers responsible for the 'Grim Reaper' campaign. Similarly, a 1989 marketing report argued:

> Our target is not going to be induced to confront unpleasant realities by the use of soft, user-friendly, humorous euphemistic advertising . . . The latter kind of advertising will not penetrate the self-protective barrier that youth has developed to reduce its fears and anxieties about catching AIDS [sic] . . . The need for hard-hitting advertising is more pressing than ever because, as time passes, youth's fear of AIDS is being sublimated rather than confronted.

Third, these documents also pointed to semantic 'noise' at the 'destination' end of the communication process. Various kinds of 'noise' were described as 'deflective mechanisms' that supposedly enabled audiences to rationalise their attitudes and behaviours, thus preventing the translation of new knowledge into new sexual behaviour.

While the terms 'communities' and 'cultures' do appear frequently in the documentation, what the documents call the 'communication environment' of the campaigns is in fact understood primarily in psychological rather than cultural terms. We can see a very clear example of this if we look at an early (1986) document produced by the advertising company which made the 'Grim Reaper' advertisement:

> It may appear that the Target Group is obvious . . . 'the community'. However, there is no such thing as a totally homogenous community. The 'community' is really a whole group of smaller communities separated from each other by streams, chasms and even gulfs of understanding. Sexual awareness and sexual practices and attitudes towards sex probably present greater differences than any other area of our society. We are separated by young and old; by hedonist and conservative; by cultural and environmental difference. Therefore targeting our message becomes a very important element of the strategy.

Many of the categories of difference familiar in cultural studies approaches are indicated here: sexual preference, age, ethnicity. Considering the community as composed of separate 'gulfs of understanding' at least potentially shifts the grounds of analysis away from essentialist notions of the 'deflective mechanisms of youth'. Yet the documents and research reports we read never systematically examined what these 'gulfs' might be in terms of our social and cultural environment.

One advertising agency's development report went on to list a number of 'target' groups that it considered important to address in the advertising campaign, accompanied by possible messages that could be used:

- Women and girls: He may be a regular guy—but he could be a carrier.
- Young men and the general heterosexual community: Why bother about safe sex when you're having such fun?—AIDS.
- Parents: How to talk to your children about safe sex without embarrassing either of you.
- Intravenous drug users and their fringe dwellers: AIDS is one habit you'll never break. Don't pass the needle!
- Legislators, politicians and the media: Unchecked, AIDS will cost the community more in health care than the last war.
- The gay and bisexual community: Why worry about safe sex when you're having so much fun?—AIDS.
- Ethnic groups (no particular strategic message suggested).

These proposed categories and messages reveal a number of cultural assumptions including: there is such a thing as a 'heterosexual community' (as well as a 'gay and bisexual community'); sex is always 'fun' and never problematic (except in relation to AIDS); parents find sexual discussion with their children embarrassing; politicians see problems like AIDS only from the economic angle. Its view of sub-cultural diversity depends on simplistic, narrow and patronising commercial media categorisations of its audience. Moreover, its analysis is not informed by any social theory of how what it calls this 'jigsaw' of cultural diversity fits together—how this diversity relates to broader structures of power in Australian society. Instead, the documents tend to reach for an eclectic and haphazard combination of conceptual models in establishing their categories. The document cited above, for example, combines opinion leader categories (parents) with categories derived from pluralist notions of power (the legislators, the media), with 'risk group' categories (injecting drug users and a totally homogenised 'gay and bisexual community'). Ethnicity is recognised but seems unworthy even of a strategic message. The report, having raised the issue of gender, ignores issues of power between genders (for example, in the area of negotiating condom use). It opts instead for non-social and grossly stereotyped categories to understand gender response. Girls will, the 1986 document tells us, want to use condoms because of 'their maternal instincts', and young men will watch any AIDS message that 'contains an element of sex' because that 'is their natural voyeuristic instinct'. The problems of individualised (in this case even essentialised) analysis of sexual practice are very clear here. The marketing discourse has regressed to little more than categories of instinctual behaviour patterns which are to be stimulated, Pavlovian-like, by advertising.

Although, then, there was a continuing interest in socio-cultural difference in the marketing material, the documents tended to psychological rather than cultural understandings of AIDS education. They emphasised, for instance, the 'self-protective barrier that youth has developed to reduce its fears', and psychological 'deflective mechanisms' rather than gender or class difference in relation to risk practices. There was also, as we have pointed out, a tendency in the research and development documents towards 'hypodermic' understandings of media messages (with an emphasis on the need for 'hard-edged advertising' that 'doesn't let them off the hook') rather than taking account of recent cultural and media theory's emphasis on audiences who are active and differentiated in their sub-cultural 'readings' of the meanings of television texts.

The 'Grim Reaper' campaign

> It was evident prior to 1986 that AIDS could be transmitted through heterosexual sex and that increasingly AIDS would threaten the whole community. (DCSH report, 1989)

The terms of reference of the NACAIDS, dated 11 September 1986, included the following: 'The design, conduct and evaluation of the National AIDS Education Program in the context of a national education strategy'. This document also included the aim, 'to advise on the development of media campaigns and appropriate application thereof'. The subsequent education campaign, the 'Grim Reaper' campaign, was based on the primary aims of the National AIDS Education Program developed in 1986 by the AIDS Task Force and the NACAIDS. They were 'to provide clear, factual information to the public, in order to raise their [sic] general level of knowledge of

AIDS and how it is transmitted; and to motivate the public to avoid practices that spread HIV infection (i.e., to avoid risk behaviours)' (DCSH report, 1988).

The original intention was to follow the awareness-raising stage of the 'Grim Reaper' television advertisement with a less alarming series of advertisements based on factual information about safer sexual practices rather than scare tactics: 'These were to run for the rest of the year, punctuated by occasional "returns of the Reaper" to keep people on their toes' (Carr 1987, p. 28). Much of the remaining funds provided for the campaign, however, were spent on upgrading telephone and counselling services in response to the unexpected demand generated by the television advertisements (Carr 1987, p. 28). The planned follow-up series of television advertisements were never developed, and the 'Grim Reaper' advertisement was not broadcast again to a mass audience.

According to a report written by one of the DCSH officials in 1987, the aims of the 'Grim Reaper' campaign were generated from a health education model of behaviour change, the 'Morin model', which suggests that a person must hold five beliefs in order to change his or her sexual behaviour in relation to AIDS, and that these beliefs can be directly influenced by educational and motivational programs. The beliefs tend to occur sequentially: there must be a belief that AIDS is a personal threat: 'I am personally threatened by AIDS'; there must be a belief in prevention: 'AIDS is preventable; certain actions will reduce or eliminate my risk'; there must be a belief in personal efficacy: 'I am capable of managing this new low-risk behaviour'; there must be a belief in the possibility of satisfaction: 'I can carry out this new behaviour and still be sexually satisfied'; there must be a belief in the existence of peer support: 'My peers will support this new behaviour'. The influence of the KAB model is also evident in these aims; that is, the assumption that knowledge shapes or determines attitudes which in turn shape or determine behaviour. As we pointed out in chapter 2, the KAB model has been pervasive in health education and underlies linear 'effects' models of communication which have also been dominant.

The 'Grim Reaper' advertising campaign was the product of five months of planning on the part of the NACAIDS and the advertising agency responsible for it. Prior to the development of the campaign a small qualitative study was conducted, reporting that 'people had only a partial knowledge of AIDS and how it was transmitted' (DCSH report, 1989). A much larger representative market research survey, sponsored by the government, of 1511 Australians was then carried out. The intention of this research, according to government briefing documents, was to provide a basis for 'designing and implementing a program of communications activities'. The survey was to be a 'benchmark', establishing findings prior to the release of an education campaign so that the campaign's effects could be evaluated. Again the influence of the KAB model is evident in the design and aims of this benchmark study. As a result, the survey focused on measuring aspects of knowledge, attitudes and behaviour related to AIDS among the sample group. Items asked respondents questions about how HIV/AIDS is transmitted, which groups were most at risk from HIV/AIDS, attitudes about homosexuality, perception of personal risk and the spread of HIV/AIDS. According to the DCSH, the results of the study confirmed its suspicions that Australians were generally apathetic about AIDS: it 'showed clearly that although most people perceived AIDS as a threat to the nation, few saw it as a personal threat. The attitude that AIDS was somebody else's problem was highly prevalent' (1989 report).

The findings of the survey led the NACAIDS to work towards an AIDS education campaign that would launch an 'assault phase' to 'make AIDS a relevant concept for all Australians . . . an inescapable part of our lives . . . not just a gay disease', as a 1987 research and development document put it. The intent was to 'deliver an emotional shock to the general community in order to raise awareness and personal concern' (DCSH report, 1989). Subsequently the advertising agency employed to design the campaign noted that its overall strategy was to 'pour a bucket of cold water over the heads of all Australians' to challenge complacency. The agency's 1986 report to the department outlining its approach used such terms in relation to campaign strategies as 'a classic pincer movement' and 'attack from an unexpected flank', suggesting a strong reliance on the 'hypodermic' model of message 'inoculation'.

The rationale for the 'Grim Reaper' campaign was also made public in official press releases. The then Federal Minister for Health, Neal Blewett, claimed that the results of the NACAIDS survey showed that 'up to 50000 Australians, most of them walking around in apparently good health, were in fact carriers of one of the most lethal viruses ever known' (*Herald* [Melbourne], 2 April 1987). The chair of the NACAIDS, publisher and editor Ita Buttrose, was quoted as declaring that the television advertisement was designed 'to stop people in their tracks and make them think seriously about AIDS'. Interviews with members of the advertising agency published in the press similarly reiterated the intention of the campaign to 'shock people out of their complacency'. The head of the team and owner of the advertising firm, Siimon [sic] Reynolds, said that his intention in using the grim reaper imagery was 'to get the message across that AIDS was a killer, with prevention the only cure' (*Daily Mirror*, 7 April 1987). The grim reaper image was one, said Reynolds, 'that I've been scared by since I was a kid: a chilling figure of death' and was chosen from 300 concepts after the firm's staff had spent months 'boning up on facts about the killer virus, under the guidance of medical experts' (*Adelaide Advertiser*, 8 April 1987). Another of the members of the creative team, Quentin Munro, was quoted as saying, 'This commercial takes people to the edge and gives them almost a sense of what AIDS is all about. Very firmly and squarely it places the responsibility of AIDS back on themselves: on the individual' (*The Age*, 7 April 1987).

Government policy documents, official public statements and research and development documents produced by the market research and advertising companies employed by the government, therefore, all agreed that AIDS was a problem for all Australians, that the public was too complacent about the risk posed to it, and that members of the public therefore required the government to deliver them an 'emotional shock' to make them confront the risk and act responsibly. The individualistic, pastoral and paternal dimensions underlying the development of the messages of the campaign are clear in these texts: the government is positioned as an authority seeking to punish its citizens for their apathy by using 'shock tactics'. Not only did these texts advocate a traditional 'hypodermic' model of AIDS message 'inoculation', but they also adopted the familiar masculine–militaristic terminology familiar in the media's construction of AIDS. Such a discourse constructs a crisis caused by human agency (rather than, for example, by natural disaster) in which the state's power and duty in taking control is supported and extreme action is justified, even to the extent of compromising civil rights (see Sontag 1989; Sherry 1993).

Sex and drugs: the 1990 television campaign

By 1990, there was evidence in the research and development documents of a belief that a universal psychological shift had occurred over the past few years whereby self-protective attitudes (and therefore complacency) had increased (after the early impact in Australia of 'hard-edged' advertisements like the 'Grim Reaper'). A 1989 research and development report describing the 'environment' in which the 1990 campaign would have to be developed noted that Australia was now in a 'chronic anxiety phase' rather than an 'acute fear phase' as when 'AIDS was new and the Grim Reaper ad was running'. Hysteria over AIDS had been replaced, the report noted, by the opposite problem—complacency. As the report stated:

> Familiarity with (and assumed knowledge about) the disease has bred the development of deflective and self-protective attitudes that most commonly express themselves in comments of the 'well, it's not going to happen to me—I'll be all right Jack' kind. If the fire of fear is left to dwindle there is no reason to expect this situation to reverse itself.

The 'assault phase' of the 'Grim Reaper' campaign had been predicated on the intention to promote the belief that AIDS was a personally relevant threat, that it could be prevented and controlled through individuals taking action and being responsible for their own health. The 1990 campaign was designed both to be sufficiently 'hard-edged' to break through complacency via a sense of personal threat and to provide sufficient guidance to establish individuals' belief in prevention and personal efficacy, thus precluding 'defensive avoidance'. Research undertaken by a market research company for the DCSH had found that some 70 per cent of injecting drug users had shared needles at some time and that a similar proportion did not always use condoms when having sex. The study also found that amongst non-injecting sexually active individuals aged between 16 and 24, only 20 per cent of the male respondents used condoms, while 7 per cent of women always requested that their partners use condoms. The emphasis of the 1990 campaign, therefore, was on 'socialising "safe sex" and "safe needle" behaviour' for young people aged 24 and under.

As we explained in chapter 3, the 1990 campaign began with the frightening 'Needle Bed' advertisement, which combined romantic images of a young heterosexual couple with frightening images of a bed covered with sharp syringes. This advertisement was linked to the 'assault phase' of the 'Grim Reaper' campaign, while introducing a new 'personal threat': the 'second/third wave' bridge between injecting drug user and heterosexual communities. The second phase of the campaign used the six 'Testimonial' television advertisements involving a man and women who were HIV positive. The campaign ended with the humorous 'Vox Pop Condom' advertisements which used excerpts from 'in the street' interviews to show how 'ordinary' people felt about using condoms.

If we examine the relationship between the 1987 and 1990 Australian campaigns as a 'problematic', we can clearly see the underlying pattern of the Morin psychological model:

1 Assault phase—the 'Grim Reaper' campaign:
   i   Belief in personal threat—AIDS is relevant: 'To make AIDS a relevant concept for all Australians . . . an inescapable part of our lives . . . not just a gay disease' (1987 document).
   ii   Belief in prevention—AIDS can be stopped: 'There are only four ways to stop the spread of AIDS' (1987 document).
   iii   Belief in personal efficacy—AIDS can be controlled: 'It must make the point that . . . individuals are responsible for the protection of their own bodies' (1989 document).
2 Socialising phase—the 'Vox Pop Condom' campaign:
   iv   Belief in possibility of satisfaction—condoms are fun: 'Protect yourself by using condoms. They're fun' (1990 document).
   v   Belief in existence of peer support—condoms are the norm: 'They're accepted, no big deal' (1990 campaign advertisement).

The idea of opening the 1990 campaign with an 'anxiety arousal' advertisement was to recreate the 'Grim Reaper's' supposed success in raising tension and anxiety about AIDS at a personal level, thus ensuring attitude change. But it was felt that raising anxiety levels alone, as the 'Grim Reaper' had done, was not sufficient. The necessary follow-up task was to encourage prophylactic behaviour: that is, 'uncontaminated needle use' and 'uncontaminating sex'.

In the research and development documentation, the 'Testimonial' advertisements were described as potentially having the power to break through 'youth's complacency and deflection barriers' by creating anxiety among both injecting drug users and non-injecting drug user heterosexuals. It was therefore argued that the 'Testimonials' should be near the starting point for the new 1990 mass media campaign. The research and development documentation had insisted that the 'Testimonial' subjects should be 'very, very different' from each other in order for the advertisements to work 'across the market'. They should include both 'the tragic victim' and the 'smart', self-protecting injecting drug user or regular condom user (thus creating both 'anxiety arousal' and a 'comfort zone' for people taking control of their own health). In the actual to-air 'Testimonials' this concept was lost; all the speakers were 'victims' (see chapter 3).

Other changes to the original conceptualisation of the 'Testimonials' took place. In its first trial, the 'Testimonial' test concept had focused on a 'real' person living with HIV/AIDS, contrasting his current physical condition (thin, ill, pale, covered in sores) with an earlier photograph of him taken as a healthy, fit young man being presented with a sports award. While being positively evaluated by the DCSH's marketing company, this suggested advertisement was eventually rejected by the department for ethical reasons related to the focus on the man's physical debility after developing AIDS and the revealing of his identity. A 1990 report noted that 'it had become evident that a modification to the original test concept was unavoidable—it was not going to be possible to *visually* identify an AIDS sufferer. Thus the revised concept uses an AIDS sufferer in shadow to preserve their anonymity' (original emphasis).

The marketing company had been much less positive about the replacement 'Testimonial' concept of lighting a series of people living with HIV/AIDS in silhouette, recommending that it was inappropriate for television. The company's report noted, 'Of particular concern is the confusion and conflict that results in the mind of the viewer when their visual image of the AIDS sufferer (usually the stereotyped victim in the terminal stages of the disease) does not match the voice they are hearing'. It was asserted that this kind of advertisement should not be used on television but might work on radio. This desire to 'personalise the message', to render it visually coherent, emerges from the professional cultural values of the media industry. The style of the face-to-face, expressive close-up is a convention of television production, the acceptable style that is only abandoned when people are 'suspicious' or 'guilty' in some way, thus requiring the hiding of their identity. It was also initially planned that the 'Testimonials' were to be followed by two different 'strands' of advertisements, which 'socialised' on the one hand condom use, and on the other safe needle practices. Unlike the tension-creating 'Testimonial' advertisements, these 'prophylactic' advertisements were supposed to create a 'comfort zone' to facilitate behaviour change. These were to be 'customised' advertisements (that is, designed to target a specific preventive behaviour) to 'socialise' clean needle and condom use. The 'Vox Pop Condom' advertisements that went to air in 1990 were designed to fill this 'comfort zone' role by using humour rather than fear as the main tactic of 'socialising the condom'. The major messages that were inserted into the advertisements were that condoms are fun, protective and 'normal'. As one DCSH document stated, these advertisements

clearly create a positive environment which encourages the acceptance of condoms as part of young people's sex life. The interview technique used presents condoms in a favourable, fun, light-hearted and unembarrassing light which tackles head-on the negative perceptions many hold, or believe their partners hold.

Part of the production strategy for the 'Vox Pop Condoms' was to use a range of 'talking heads' in the 'on the street' interviews: 'a wide cross-section of opinions from people of different ages, of both genders and a variety of backgrounds' in order to 'maintain the involvement of the viewer' (DCSH document, 1990). This 'wide variety of backgrounds' included both 'ethnic' (non-Anglo–Celtic) voices and an older woman (a 'grandmother type').

Again we should note the individualised focus of this psychological model, including the overall campaign 'map' which drew closely on the Morin model of behaviour, and the emphasis on socialising individual viewers with a series of personal beliefs while highlighting the importance of personal responsibility. There is no recognition here of the social location of beliefs and therefore of the process of social interaction in the context of power negotiation and the ensuing perceptions of the behaviour of one's sexual partner. Again, in the 1990 campaign, we can see the same linear development from the 'assault' to the 'socialising' phase. Yet, as with the Australian campaigns generally, so too the 1990 documents made reference to ethnographic and cultural intentions. Despite the obvious influence of the KAB model of behaviour change, different sub-cultural responses were recognised; at least to the extent that the Australian documents argued strongly for two 'strands' of the advertising campaigns:

> one directed at IVD [intravenous drug] users within their culture—with messages that are clearly relevant to them (i.e. ruined lives through drug use and poor needle hygiene). And another directed at non-IVDU youth and parents within their culture—with a message of protection from sexual transmission of AIDS via condom use.

It was argued that since young people are very discerning about communication, each advertising strand would have to be 'just right' culturally, or else it would be read as 'the outside world giving us another lecture or rave', in which case young people would 'switch out/turn off'. In other words, this 'just right' cultural effect would eliminate the risk of semantic 'noise' and therefore ensure efficient transfer of knowledge to attitudes and behaviour. However, it should be noted in this research and development documentation that, despite the sub-cultural thrust of the thinking behind the campaign, injecting drug users were sometimes constructed for non-users as 'exotic others' rather than cultural 'insiders'. The documents, for instance, highlighted the importance of emphasising the 'insidious' spread of the disease 'from the world of the IVDU ("them") to non-IVDUs ("us")' via sex. Sexual activity was to be seen as 'the bridge between the world of "them" and "us"' and the 'Needle Bed' advertisement was designed to emphasise this 'bridge'.

Thus, although these documents suggested that it was important that the campaign should not 'perpetuate a "them" (druggies) and "us" (normals) division in the community', that stereotyped opposition was quite potent in the assumptions expressed in the same documents about how 'complacency' would be broken down psychologically. Moreover, the documents' understanding of 'us' ('non-IVDU youth and parents within their culture') is quite hopelessly homogenising, ignoring differences in generation as well as gender, class and ethnicity. The actual to-air 'Testimonial' advertisements, however, were careful to avoid this 'us/them' dichotomy. The three needle-sharers featured—'Chris', 'Debby' and 'Emma'—were all profiled as either into shooting-up only at parties, or else using injecting drugs casually (for example, privately within an otherwise 'normal' marriage). They were explicitly *not* presented as part of a 'junkie' culture. Indeed, the 'clean needles' strand of the campaign was targeted entirely at the recreational injector.

Inevitably, the campaign's emphasis on both 'needle' and 'sex' narratives simultaneously led to more complex messages than, for example, the 'Grim Reaper' campaign which focused on safer sex only. The 'Needle Bed' advertisement was always intended to illustrate the bridging process between needle-sharing and sexual transmission. In its original storyboard form it began with showing images of needle sharers, but this was changed after the advertising firm conducted some developmental audience research and found negative responses to using these images. In the final 'Needle Bed' transmitted form, the initial visuals emphasised heterosexual sex without showing any direct image of people injecting drugs. The only obvious 'bridge' between the couple and injecting drug users was represented by the male and female hands placing syringes on the mattress towards which the couple were moving (the bed image signifying 'sex' and the syringes 'drug use').

The actual 1990 television campaign was not directed towards the two distinct strands (heterosexuals and injecting drug users) initially suggested in the research and development documentation. It certainly did carry messages exclusively aimed at heterosexual transmission—the 'Vox Pop Condom' advertisements which used naturalistic interviews with (mainly) young people on the street, in shopping malls and on the beach to emphasise the 'fun' side of condoms. The separate 'Vox Pop' advertisements for injecting drug users that were initially planned were never developed. The 'Testimonial' series also included interviews that emphasised sexual transmission of the virus, thus carrying a 'use condoms' message; in the case of two of them a needle-sharing past was not even suggested. Consequently all three parts of the 1990 television campaign ('Needle Bed', 'Testimonials' and 'Vox Pop Condom') in fact addressed the broader 'heterosexual community' as the 'implied reader' of their texts, even though some of the Testimonials ('Chris', 'Emma' and 'Debby') were aimed at (casual) injecting drug users as well.

CONCLUDING COMMENTS

In this chapter we have begun to move from analysis of the content of television texts to production analysis. Our focus here has been on the interface of health bureaucracies and commercial advertising/marketing companies in producing government-sponsored television advertisements. To a significant extent, of course, the analysis of this chapter has been textual, seeking to expose the underlying paradigm assumptions—in relation to models of communication, construction of audiences and notions of behaviour change—of these Australian research and development documents. By examining the assumptions stated in these texts, we have been able to point to the primary importance of the KAB and 'effects' models of communication and behaviour change and yet, at the same time, to the cultural concerns that were also symptomatically evident in these texts. Those cultural concerns were sometimes quickly tokenised and lost as in the documentation relating to the 'Grim Reaper' advertisement. At other times they led to plans for meeting the needs of 'distinct target audiences', as in the 1990 AIDS television campaign which emphasised two different strands or sub-cultures: injecting drug users and non-injecting heterosexuals.

The dominance of 'effects' models together with concern about 'community response' (especially on the part of parents) led to a conceptualisation of 'culture' in the documents either instrumentally (in terms of identifying 'at-risk groups' or 'target cultures'), or strategically (in terms of 'pressure groups' or 'cultures'). The result of this instrumental and strategic definition of cultures meant that the AIDS evaluation reports were caught in the trap of trying, on the one hand, to reach what they called 'target cultures' or 'at-risk groups' from the 'inside' and, on the other hand, not offending significant pressure groups such as 'parent cultures'. AIDS advertisements were therefore considered to be most 'effective' when they least offended both instrumental and strategic groups.

One problem with this type of 'production' analysis is that it relies only on written documents. Not all decisions, and certainly not all planning and policy negotiation, are in written form, but are part of the routine daily activities of professional practice. We do not know, for example, from a perusal of the available documentation, why the two proposed strands of the 1990 AIDS campaign did not go to air.

To gain access to those dimensions of professional culture as lived or embodied experience, we need to adopt more ethnographic methods. Ethnography starts from an assumption that behaviour, rather than being the end effect of a KAB linear process, takes place within a cultural context. AIDS television advertisements and the research and development documentation surrounding them are produced in a context of professional interpretation and negotiation, where assumptions about 'what are the crucial health issues of today?', or 'what makes good television?' become the daily practice of professional workers. More often than not these values of practice are not made discursive; they are not written down and often are not even overtly articulated. Yet they undoubtedly have effect on the style, discursive structure, form and therefore the meanings of television AIDS texts. In the next two chapters we will go much further into an ethnography of the production of such texts.

Meanwhile, in this chapter we have begun to show some of the complexities and 'multiple subjectivities' working at the bureaucratic/commercial interface, in particular the uneven mix of individualist–psychological and cultural models and understandings of social behaviour in relation to health threats. The issue here is not one of intention, for there seems little doubt that both health bureaucrats and commercial advertisers want to employ cultural concepts in their campaigns as part of the objective to 'get the message across effectively'. At present, though, the research paradigms they employ often work actively against that intention.

6

THE 'THREE WAVES' OF AIDS:
INTERTEXTS AND EXPERTISE

Daily access to high level government and bureaucratic offices was denied us in evaluating the development and production of government AIDS campaigns. Although that kind of access is always unlikely to occur in government circles, it is sometimes possible in the commercial media. Just a year prior to the release of the 'Grim Reaper' campaign in Australia, one of us had produced with a colleague an 'ethnography of production' study of the television series *A Country Practice (ACP)* (Tulloch & Moran 1986). Because good relations with the *ACP* production team had been established through that study, it was possible to carry out further field work when *ACP* decided to produce its first AIDS story in 1988. Thus we were able to follow the production process from its first planning stage to studio and post-production. This story became the four-part series of episodes entitled 'Sophie', that we described in chapter 4. Our access to the *ACP* production of their first 'AIDS story' gave us the opportunity to trace the way in which commercial television professionals engaged in the shifting metaphors and narratives of AIDS available in the late 1980s. Which did they choose to promote in constructing their own narratives? Why choose the ones they did? And with what effect: both on their familiar characterisations and on audiences? The only way to answer some of these questions was to undertake an ethnography of production.

ETHNOGRAPHIES OF PRODUCTION

Ethnography is concerned with human behaviour that occurs within a context of space/time coordinates. In terms of spatial context, for example, a television production house never makes its meanings in isolation from a larger context which includes television channels, audiences and professional organisations. In terms of time coordinates, these meanings are constructed in the context of forward planning, master plans, ratings periods, actor availability, networking scheduling demands, timing of commercial breaks and so on. So when an AIDS text is constructed within this particular socio-cultural group, its messages are 'processed' and its meanings are made according to the production strategies generated by those broader contexts of space and time. It is those rhetorical strategies which put in place (*mise en scène*) textual meaning as understood within production cultures. All of the familiar research emphases of ethnography are implicated in this analysis of production strategies within time/space coordinates: the emphasis on understanding (and subjective reflexivity); on process (as the competing discourses and intertexts that define social situations); on natural settings (the study of people in their own daily milieu rather than in the analyst's laboratory); on holism (the understanding of everyday interaction within its broader, socio-cultural context). Ethnography's familiar methodological strategies also arise from this emphasis on inter-subjective experiences and discourses in a natural setting. The use of observational techniques, for example, allows the recording of behaviour as it occurs—as daily practice—rather than relying on people's retrospective accounts of it.

When we analyse ethnographic data we are also performing textual analysis. The interviews and other observations that emerge from ethnographic research are texts just as are television programs or the policy and research and development documents that we examined in chapter 5. The production interviews quoted in this and the following chapter were conducted during early production of the 'Sophie' episodes. They reveal the ways in which narratives of AIDS (from the medical profession, social workers, conventional soap opera and medical drama genres and the personal concerns and lived experiences of the television workers involved) circulate and are made to cohere in the context of commercial television. In conducting this analysis, we challenge the linear model of health communication in emphasising the multi-layered processes of constructing meaning in the television text which stem from the professional practices of television workers, including directors, writers, actors, set designers, audio directors, lighting technicians, incidental music composers and so on. These practices operate according to the cultural knowledge of media professionals. An ethnographic approach involves entering the 'world' of these professionals, both by participant-observation and interview, and by 'making sense' of the cultural knowledges and assumptions that underlie their everyday activities. We were interested in studying the process by which the intended or preferred meaning of the text was constructed and converted into the actual text; that is, the transformation and transcodification of meaning.

THE 'THREE WAVES' OF AIDS

The first wave of AIDS deaths hit the homosexual community. The second, IV drug users. Now women and their babies are becoming infected. The third wave looms over Australia. (*Sydney Morning Herald*, 21 May 1988)

The 'Sophie' episodes were recorded and screened in 1988, some six years after the first mainstream news media report about the epidemic that was to be called AIDS and five years after the first Australian with HIV/AIDS had been diagnosed. For the producers of *ACP*, the decisions made to introduce injecting drug use and AIDS issues in the context of the Sophie character were based on a number of considerations that went beyond merely wanting to canvass those health issues. Financial considerations were also important in this decision. The producer, Forrest Redlich, commented that new management policy at the channel and a drop in advertising revenues had required more planning to save money and attract audiences. This meant 'tighter' storylines and careful plotting of character development. As the executive producer, James Davern, said, 'You're battling for an audience all the time. The other commercial channels are throwing everything in the book they can at us . . . to attract the audience you've got to be cleverer than four years ago. And cleverer means you've got to work harder'.

The actual HIV/AIDS angles of the 'Sophie' story were not the generating point of that episode. At that time, the Terence Elliot character had recently married Alex Fraser. The character of Sophie, Terence's only daughter, had originally been introduced some years earlier as an adolescent and then disappeared from the series for a time. The 'new' Sophie reappeared as a heroin addict who had returned from overseas travelling as a journalist. As noted in chapter 4 the advantage of using the Sophie character to embody the person at risk from injecting drug use and HIV was her links with the major characters of Terence Elliot and Alex Fraser. The reappearance of Sophie was designed to provide a point of conflict (as is symptomatic in the soap opera genre) for the newly married Terence and Alex, to 'throw a spanner in the works' and to 'rip the marriage apart' for dramatic effect, as Forrest Redlich and James Davern described it. Redlich commented that 'It's very character-determined, because the bottom line of that episode was not an AIDS story. It was not even to do a heroin story. It was to throw something into the ring for Terence and Alex'. A warm reunion was planned after some weeks of this conflict between Terence and Alex, demonstrating their love for each other (prior to another point of conflict being introduced—Terence and Alex do, finally, separate). To help provide this (temporary) romantic closure, it was decided that the character of Sophie had to be written out of *ACP* by having her die.

There was also a more direct commercial consideration for producing the 'Sophie story', including her death. Marriages and deaths among the regular characters help boost the ratings:

> *Redlich* There's got to be an eight or nine-month master plan where you plot your year, and you've got your highs and lows. You don't know what they're going to be specifically, but you know that around this time when everything's been going really nicely, it's about time we threw a spanner in the works. Because the audience wants to see this kind of stuff happening. So everything's on a master plan. The content of the particular episode comes through research—but the master plan was already there. The dilemma was *how* Sophie should die.

If it were not for the success of the previous episodes dealing with Sophie's addiction to heroin, the 'Sophie' AIDS story would not have been developed. The actor who played Sophie, Katrina Sedgwick, had immediately produced such 'chemistry' with Shane Porteous (playing her father, Terence Elliot) in the previous episodes that, as story editor Stephen Measday said, 'We suddenly thought we've got a terrific character here, and we must have her back to do another story'. 'Q' ratings (measuring the popularity of individual characters) confirmed the success of the Sophie character. But for these economic and production determinants, it is likely that some other plot device would have been used to create conflict in the relationship between Terence and Alex. Producer Bruce Best confirmed that if this acting 'chemistry' had not occurred, there would have been no thought of doing a Sophie/AIDS story: 'It was just a thought at that stage—a forward projection—if we could get her while the idea was still hot'. The reason for incorporating storylines based on heroin addiction and the risk of AIDS also emerged from a sense of social responsibility. The writers and producers harboured a strong belief in the role played by *ACP* in bringing to the fore medical and social issues, and in getting the details 'right'. Personal experience often had a part to play in the way the show tackled such issues. As one of the regular writers, David Allen, had noted some years earlier:

> *ACP* impresses me because the stories seem to come basically out of what somebody involved in the production has personally experienced. Like the alcoholism one that I'm doing now—I'm not an alcoholic, but I drink too much . . . That way you tend to want to be more truthful than you normally would be. And you feel as though you are doing something worthwhile . . . A lot of good has been done making the public aware of the basis of some diseases that people may well be frightened of when they see it in others. (quoted in Tulloch & Moran 1986, pp. 37–8)

Television dramas like *ACP* 'need' expert knowledges to lend 'reality' to their productions, while medical and public health workers court such media to publicise their concerns or research findings. *ACP*, however, was made by a commercial production house which is highly aware of the need to entertain and not 'preach' or appeal only to a minority audience. The object was to reach a diverse audience, to strike the right balance between social relevance and entertainment, naturalism and melodrama, comedy and tragedy. The use of the Sophie character encouraged audiences to respond to the issues around heroin use, needle-sharing and HIV/AIDS on a more sympathetic and empathetic level. The lessons of 'Sophie' were aimed at all families, attempting to show audiences that they could not close themselves off from the problem by engaging their emotions:

> *Davern* You can watch a television commercial from afar and you can distance yourself. Or like when you're watching *Dallas*, you really distance yourself a little bit. It's a comic strip because you have no experience with those people. But you *know* Alex and Terence: they've been around for a long time, they're familiar. They're happily married, everyone has experienced what they're experiencing—they relate to them.

Happily married people distance themselves from AIDS—it's somebody else's problem. But it's not if it can happen to Terence Elliot.

In the 'Sophie' episodes, producers Davern and Redlich felt that they wanted to show the outcome of young people becoming addicted to heroin and becoming vulnerable to HIV infection through sharing needles and having sex with HIV-positive partners. They were keen to emphasise how easily any young person, regardless of their social background, could become addicted to heroin and contract HIV:

> Redlich What you've got is little fifteen-year-old kids out in the streets sharing needles with AIDS positive junkies, and then turning tricks in back alleys, right? It's scary stuff.

> Davern It's also the kids, the young kids who are a bit wild who go to parties and someone's got heroin in a needle, you know? And I know kids who have tried it once and they say, 'Oh, you don't become an addict if you try it once'. That's the danger.

Despite the talk of 'fifteen-year-old kids . . . turning tricks in back alleys', the imputed audience for 'Sophie' was not high-risk street kids at all. Rather, 'Sophie' was aimed at 'our own teenagers at parties' as suggested by Davern. Beyond this target audience of seventeen and eighteen-year-olds who are part of *ACP*'s family demographics, it was also aimed at Redlich's other target of 'second marriage adults'. This was to become a major focus for the writers as we discuss later in this chapter.

The Australian Medical Association (AMA) had had close and productive relations with the *ACP* producers over the years. According to James Davern, the AMA had been putting 'some pressure' on him since 1987, trying to persuade him to produce an AIDS story in *ACP*. At first Davern was reluctant to devote a storyline of *ACP* to AIDS:

> We have given it a lot of consideration, and we find that, at this date, February 1986, still not enough is known about how the disease is transmitted, and I don't believe in scaring people. And the fact that it's linked so strongly with homosexuality makes it very difficult to make a homosexual AIDS victim a 'goody' and sympathetic. (quoted in Tulloch & Moran 1986, p. 291)

Davern wanted to wait until he could find a 'new angle'. At that time (1986–87), the Australian news media had been directing an intense focus on the risk posed by AIDS to heterosexuals (Lupton 1994a, ch. 4). Although the apocalyptic visions conjured up by the 'Grim Reaper' campaign were circulating in 1987, this metaphor of the 'silent, stalking killer' was more appropriate to the horror genre than the naturalist soap opera format. Soap opera deals with human relationships; and in 1987, at that particular moment of transition between the depiction of AIDS as the 'gay plague' to the 'danger to all' representation, the most obvious way of linking these two depictions interpersonally—through 'prejudice against gays' stories—was appearing in television drama, including those made in Australia (for example, the 1986 *The Flying Doctors* episode described in chapter 4). Davern was also aware of the controversy among the medical profession over whether heterosexuals were at risk from HIV/AIDS, and wanted to wait until the profession had 'got its story right'. He decided to put off producing an AIDS storyline until a different angle could be found and the 'story' of heterosexual transmission had been confirmed.

In 1988 the 'second' and 'third wave' narratives that were beginning to be reproduced in the news media provided an entree into a new type of AIDS drama. In these discourses, the 'first wave' of HIV infection was represented as constituted largely by gay men contracting HIV via sexual interaction. The 'second wave' was the spread of HIV to injecting drug users via the sharing of needles, and the 'third wave' was the movement of HIV from injecting drug users to their sexual partners, thus spreading HIV to the non-injecting drug using and heterosexual population. Symptomatic of these new narratives was a feature article published in the *Sydney Morning Herald*, entitled 'AIDS: The Third Wave' (21 May 1988). The article described drug use and prostitution (male and female) in New York City's red-light district, going on to compare this scenario with Kings Cross, Sydney's red-light district. A doctor in New York was quoted as saying:

> In my opinion the AIDS epidemic in New York is now in its third wave. A group of young, non-needle using but very sexually active—even promiscuous—inner city teenage girls is catching the virus. Basically it's sexually transmitted from boyfriends who are IV drug users, or who have been prostitutes when the girls are not.

The article was headed with a cautionary 'real life' narrative on the ease of sharing needles from the point of view of a drug user: 'It happened to me just last month. It was about eight at night and all the pharmacies were closed. In the end I went around and saw a friend and we shared an old needle. I didn't really care if he had AIDS or not and at the time I didn't really care.' The article also quoted an Australian researcher in HIV/AIDS epidemiology who cited eight cases where Australian heterosexuals had contracted HIV, including a woman whose boyfriend was an injecting drug user. The moral of these cases was clear—'Always use condoms. Never share a needle'—as a doctor who worked in Kings Cross was quoted as saying.

The narrative constituents of the 'second' and 'third wave' of infection provided *ACP*'s required 'new angle'. Indeed some months before this newspaper article appeared, *ACP*'s social worker adviser, Virginia Foster, who worked at the Wayside Chapel at Kings Cross, had already passed on to the production team the 'second/third wave' narrative. She knew that the team was planning to write the character of Sophie out of the series, and so she suggested that Sophie could die of AIDS contracted from sex with an injecting drug-user boyfriend or by sharing a needle. Foster was also concerned to get the message across to the *ACP* audiences that women were at risk of HIV infection:

> I thought it would be good to 'knock Sophie off' with AIDS because then it would show people that she was a drug addict, she was also a prostitute, so there was a whole combination of ways that she could have got AIDS. *And* she was a female, because despite all the educational material and a lot of brochures, I think a lot of people still have in their minds that it's a homosexual disease and we've really got to get rid of that. So that's why I pushed that point.

Official and 'expert' discourses had provided an agent of villainy: drug addiction and the shared needle. They also provided the human relationship victims of a soap opera tragedy: young friends sharing needles or the trusting partners of drug users or prostitutes. The narrative scenario was also provided: the city red-light district, hotbed of injecting drug users and prostitution. Forrest Redlich, after speaking with Foster, quickly saw the potential of turning the threat of the 'second/third wave' into drama by avoiding the 'gay angle':

> Everyone had done the prejudices against AIDS. Even American comedy had done the 'sweet little boy who comes in and declares himself a

'Turning tricks in back alleys': Terence (and social worker) encounters the agent (needle-sharing), victim (Paul) and scenario (Kings Cross) of AIDS.

homosexual with AIDS' and we all cry a lot. So what we were constantly trying to come up with was a new angle, and we fell on to it inadvertently while researching a heroin story at the Wayside Chapel—from a dramatic point of view it gave us an angle that nobody had exploited yet. It's the indiscriminate kids who experiment with heroin, or who use needles communally, who can transfer the disease. And if you're talking about a way to get into the heterosexual community, your examples are things like a strung-out prostitute who's looking for a quick fifty bucks to score some heroin, who has AIDS antibodies, who then turns a quick sort of 'rough bang' in a back alley, cops her fifty bucks, and away she goes. The guy goes home, you know, with AIDS positive.

One of the writers of the 'Sophie' episodes, Tony Morphett (who had also written the *The Flying Doctors* episode on AIDS two years previously), was similarly enthusiastic about this approach in terms of the 'health information' and 'raising public awareness' aspects of the story:

It's a good time to be telling this needle-sharing story in Australia, because at the moment AIDS owing to needle-sharing is quite rare here, compared with, say, New York where they've got a higher rate of it. In Australia you are still looking at a situation where 87 per cent of AIDS cases are homosexual males or bisexual males. You've got 6 per cent coming out of the blood transfusion window before the blood started to get tested well. Then there are two areas—heterosexual transmission and shared needle transmission which are quite low at the moment in Australia. So it makes sense to bore in on these areas at the moment in terms of giving the public information—these are the areas which are now going to balloon.

Clearly Morphett was well informed; *ACP* always took pride in 'getting the facts right', and employed a trained nurse to make sure it did so on the medical side as well as taking advice from 'experts' like Virginia Foster on the construction of storylines.

Forrest Redlich's and Tony Morphett's descriptions are similar in narrative detail to the newspaper article on the 'third wave', suggesting intertextuality. But this is not simply a case of one media form 'influencing' another. The interviews with Redlich and Morphett were in fact carried out a few months before the newspaper article was published. This indicates that a dominant discourse on AIDS, emphasising the 'second/third wave' threat, was becoming available from commonly accessed 'expert' sources and then was transformed for the public via a variety of media forms and genres: in this case, soap opera and 'hard' news. When we speak of 'intertextuality' here, we are not suggesting that one media producer gets his or her 'ideas' from another. Rather, we are examining the ways in which dominant discourses circulating in different cultures—for example, in the 'expert' cultures of the medical profession and its ancillary industries (like social work and health promotion), as well as in the commercial sector of the media industry—mutually coalesce and reproduce each other.

As this suggests, the medical profession 'gets its facts right' not simply in relation to some 'objective' statistical or clinical norm about the modes of HIV transmission in Australia and the United States, but as a *communication* norm, potentially attractive to audiences, via the production and reproduction of new narratives and metaphors in a variety of media. In this sense, the various narratives—of AIDS 'experts' and authorities, of the news media, of public health advertisements and of television drama such as *ACP*—are mutually reinforcing fictions which construct 'AIDS' in a conjunction of professional domains. The 'three waves' narrative could now, it seems, 'bore in' (we note the hypodermic-style metaphor) on *ACP*'s audiences. However, as we have emphasised, neither television drama nor any other media form works this way—neutrally 'transmitting' messages. Nor do the producers of commercial soap opera see it as purely a pedagogical medium. 'Research' (derived from medical and other 'experts' and other sources) and 'master plans' are the warp and weft of a program embedded in the institutional and economic structure of new networking arrangements, lower advertising revenue and strong competition for ratings from other channels. Commercial soap opera is not designed simply to 'educate' audiences but to attract their attention, entertain them and sell advertising space. As Hugh Stuckey, an *ACP* story editor, observed, 'The drama *really* comes first. If that doesn't entertain, there's no point putting messages in'. There is also the imperative to manipulate storylines so that regular characters are featured as much as possible: 'we don't believe the audience has as much interest in people they see for only two nights as in the ones they have come to know and love' (quoted in Tulloch & Moran 1986, pp. 66–7).

At this point of transmission of the AIDS and drug use 'message', the 'current reality' (the three waves narrative) had to be translated into dramatic writing. This was a process of transformation from one verbal text (that provided by social work adviser, Virginia Foster, for instance) into another—that of the writer, where, as we shall see, a range of other commercial, aesthetic, personal and social intertexts operate.

WRITING THE 'SOPHIE' TEXTS

As noted above, the 'Sophie' story ran over four episodes (two weeks) and, as was usual with the *ACP* production process, each episode was written by a different person. In the case of the 'Sophie' episode block, Forrest Redlich's 'master plan' of the storyline was taken into a two-day story conference with the writers: David Boutland (part one), Tony Morphett (part two), David Phillips (part three) and Judy Colquhoun (part four). Each writer was given a two-page plot summary for the episode they were writing, from which they had to construct a 15-scene episode. Writers were also provided with information about heroin use, youth work related to injecting drug users, medical information about drug use and HIV/AIDS, and the geographical setting of Sydney's Kings Cross. For example, Tony Morphett, the writer of the second episode, was given 'basic stuff about Kings Cross, about the Wayside Chapel, about how we'd go about the search, medical details . . . I knew that my episode would end up on the revelation that Sophie has AIDS'. The task of each writer was to take the basic master plan and 'flesh it out'. This process takes place as a series of discussions and sometimes arguments within the production team. As Morphett observed: 'When you go through that two-day process of thrashing the story out and breaking it up, the writers have a very large input. I'm often teamed with David Boutland, and David argues every point. There's a lot of creative dispute and argument goes on there'.

New constructions of AIDS emerged from the need to find a 'new angle' that went beyond having Sophie return to Wandin Valley to overcome her heroin addiction, as previous episodes had already covered this angle. The transformation from two-page plot summary to 15-scene episode was thus a process of negotiation between intertexts: working out of 'master plan' texts, avoiding narratives 'we've done before' and accessing 'new angles' for other, pre-established narratives and texts lodged in personal and cultural memory.

Tony Morphett was particularly interested in highlighting the marital problems between Terence and Alex in dealing with Sophie's effect on their relationship. He himself was in his second marriage, with stepchildren, and drew on his personal experience to write about the situation. He was anxious to avoid sentimentalisation (using the American series *The Brady Bunch* as an example to be avoided) and to construct 'real' characterisation:

> Terence's primary impulse is ruling everything at the moment, and that is 'get my daughter back to Wandin Valley, straighten her out, get her clean again'. Meanwhile we're looking at the fear of the second wife, Alex—of what the intrusion of this heroin-addicted adult is going to do to her marriage with Terence. She's finding out what everybody involved in a second marriage finds out, and that is that you marry the person's past. That sub-plot of Alex's reaction to the idea of Sophie coming back was roughed out in a line or so of the given material, but it wasn't

elaborated. It seemed to me to be very important to elaborate because so many people these days are in second and third marriages, and it's an area that we don't look at dramatically, or alternately it's an area that tends to be sentimentalised a lot. You know, everyone is a saint and welcomes stepchildren with open arms. It interested me a lot. I have two stepchildren from my wife's first marriage, and my wife has three stepchildren from my first marriage, so I've been through that 'stepping' situation a lot. And it's always seemed to me that in drama it's been either ignored or sentimentalised in the way that, say, *The Brady Bunch* sentimentalises it.

Here stories from personal memory are compared with other intertexts (sentimentalised tales from American television) and the latter found wanting. As we go on to demonstrate, however, the transformation that Morphett worked on the two-page summary was not through contrasting the 'real' with unelaborated or sentimentalised fiction. In fact, Morphett's '15 scenes through the hour', which were already embedded in commercial narratives (for example, the need to find 'new angles') continued to be constructed intertextually in a number of different ways: by way of other, fictionalised texts (or 'back-stories') invented prior to 'Sophie', by way of high cultural models like Shakespeare, by way of stories heard at Alcoholics Anonymous, by way of urban myths about work and exploitation, by way of *The Brady Bunch*. All of these provided intertextual context for the writing of the 'Sophie' episodes.

For *ACP* to be not 'sentimentalised' meant to be 'responsible', to deal with 'real' social issues through 'real' characters. This understanding of 'real' character is, of course, very much in the tradition of two high cultural concepts. The first is the Stanislavsky Method which requires actors to bring with them to their parts the details of character in the unscripted 'off-stage' scenes (thus requiring a concern for 'back-stories' and character 'density'). The second is the 'Shakespearian balance' (as Morphett put it) between 'light' and 'heavy' plots, and between parallel stories: 'It's absolutely axiomatic that the subject ought to be related to, or parallel in some way, the main plot. You can see it working in *Othello* where you have jealousy played out at all levels' (Morphett). In the case of 'Sophie', producer Forrest Redlich was most concerned to emphasise (via a series of 'parallel' sub-plots across the four parts of the episode) that young people are not only prey to drug addiction but are also subject to other problems, including being exploited at work by adults, experiencing the despair of unemployment and suffering family breakdown. Subsequently the 'Sophie' episodes were also planned to include scenes portraying a young girl in her first job serving fast food being fired by her employer when she turns eighteen, unemployed young people drinking in a squat, and the story of a father who deserts his children while looking for a straying wife (this story itself parallelling the back-story of Sophie abandoned as a child by Terence).

In implied contrast, of course, is the method of popular drama. Not for these writers the 'invention' of characters simply to populate a scenario motivated by car chase or gun fight. For Tony Morphett 'it's basic to my approach to writing that action grows out of character'. Stephen Measday, the script editor, was also concerned to deal with 'real' social issues through 'real' characters, ensuring that characters are not 'shallow', appearing to have a believable personal history:

> One of the things that the script editors often talk about is not having shallow characterisations. Each is somebody who had a life before and will go on afterwards as well. That's all very well established for the regulars, but where a main character [like Sophie] comes in as a guest a lot of the conference time can be spent discussing those aspects: where was this person before they arrived? Where would they go now? Do they have a family? What records do they like? Are they interested in the theatre? Do they drink? A lot of that stuff then bears on how the writers go away and fill out the characters in the episode.

In the writers' view, however, the success of the character was due to the 'realism' of the back-story of Sophie's heroin addiction as well as the acting. Morphett was also concerned to emphasise that middle-class people could become addicted to heroin and therefore render themselves susceptible to HIV/AIDS. In the case of Sophie, a young woman from a privileged background, the move to the squalid life of a Kings Cross junkie was partly achieved through the 'back-story' constructed of her life as an investigative journalist visiting the world's 'trouble spots' and using heroin as a means of coping with the pressures of her job. She was positioned, therefore, at least initially, as a 'society user' of heroin rather than a 'street junkie'.

Sophie's transition from 'society user' to 'junkie' was based on a personal experience Morphett had of attending an Alcoholics

Anonymous (AA) meeting. At that meeting, he recalled, a 'respectable' middle-class woman explained how she felt about her own secret alcoholism by detailing her experience of seeing a 'derelict' sitting on a park bench with his bottle. For this woman, the old alcoholic had 'come to terms' with his addiction; he knew what was important in his life and had pared his life down to drinking. She found herself envying the man and his honesty. Morphett went on to use this experience to justify Sophie's decline into full-scale heroin addiction:

> I was thinking about this lady as I was thinking about Sophie being surrounded by people with high income levels. She went to the Cross to score and saw a boy shooting up in an alley. And she said 'I realised that he'd come to terms with it, that he knew what was important'. It was a revelation to her, and so she befriended the boy. This was Paul. Paul had been up at a pub, he'd just sold himself for fifty bucks, he'd just gone round the corner, bought his little baggy, and shot up in an alley outside the place where he lived because he really didn't want to spend the time going up the stairs. And this to Sophie was the revelation. This was the window into reality, that you could actually stop worrying about all the other stuff and give yourself over to heroin. And this was the moment I was looking for, which turned the middle-class society addict into the street junkie. It was the embracing of the street junkie culture, which is about nothing except finding the money, borrowing the money, cracking it to get the money, stealing the money, stealing the stuff to get the money, to get the smack to put in your arm, or leg, or eyeball, or wherever you happen to be using at the moment. That was the moment I was looking for, and that actually came out of the woman at the AA.

Another, more psychological, dimension of Sophie's addiction was her experiences in early childhood. At the story conference, Morphett emphasised the importance of the scene where Terence, after finding Sophie in a flat in Kings Cross, hears her memories of childhood: memories of the death of her brother David and Terence's subsequent retreat into alcohol before he left his family altogether. Stephen Measday's story conference notes for this episode contain an important comment from Morphett:

> Where did things start to go wrong? Secondary school—everyone was too busy—Dad working—12 when Terence left home—year after David died. Her life stops at 11 . . . He spent a year being drunk, shouting

at Mum—The year he drank he destroyed her hero worship . . . NOTE 'I woke up in the middle of the night—I came downstairs—I wanted to talk—and I saw you drunk in a chair with a bottle—and I thought you were dead. You were so ugly, face drawn, head down. You looked worse than I do now'.

Later, in an interview, Morphett commented on his thinking behind the story conference note:

> In terms of accidents on the road, in terms of the percentage of people who are in gaol, in terms of crimes of violence, alcohol is implicated far more than heroin. And, indeed, medically speaking, is more dangerous to withdraw from. I was conscious of the fact that Terence was a person who'd had a drug problem himself in the past, and this had to have had an effect on his relationship with his daughter, and had to have had an effect on his daughter's view of how you solved your problems. I said to Stephen 'put this down', and I just had this picture of the girl, waking in the night, going downstairs and finding her father unconscious because of his drinking. Because it struck me that you were looking at two things there: the drug addiction story and a lack of communication story. It was just an important picture that I wanted reflected in the notes, so that when I sat down to write it'd be in front of me.

The specific comparison between heroin and alcohol addiction, however, that Morphett had inserted in the story conference notes ('you looked worse than I do now') was missing from the final script—and with it, arguably, the most overt marker of the societal, all-age problem of addiction that was contained in his original script notes. On the other hand, Tony Morphett's 'street culture' slant had an unexpected ally in the precise time demands of network television, through the agency of script editor Bill Searle.

SCRIPT EDITING

The major task of the script editor on 'Sophie' was to maintain unity between the style of the different writers. This was made more difficult on this occasion because, as a result of the recent ratings success of various mini-series on Australian television, it had been decided to do a four-part (instead of the usual two-part) story, and run 'Sophie' over two weeks. Thus there were four (not two) different writers. Morphett was disappointed that they had not taken the mini-series concept further, to enable Sophie to develop a 'living with AIDS' inflection:

> I really believe that we killed Sophie off too fast. We reveal that she has AIDS and then two episodes later she dies of an overdose. I think that this is a bit too easy by far. I would have liked to have watched the effect of having an AIDS patient in Terence and Alex's house, the effect that would have on their practice, the effect on their marriage. I think it would have been a very interesting story to have run for maybe six weeks.

The in-house producers' rejection of this idea was mainly on commercial grounds. As Stephen Measday put it, there were worries that 'we've got a couple of great stories here [but] if we keep it going for three weeks, will the audience switch off?' However, Morphett's other idea of giving 'junkie culture' more of a profile in the 'Sophie' episodes was given a nudge by the script editor, Bill Searle, who isolated a significant timing problem after the rehearsals. Episode two was running short. To deal with this, Searle wrote an entirely new scene for 'Sophie' to add more time to the episode, centring around a discussion between Terence Elliot and Maggie Sloan about the legalisation of heroin. As Searle notes, this scene came about because:

> We needed something in there, and I didn't want to write another sub-plot. I also thought that maybe there was another angle to this whole thing that we hadn't looked at, and I knew the heroin legalisation idea was one that Jim Davern wanted to feed into an earlier script, and it didn't fit in that script. It occurred to me, knowing that we would need a little bit more time, that this was the perfect hour to stick it in.

In the scene with Matron Sloan, Terence moves towards the idea of legalising heroin precisely to break the nexus of the junkie economy that Morphett describes: 'about nothing except finding the money . . . stealing the money, stealing the stuff to get the money, to get the smack to put in your arm'. Notably, here again the story came from another text (from an earlier *ACP* storyline and 'an idea that Jim Davern was keen to have floated'). It was discarded there and inserted instead in the Sophie episodes in the context of a need to 'pad out' an episode without introducing another subplot.

A further text influencing the shooting of this 'legalise heroin' scene was that of a news report. The director of the episode, Leigh Spence, had originally thought that the scene was 'preachy' and that it might come across too much like a government health campaign. Spence's opinion changed, however, when he heard an item on a radio news program about the issues around the legalisation of heroin, which 'really pointed that scene up as real to me. Because then I realised it was a lot more important—what [Terence] was saying—than I originally thought'. This change of heart had an effect on camera angles and how Spence directed the actors in the scene, with a greater emphasis on Terence's face as he spoke the words announcing his belief that heroin should be legalised.

CONCLUDING COMMENTS

In this chapter we have seen that the transformation of an AIDS story from its 'three waves' focus in the 'expertise' discourse of professional social workers to the finished script is a continuous play of intertexts, in which new AIDS meanings and narratives are continuously added to the production agenda. Some (for example, the legalising heroin narrative) stay on the agenda. Others drop off: for example, the teenage alcoholism/rural unemployment subplot (which would have extended the 'class' debate of 'Sophie') was edited out after recording, leaving as its only trace the country squat where Sophie dies. Still other stories temporarily drop off (for example, Morphett's parallel between Terence's alcoholism and his daughter's heroin addiction), but are reintroduced later in the transcoding process (see chapter 7). None of this is just happenstance. Deeply embedded in commercial requirements of planning, budgeting, attracting and maintaining audience interest, these values of practice amount to a structure which underpins a text that, as well as being 'quality soap', is also a 'commodity'.

PASTORAL SPACE AND COMMERCIAL TIME:
'SOPHIE' IN IMAGE, MUSIC AND SOUND

In the previous chapter we looked at writing an AIDS television text as a process of intertextual transformation. We observed the ways that AIDS and other social messages additional to that of the 'three waves' become text as the result of a series of relatively separate verbal and written institutional practices. These included forward-planning meetings, receiving advice from 'expert' sources, research at the Wayside Chapel, in-house two-page narrative plotting, story conferences, script writing and script editing. Overall, we can see these practices as a series of specific institutional sites where specific professional tasks are performed (for example, script writer Tony Morphett finding the narrative device to translate Sophie from middle-class journalist to Kings Cross 'junkie'; script editor Bill Searle timing the script and adding a new scene) before the text is passed on to the next stage of production.

All of these practices are, as we began to see in the last chapter, embedded in commercial and aesthetic reading formations that provide some coherence as new stories about AIDS and other issues wax and wane. Reading formation has been defined as 'the product of definite social and ideological relations of reading composed, in the main, of those apparatuses—schools, the press, critical reviews, fanzines—within and between which the socially dominant forms for the superintendence of reading are both constructed and contested' (Bennett & Woollacott 1987, pp. 64–5). A reading formation, then, is a semiotic institution that is determined discursively and intertextually. It serves to organise the reading practices of audiences, constituting readers as certain types of subjects and shaping the particular ways in which texts are read.

By the time that the completed script reaches rehearsal and studio, all of these practices are encoded as written text. The two-page summary narrative and research notes have been transformed, but not yet transcoded. This scripted text is still in the form of written language. In the process of studio production and editing it is, of course, transcoded from a verbal language into an audio-visual one. It is performed, shot, and edited for image and sound. Together these different coding systems (of gesture, space, language, image, music and sound) create what Roland Barthes called the 'real informational polyphony', the 'density of signs' (cited in Elam 1980, p. 19) of the performed text. As performance semiotician Keir Elam notes:

> At each moment the spectator will have to assimilate perceptual data along diverse channels, perhaps conveying identical dramatic information (e.g. simultaneous pictorial and linguistic references to the scene of action) but transmitting different kinds of signal-information. The first characteristic of this discourse is thus its semiotic thickness. (1980, pp. 44–5)

From the point of view of textual meaning, this semiotic 'thickness' is obviously a complicating factor. One of the main features of the semiotically 'thick' text is what Elam calls its temporal unfolding: 'Not all the contributory systems will be operative at every point in the performance; each message and signal will at times fall to a zero level' (1980: 45). For example, the Sophie/Terence addiction parallel (he to alcohol, she to heroin) that story editor Stephen Measday was keen to emphasise at the story planning stage came close to 'falling to zero' between Measday's story conference notes and Morphett's written script, because the link is implied in the script rather than directly referred to. However, this parallel was eventually taken up overtly, as we shall show later, by a musical cue.

LIGHTING 'THE DARK SIDE'

As Elam notes, a major responsibility for the overall semantic and stylistic coherence of the performed text lies with the director, as well as with the actors who 'show forth' the text. All the television professionals responsible for the images, music and sound, however, are also responsible for the coherence of the text. In *ACP* and other popular television performances, each professional works within a dominant naturalist paradigm, establishing 'psychologically plausible' gesture, lighting mood, music sound effects, set design and so on. In *ACP*, for example, a 'glow' and 'warmth' are routinely constructed in the effort to represent a pastoral setting. This 'warmth' is an

Pastoral overcoding: the 'warmth' of lighting and human interaction in the country. Terence and Sophie at 'Camelot'.

important unifying feature of the house style of *ACP*. It permeates not only its narratives (as we discussed in chapter 4), but also its visual and audio style. This pastoral 'overcoding' is very important in maintaining the semantic and stylistic coherence of the semiotically 'thick' *ACP* text; and strongly determines the textual meaning of any AIDS story inserted therein.

For the 'Sophie' episodes, director Leigh Spence intended to use lighting to contrast the city scenes with the country scenes. He gave instructions that he 'wanted sunlight in "Camelot" [Terence and Alex's house]. I wanted it to be warm and pleasant, so that it would contrast with the dark side that was being played. Had I done those scenes in dark rooms and shadows, I thought it would be melodramatic'. 'Camelot' would be the setting for Sophie's revelation to Terence that she is HIV positive, and also where Terence and Alex would argue bitterly over her. Human tragedy here, in the country, was to be played out in the sunshine, while the *visual* 'menace' in 'Sophie' was confined to Kings Cross and to the derelict house where

Sophie would die. This house, as the squat of unemployed alcoholic youths, was an extension of 'city problems' into the country.

In fact, the 'sunlight in "Camelot"' visual concept was deeply embedded in *ACP*'s 'laughter and tears' formula, according to the lighting director, John Norton:

> When the show was first started, it was very important to have an overall concept because most of the show was being shot in and around hospitals. We gave it that clinical hospital look, like fluorescent light, coldish light. At the same time, to get the contrast between the hospital and the farm houses that we do as studio interiors, we wanted to see the sunlight coming through the windows. We wanted to see it nice and bright outside so that we could get the contrast between the hospital and the farm areas. Because it's out in the country, we felt that people want to see the country atmosphere as nice bright windows and sun streaming through them.

As Norton described it, with the established lighting concepts laid down, they could be adapted slightly for particular stories and directors: 'As in this block, with Sophie dying, we've got to be a little bit more dramatic. And that means a lot more shadows, a lot more treatment on the walls, seeing shadows, seeing lines, and making it a little bit more contrasty than normal'. Consequently, when the other 'Sophie' director, Bob Meillon, asked his lighting director Bob Miller to give him pools of light in the dingy Kings Cross set 'to get mood, a bit of feeling into it', he was simply extending and adapting lighting conventions based on the 'warm' country's Other places: those places such as the city where 'problems' were encountered.

In the 'Sophie' episodes the 'softness' of country light was used to suffuse whole scenes, as where Terence and his daughter talk about her problems at 'Camelot':

> *Norton* 'Camelot' had beautiful stonework inside the kitchen and lovely timbergrain shelving and woodwork. Our scenic artists had one window over the sink, in the back of the set. So we decided to add to the general softness of the whole set. It was in very dark tones and beautifully textured brickwork; we put a big scrim over the back window and lit it all from that window. So that no matter where they're standing, the cameras get all the light appearing to come from the window, even though it's coming from just above the window, just out of sight.

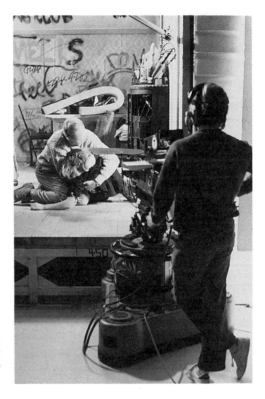

The squat as the country's 'other dangerous place': Terence finds the dead Sophie.

This softening light was also imported to the 'city' scenes, where appropriate. For instance, the scenes in part two when Terence and Sophie talk nostalgically about her childhood, with Terence staring out the window of her flat:

> *Miller* Terence was staring out of the window. Bob Meillon wanted a bit of feeling in there; which is good for us because we use a lot of source light. If there's a window we'll use it as the source, like natural light; and we'll push a big soft light through there. And over that window we'll put a rolex diffuser and put a light through that so it covers the whole set as well as coming through the window, so that it gives the feeling that it's all coming through there.

Even that window in the squalid Kings Cross flat, then, resonated with the softer, brighter light of the country. Or more precisely, it resonates with the illusion of something better as Terence turns his back on Sophie's room and on her memory of his own drunken past.

If, in the semiotic density of the 'Sophie' text, the 'country' is primarily signified by light, the city squalor of Kings Cross is conveyed by set design and sound. Art director Steve Muir had already read the scripts of 'Sophie' before the first studio production meeting and so had established his own perception of what was needed for the Sophie/Paul room in Kings Cross:

> I read the scripts; they told me how it was really seedy, the sort of conditions that junkies live in. And although I've never seen it myself, I just established the fact that it would be a pretty derelict sort of place, because they don't have that much, they don't have money for rent. There wouldn't be very much furniture because [Sophie and Paul] have probably hocked it for their heroin habit. So it was just basically a pretty run-down building that they were living in. For a set like that the colours are better if they're dull colours with not a lot of reflectants, because the whole mood of the story is quite drab and sad. So the colours I used were mainly greys and tones of beige in the set—no vibrant colours whatsoever. There was graffiti in the hallway, which was just to indicate that the kids come into the place and vandalise it. Just to show that it was really in quite a state of neglect.

For director Leigh Spence, Muir had to design the interior of the derelict house in the country—again squalid and vandalised—where the alcoholic teenagers squatted, and where Sophie would finally shoot up with Paul, overdose and die. If the window light in Sophie's room in King's Cross was an illusory extension of the country, this squat, signifying 'menace', was an extension of Kings Cross addiction into the country. As Muir said, 'Sophie was going to die in it, so again all the colouring had to be really sombre. Because of the fact that she was going to die there we used the grey floor and the dark stone fireplace, which helps to give the mood'. As with the 'serious' hospital scenes, as with the Kings Cross flat, so with the squat where Sophie would die: visually it was that Other dangerous place designed in contrast to the sunshine of the country.

Yet it is at 'Camelot' that, at the end of part two of 'Sophie', Terence learns that Sophie is HIV positive. It is in that bright kitchen, with its friendly kitchen table, warm sandstone walls and homely furnishings that, in the immediately previous scene, Terence makes his last attempt to, as it were, bring Sophie safely home to the country. Terence and Alex argue in mid shot about Sophie, then Alex exits and Bob Meillon's camera goes wide as Sophie enters with the words, 'I don't blame her—if it were my house and marriage I wouldn't want a junkie daughter barging in'. The shot cuts to Terence, busy getting breakfast at that friendly table, saying, 'I want you to try and stop thinking about yourself in those terms', as the light streams through the window behind. Then the camera moves so that Terence blocks out the light; the phone rings, and he goes into the hallway, learning there about Sophie's news. This final interaction between Terence and Sophie is shot in extreme close-up, and contrasts with the comfortable 'country' *mise en scène* of the earlier wide shot in the kitchen. Camera style, lighting format and set design all work together here to play out the *ACP* text of warm and cool light, laughter and tears.

'A KIND OF MENACE': SOUNDING 'SOPHIE'

Over those two scenes at the end of Tony Morphett's episode of 'Sophie', audio director Howard Fricker incorporated two sound effects. Over the kitchen scene, Fricker ensured simultaneous trans-coding by matching the work of the lighting and scenic personnel with his own peaceful country sounds: bird noises, a cow, the distant sound of geese—all very soft and quite difficult for an audience to hear. This background sound continues beneath Terence's phone conversation with Dr Black from the city hospital, and stops suddenly as Sophie takes the phone. The brief, almost subliminal pause in background sound introduces the ominous 'Kings Cross' music, menacing, pulsating, and prefiguring the extreme close-up of Sophie, and moments later her words, 'He's telling me I'm AIDS positive'. This example indicates a central feature of Fricker's sound style: that music travels, sound does not:

> The music carries her drug abuse problem, the sound effects don't. The
> sound effects are typical Kings Cross effects. The overuse of sirens—and

I will admit they are overused—is basically to add a feeling of pain, a feeling of ongoing crisis. There were police sirens and ambulance sirens to add an air of urgency. I don't want you to forget where you are. I made the sirens as repetitive as I could because I wanted it as though the Cross is a continual whirlpool, which is basically all the same, nothing ever changes, week in, week out, and it's an ongoing problem. Sophie's only one of millions, over a period of years. She's one of many people who has run into the same problem.

With his sound effects, Fricker was wanting to emphasise that 'they were in the Cross', whereas the music—wherever it was played (including at 'Camelot')—needed to bring 'you right back into the Cross every time—it needed to hurt'.

'Sophie' producer Bruce Best went to the unusual length of employing a special incidental music composer, Rhys Rees, for this important 'mini-series' version of *ACP*. Rees first saw 'Sophie' after the producers' preview (in other words, after the studio and off-line editing stages).

Rees It was obvious that there had to be a Sophie theme, but also something for the Cross, two totally different fields. The Sophie theme was more orchestral: strings, piano and oboe. I thought the Cross had to be more modern instruments or modern sounds, and also a kind of menace, whereas Sophie's theme I wrote down in my notes as 'a sense of loss'. Terence wandering around looking for his daughter who was obviously from a good background, somebody who had everything going for her, but has lost direction, or basically was throwing her life away through being a heroin addict. So I actually wrote down 'a sense of loss' as a sort of inspiration, although, funnily enough, the theme I used I had already written some time ago. It was a kind of sad tune, and it just fitted that 'loss' idea.

The 'lonely' and 'nostalgic' pipe and oboe are, of course, conventional instruments signifying the pastoral, and Rees' use of an already recorded piece in this style for Sophie's theme was therefore not particularly surprising. Also conventional were the sounds of police sirens to invest the Kings Cross setting with 'a kind of menace'. The shepherd's pipe, or in this case the 'nostalgic' sound of the oboe, was carrying the sense of loss of a better, purer past (in the country/in childhood) to the degenerate city.

Music, then, as Fricker says, is portable in 'Sophie'. The oboe of Sophie's theme goes to the city and the 'music that hurts' of the Kings Cross setting returns to the country. In particular, for his transportable Kings Cross music, Rees made use of the ominous tinkling sound of a bell-tree:

> *Rees* It's a stick with lots of bells on it. I used that a lot. I tried to use it whenever the dialogue was talking about heroin. There were a couple of places where I used that specifically where heroin is mentioned: when Paul reappears at 'Camelot' and when he and Sophie go into the hut.

The bell-tree and musical cello drone is used most obviously in association with Paul. In coming from Kings Cross to the country to lure the reformed Sophie back to her heroin habit, and therefore to her death, Paul is the physical agent of movement from the risk-laden city. As Rees commented, there are two particular locations where the bell-tree and drone are used with 'Kings Cross heroin' effect in the country. The first is at 'Camelot', when Paul actually comes back and takes Sophie away. The second is at the squat Paul and Sophie visit to use heroin. The 'heroin' sound is used in this scene instead of visual images of 'shooting up', since this would not have been accepted by the television channel during family viewing time. This 'shooting up' musical analogy was one case where the visual channel literally, in Elam's words, 'falls to zero', while a 'sudden burst' from the audio channel picks up the meaning.

As well as this 'second/third wave' heroin signification, Rees used the bell-tree in another way in Morphett's long Terence/Sophie scene set in Kings Cross. In this scene there are three distinct musical interludes. Sophie's theme opens the (briefly happy) family nostalgic discussion of Sophie's childhood. The second musical interlude mingles the cold cello drone of 'the Cross' with the nostalgia of Sophie's theme as family memories become suffused with the pain of death, betrayal, addiction and loss. It is here that Sophie's comment about Terence's alcoholism is made; and the parallel between her addiction and his which was lost in Tony Morphett's final script is restored by Rees using his bell-tree over Sophie's lines, 'You fell asleep and your face was sort of collapsed.' Here again, where words 'fall to zero', the bell-tree sound effect picks up the meaning. The third musical interlude, which premises Sophie's return to Wandin Valley and the lost potential of her past, which she will attempt to put right by becoming a serious journalist again, restores Sophie's musical theme. As we argued in chapter 4, there is an *ACP* ensemble (of writing, characterisation, set design, lighting, sound and music) that is recognisably 'pastoral' in its style. It is the sharing of semantic content (this overcoding of the text as pastoral) by the various channels of audio-visual communication that establishes the dominant meanings and coherences of the transcodified text. It was into this audio-visually over-determined series text that the 'three waves' AIDS message was inserted. Far from moving smoothly in a linear direction from expert 'source' through 'transmitter' to 'destination', the 'expert' message linking injecting drugs, heterosexuality and HIV/AIDS risk had to encounter a pre-existing text, and a 'transmitter' with strongly established formulae and idiolects of its own. By idiolect we mean a professional subcode: for instance, *ACP* set designers far prefer sets with 'character' (an old house interior in the country rather than a modern gyprock city flat). Different set designers, however, will inflect 'character' in different ways; one emphasising 'natural' interiors in stone, brick and wood (as at 'Camelot'), another working with 'heritage' colours, and so on.

One example of pre-existing formulae was the choice of Sophie as the vehicle for a 'second wave/third wave' story. In the context of the Kings Cross, homeless kids and drug addiction scenario, Sophie was much too old. The needle-sharing 'street kids' who Virginia Foster encountered as part of her work as a youth social worker were usually in their mid-adolescence or younger. Sophie, however, as an already established character in *ACP*, pre-existed this narrative. She was part of the *ACP* dramatic master plan, introduced to create conflict and dramatic tension, 'throw a spanner in the works' of the soap opera's happy family. Because of this age problem, Paul was designed as a younger lover for Sophie. Paul would thus represent the 'street kids' in Davern's view; and as lover and friend of the 'regular' character Sophie, as well as a 'young rebel', would attract audience empathy. In our view, however, this intention did not work, for the program's pastoral overcoding constructed Paul as Other—from the dirty, degenerate city (see our discussion of audience responses in chapter 10). This was emphasised by the music scorer's own idiolect of contrasting the abrasive 'city' bell-tree used in Paul's appearances with the nostalgic 'country' oboe.

SEQUENCING AIDS: TIME COORDINATES

Most of our production analysis up to this point has focused on the space coordinates of 'Sophie'; on the way in which HIV/AIDS narratives are contextualised and given meaning according to professional idiolects and intertexts that represent negotiated strategies in the broad context of commercial television. The emphasis has been on the individual writer, set designer, director, music composer, lighting director and so on within their particular context, and this in turn contextualised within a broader commercial aesthetic. The process has been to work outwards from individual practice to global commercial space. In this section we will focus more directly on the time coordinates of making AIDS television in this commercial context.

A relatively short time before the 'Sophie' episodes were made, Australian commercial television had been networked nationally. This, as producer Bruce Best explained, had made the process of 'timing the product' much more difficult:

> Because of networking you have to hit the half hour exactly. Because they put their news out at 8 o'clock we have to cut the program to a fairly precise time at the halfway mark. And in the actual overall duration there's no tolerance anymore at all. It just *has* to come out at 46 minutes. If it's more than 46 minutes they simply cut it off. It simply doesn't go to air.

Exact timing, then, is crucial: an episode must not be longer than 46 minutes. The script has, of course, been timed by the script editor for rehearsal; and the director's assistant has timed every take during recording. So, by the time of the first edit, the director has a fairly clear idea of the size of the problem. It is at the producers' editing preview that the hard decisions about timing are made. Two of the four episodes had very major cuts finalised at this stage. It was at the producers' preview that Best began by saying of 'Sophie' part four: 'This one's a minute over, so we'll pull a minute out of the cemetery scene. It's too long'. That comment marked the closing stages of a professional tussle which had begun just after the location edit two weeks earlier. It also marked the predictable collision between 'visual style' and commercial demands of timing.

The cemetery scene was the denouement of the 'Sophie' episodes, closing part four, in which Terence is shown reading Sophie's account of her life as a journalist and 'junkie' (detailed in chapter 4). Two production workers were particularly committed to this scene. The writer of this episode, Judy Colquhoun, regarded this scene as 'the favourite thing I've written in the last fifteen years. They rarely come off the way you want them to. But that one came off'. For her, the lines marked the fact that the 'only thing that Sophie had left at the end was that she was a good journalist. That's her tragedy as I see it. Here she is dying of AIDS at twenty-three, when she could have been on the front cover of *Time*'. Leigh Spence chose these lines as the *pièce de résistance* of his 'visual style' as director. The sequence was filmed at a churchyard in the countryside west of Sydney. It was a fine morning, mist was rising from the nearby river, and Spence took the unusual step of shooting earlier than usual, before breakfast at 7.30 a.m.. This was to catch the last of the mist rising in the valley beyond Terence. His opening camera position was high on a ramp, and from there the steadicam was to move down and towards Terence as he holds Sophie's letter over the rose-strewn grave:

> *Spence* My feeling about the scene—and I thought it was beautifully written, I kept getting lumps in my throat when I read it—was to do it all in one continuous shot, so that the vision was following the audio. What I wanted was the audience to get the loneliness of this man, and that's why you go back wide, and slowly just go further and further into his emotion as you come forward. So it was almost three minutes of continuous moving around him.

Spence directed Katrina Sedgwick, the actor who played Sophie, to read the letter in a flat, unemotional voice: 'I thought, being a journalist, she would read it as a journalist, without emotion, as just a reportage of what she had written'. The emotion was to be carried neither by her voice nor by Shane Porteous' (Terence) acting, but by the camera.

Predicting problems with this scene, Bruce Best gave quite specific briefings at the directors' meeting about how to shoot it. He advised Spence to use camera tracks to achieve 'a very still look'. But time considerations were important here. It would have taken much longer to shoot the scene using tracks; and Spence would certainly not have got the early morning mist effect had he done so. Writer Judy Colquhoun supported Spence's visual ambition with this scene, saying that *ACP* 'doesn't take enough chances stylistically. I don't think anyone's going to turn off because now and again we stretch the boundaries a bit more than you'd expect in a television serial'. For her, it was crucial that Sedgwick read the letter while Porteous silently 'folded it over and over until it wouldn't fold anymore. I think the actor's good enough to get away with it. He can stand there for a minute and a half with a camera on him. They don't trust the actors enough sometimes'.

The problem for Best was the timing, and maintaining the audience's attention for such a long scene (three minutes, ten seconds). Keeping the audience's attention is, of course, a most important value of practice in commercial television. Sound director Howard Fricker, for instance, told us in detail about his closing sound edit for part one of 'Sophie', which included both reverberation and echo as he blended the slow motion sounds and visuals of the prostitute Sophie running away from her father in Kings Cross with the familiar 'pastoral' closure of the soap opera. As with theColquhoun/Spence graveyard scene, the aesthetics of this gave Fricker enormous satisfaction. But more important for him than the aesthetics of 'probably the best scene I've ever mixed' was the tying in of the audience to keep watching *ACP*:

> What I'm after is to draw people *in* to their television sets, so that they become *part* of that television set, of that show. There are many reasons for doing it. One of them is for artistic reasons. But the *main* reason is to keep people glued to their sets so that the result is the show rates well and we have a saleable product.

Unlike Fricker's concluding scene to part one of 'Sophie', in the case of the graveyard scene Bruce Best believed there would be a conflict between aesthetics and audience attention. Although thinking that the scene was 'beautifully written', he was concerned about its length and emotionality: 'right from the time I first read it, I had a lot of warning bells ringing. I was having trouble right from the word go working out how we were going to convince the audience to hang in. It probably worried me it was a little indulgent, the length of it, the style of it'.

Persuading the audience to 'hang in' and not to change channel was, as always, a central strategy. The audio-visual rhetoric and timing of the scene had to achieve that consuming goal. Best decided that as the finale of the four-episode sequence of 'Sophie', such a long scene would not work, particularly with the 'voice from beyond the grave' implications:

> When the scene came back from the location cut I knew that it couldn't play at the length it came in here. You've got a girl from the other side of the grave reading a story. Now sure, the story has a strong message and there's a lot to be learnt from it, but it was a lot closer to radio than television to put it to air as the wrap-up of the show, of four hours, the last act—I just didn't believe it would work at the full length. The voice from the other side of the grave worried me. I couldn't really see how at that stage of the play, in the final act, we could spend three minutes having a deceased character read us a magazine article. What you are saying is that you are going to try and sustain a scene for three minutes on an actor's face.

In addition, Best complained about the degree of camera shake and he worried about the 'rather timeless' positioning of the scene (was it straight after the funeral or not?) which, together with the 'voice from beyond the grave' gave a rather otherworldly feel to the sequence. A number of assumptions are evident in Best's judgement that this scene, as shot, would lose an audience. They included assumptions of naturalism (camera shake and an undefined time frame), of what makes good television (not 'radio with pictures'), and of what emoting through pictures means (individual, psychologised performance rather than camera style). To deal with each of these 'problems' Best asked that Shane Porteous dub his voice over Sophie's lines during the recording week that followed. Porteous was asked to give 'not a flat delivery, but a more emotive delivery'; and in fact recorded five versions.

After some rather desperate re-editing by Leigh Spence (given that his entire principle of one continuous take had been abandoned), the new version came to the producers' preview, and encountered Bruce Best's opening comment that 'we'll pull a minute out of the cemetery scene'. The producer was still very uneasy with the new version, commenting on its 'self-indulgence' and overly emotional style. He was inclined to 'pull the scene out altogether'. It was eventually kept, but its length was cut down, much to the dismay of the writer, Judy Colquhoun and the director, Spence. Best was unrepentant, though he would have preferred to have gone back and reshot the scene had the urgency of producing 'two hours a week television' allowed it: 'I hate doing that to something that's as well written as that. You do feel like the butcher from wherever at that stage. But in the end you have to trust your instincts'.

CONCLUDING COMMENTS

We want to make two important points by way of our field study of the production of an AIDS television text. First, rather than the linear progression from 'expert' source via neutral receiver to passive destination that the American 'effects' communication tradition perceived, 'facts' and 'expertise' are frequently constructed jointly with new narratives and metaphors circulating in the public domain. Second, the actual process via which health messages enter commercial television narratives is not linear either. In the case of public health television advertisements, there is at least a semblance of a linear sequence as major health problems are specified by health experts, then represented audio-visually by advertising agencies and finally viewed by the public. This sequence is far from clear in commercial television, in which the pedagogic function is secondary to the need to consider budget and timing implications, attract and keep audiences and please advertisers.

Professional 'creativity' is thus all about intertextuality, about accessing, using and recreating existing narratives. Stories (as intertexts) overpopulate 'Sophie'; and they become the produced text of 'Sophie' (or linger as subtexts in the back-story, or disappear altogether) according to the professional culture and idiolects of commercial television. These include the master plans detailing long-term plot and character developments, *ACP*'s 'audience empathy' policy of linking health issues to major characters, its self-conscious position as 'responsible soap' seeking to highlight important social issues such as drug using and AIDS, its emphasis on timing and audience attention, and so on. These are the time and space co-ordinates of popular television. They often operate synchronously, and seldom in the strict linear fashion conceived by 'effects' theory. It is these narratives, these intertexts and these strategic discourses with which a health message must engage; and in the process it is inevitably transformed.

By using a case study we can see clearly how professional, commercial and audience cultures interact. Many references to the responses of 'the audience' have been made by television professionals in this and previous chapters. To what extent *do* audience members read popular television products in the way that their producers intend? Equally, we should not expect a linear flow from knowledge to attitudes to behaviour among audiences. As we will go on to demonstrate, viewers, too, work from within their own sub-cultures with the meanings and narratives of AIDS. We turn to audience research in Part IV.

PART IV

VIEWING AIDS
TELEVISION: AUDIENCE
RESPONSE

READING THE 'GRIM REAPER'

How do television texts contribute to individuals' understandings of phenomena such as AIDS? As we have noted in previous chapters, research emerging from the cultural studies perspective has emphasised that audiences do not respond in a particularly predictable or linear fashion to television texts, whether they are advertisements, documentaries, news reports or fictional programs. While the producers of the television text have specific intentions in shaping the tenor of the text, in encoding a 'preferred' meaning, there are numerous ways in which audiences may respond to the text. It is now generally accepted in communication research that through sheer audience reach and repetition, the mass media may influence individuals, but in largely indirect and cumulative ways. The mass media are viewed as important in disseminating information but less influential in changing attitudes or behaviours. Some researchers have described the 'agenda-setting' function of mass media, or their role in highlighting some issues or events in the public domain and therefore 'heightening public sensitivity' to these issues and events (for example, Bush & Boller 1991). Research has suggested that media products such as television texts are able to raise awareness of health-related issues on a mass scale. To demonstrate, however, that audiences are aware of a specific text is merely to show that they have seen it and, to some extent, remember aspects of it. Whether this 'awareness' translates into changes in the ways that individuals think about or respond to the issue is a completely different question.

In this chapter and the next, we explore in detail audiences' responses to AIDS advertisements sponsored by the Australian government. In this chapter, we focus on responses to the 'Grim Reaper' campaign, drawing upon data from qualitative research using interviews and focus groups. The following chapter uses findings from projects which explored in far greater detail young people's responses to the 'Testimonial' and 'Vox Pop Condom' advertisements, combining both quantitative and qualitative methods.

GENERAL RESPONSES TO THE 'GRIM REAPER'

The official consensus on the effect of the 'Grim Reaper' campaign, according to a glossy publicity pamphlet published in 1991 by the Commonwealth Department of Community Services and Health, was that: 'The "Grim Reaper" achieved the intended result, to shock viewers out of a dangerous apathy'. Furthermore, the pamphlet asserts, 'Media reaction was generally favourable and supportive. Without exception, every newspaper in the country took the view that AIDS was a sufficiently serious threat to warrant the shock tactics of the Reaper advertisement'. As this suggests, the intention of the campaign, therefore, was not simply to stimulate high levels of awareness among the population, but *also* to achieve support among other media as part of a public relations exercise. This is all part of the 'technologisation of discourse' and the promotional uses served by health campaigns to which we referred in chapter 3.

Judging by the coverage given the 'Grim Reaper' campaign by the Australian print media, this latter aim was definitely achieved. The tenor of the campaign was the subject of much debate in the print media, particularly in the week following its launch and first appearance on television, for its use of 'horror-movie' imagery and shock tactics to frighten individuals. Newspaper coverage of the campaign, however, was largely positive. The majority of editorials and feature articles supported the intention of the NACAIDS to warn the Australian population about the threats posed by AIDS. This support on the part of the press is vastly different from the divided response of the British press to that country's AIDS media campaigns, where the conservative newspapers decried the Health Education Authority's attempts to present HIV/AIDS as a threat to heterosexuals, insisting that it was a risk only to gay men and injecting drug users (Murray 1991; Beharrell 1993). According to the Australian press, the use of shock tactics in the 'Grim Reaper' television advertisement was entirely appropriate, given the potentially serious nature of the epidemic. As an editorial in the *Newcastle Herald* opined, 'It was reasonable for the opening government advertisement to emphasise fear, for AIDS is a swift and brutal killer' (15 April 1987). The image of the 'Grim Reaper' itself became used by newspapers as a symbol for the AIDS epidemic, as well as the campaign. A photograph of the 'Grim Reaper' as it appeared in the television advertisement was often employed to illustrate articles about AIDS, as were stylised drawings of the figure (see Lupton 1994a for further details on the press coverage of the campaign).

So too, the objective of attracting a high level of public awareness to the 'Grim Reaper' advertisement seems to have been achieved. A Morgan Gallup poll conducted in September 1987 (five months after the 'Grim Reaper' advertisement was shown), reported that more than half the respondents saw AIDS as the most urgent health problem facing young Australians at that time. Fewer people, however, were concerned about actually contracting HIV themselves than they were at the time the campaign was screened (49 per cent, down 10 per cent), suggesting that the effects of the shock tactics may well have worn off quite quickly. The vast majority of respondents surveyed in September 1987 (82 per cent) did not believe that they needed to change their behaviour because of the threat of HIV/AIDS (Morgan Gallup 1987).

A representative survey of people living in Sydney and Melbourne conducted by the NACAIDS in the month following the release of the campaign found that 97 per cent of respondents had seen the television advertisement, with 95 per cent agreeing that the campaign had increased public awareness of HIV/AIDS and 81 per cent agreeing that it had increased people's knowledge of the syndrome (Taylor 1987). In another random survey of people living in the state of South Australia, 94 per cent of the respondents recalled having seen the 'Grim Reaper' television advertisement; 64 per cent thought the advertisement was a 'good way of campaigning against AIDS' (13 per cent were unsure and 23 per cent thought it was not); and 34 per cent said that they had 'personally been influenced' by the campaign (Ross et al. 1990, p. 343). The campaign remained memorable some years after its brief appearance. One survey of audience response to AIDS in the media carried out in Sydney found that 73 per cent of respondents in 1988 and 72 per cent in 1989 still had unprompted recall of the 'Grim Reaper' television advertisement (Bray & Chapman 1991).

Following the release of the 'Grim Reaper' campaign, AIDS and STD clinics and general practitioners were initially swamped with demands from people seeking HIV tests and information. The number of women attending one clinic for HIV tests increased by 127 per cent and the increase in the number of heterosexual men attending was 154 per cent. During the two weeks that the television advertisement was screened, approximately 40 000 telephone calls were received by the hotline established to deal with inquiries (Commonwealth Department of Community Services and Health 1988). The AIDS information hotline at a Sydney AIDS clinic received an increase in calls of over 300 per cent in the month of the campaign compared with the seven-month period before it had been released. These calls included a marked increase (doubling) in the proportion of women seeking information and in the number of inquiries about HIV testing (Morlet et al. 1988, p. 284). The majority of people seeking testing and information, however, were judged to be at very low risk of infection and appeared to be demonstrating unfounded anxiety. Indeed, it has been claimed that those individuals *most* at risk from HIV infection were discouraged from seeking an HIV test in the months following the 'Grim Reaper' because of the stigmatisation they felt the campaign had engendered (Rosser 1988, p. 368). Furthermore, some people living with HIV/AIDS found the tenor and imagery of the campaign and the accompanying publicity upsetting. As some health workers remarked,

> it was our subjective experience that, during the campaign, some HIV-infected patients who were attending the [clinic] became distressed at the perceived 'remystification' of AIDS by the use of the 'Grim Reaper' analogy. They felt that their social ostracism was being exacerbated by a rising fear of the disease in the community. (Morlet et al. 1988, p. 285)

These statistics suggest that the 'Grim Reaper' television advertisement appeared to have achieved its main objective: to stimulate awareness and concern about the threat posed by HIV/AIDS amongst a wide range of people. Some heterosexuals were frightened enough by the campaign and the associated publicity to request an HIV test or further information about HIV/AIDS from AIDS agencies and clinics. By these measures, the campaign could be broadly considered a success in terms of the aims articulated by its producers. As we noted above, however, these types of surveys are at best blunt instruments if we want to understand the complex ways in which audiences respond to health campaigns. Why has the 'Grim Reaper' advertisement proved so memorable? Why did some people respond with personal concern, while others did not? What were the 'after-effects' of this short-lived campaign? What were its cultural resonances?

While we have not conducted research explicitly focusing on audience responses to the 'Grim Reaper' television advertisement, two projects we carried out in 1993–94 incorporated discussions of HIV/AIDS education campaigns. We asked participants about television campaigns that they recalled having seen over the past years as part of their everyday viewing habits, and what they thought of them. As a result, we were able to explore participants' responses to AIDS television campaigns over the long term, allowing them to reflect on their attitudes in the context of other dimensions of their lives. One study, involving one-to-one interviews with 50 adults living in Sydney, specifically explored the reasons they had decided to have one or more HIV tests (for more details of this research, see Lupton et al. 1995a, 1995b). The other was a project looking at the thoughts and experiences of young people aged 16–17 years in Sydney and rural New South Wales in relation to school-based AIDS education and other sources of information about AIDS. This study used both qualitative and quantitative methods, including focus group discussions with 138 participants, upon which we draw in this chapter (see chapter 11 for further findings from this study).

THE HIV TEST STUDY

The project exploring participants' reasons for having an HIV test involved individuals aged, from 18 to 65 years, from a range of occupations and areas in Sydney. They were invited to participate in an interview if they had had at least one HIV test in the preceding six months. We assumed that such an action indicated, at some level, a personal concern about HIV/AIDS.

One of the questions in the interview asked about the media campaigns participants remembered seeing, and what they thought of them. The 'Grim Reaper' advertisement was remembered by most of the participants, several of whom commented on the personal impact the advertisement had had upon them because of its frightening imagery. The younger participants, at the time of interview in their late adolescence or early twenties, remembered the 'Grim

Reaper' advertisement from their early adolescence before they had become sexually active. As two young female university students said:

> . . . when the 'Grim Reaper' came out it scared me half to death. I thought, 'My God, I should never have done all those things I did in my teenage years!'.

> The 'Grim Reaper' ad, that was one of the things that got me thinking seriously about AIDS, I was about 15.

Several older participants said that they were persuaded to have an HIV test because of this advertising campaign. For example, a 31-year-old female university student said that the 'Grim Reaper' had aroused strong feelings of anxiety and fear:

> . . . the 'Grim Reaper' one, that was in '87. Yeah, that absolutely terrified me, because I'd never had a test, I'd engaged in multiple risky behaviours for a period of about six years . . . and I was just horrified and I thought, 'That's me.' And when I went and had the first test I was 100 per cent sure I was positive before it came back and I was ringing the doctor every day.

Another participant referred to 'this image of this big bowling ball coming down and hitting you into the AIDS alley', approvingly noting that the fear aroused by such advertisements is 'extremely effective' (male professional, aged 26).

Not all those who remembered the 'Grim Reaper' advertisement, however, were positive about it. Indeed most of the members of this group were cynical about the 'scare tactics' employed in the advertisement, with several offering highly derisory or negative evaluations of its crudeness. As one participant said: 'I saw the 'Grim Reaper' one once—I heard a lot about that. It was just too much, it was ridiculous. If you get a message *that* heavy your natural reaction is just to laugh at it' (male professional, 42). Another similarly commented that she found the 'Grim Reaper', 'a bit of a joke . . . I remember laughing at it' (paraprofessional, 20). This person also asserted that the advertisement 'didn't tell me anything—all the ad said was that there was this thing and it was killing people, bowling them over with a ten-pin bowling ball'. A third participant commented that while she had found the 'Grim Reaper' advertisement memorable and controversial, it 'didn't do anything for me, though, I thought it was silly' (paraprofessional, 32).

Some participants suggested that the advertisement may have persuaded people that they were not personally at risk through the dissociation provoked by the horrifying images. One woman said that while the advertisement had an impact on her because it was so shocking, she thought at the time that the campaign was a good idea for 'others', for those 'really at risk':

> At the time it was so distant from me . . . That thing of, you know, it can't happen, it doesn't happen to you, it didn't connect. It was another campaign thing, you think it will be great for the people it needs to get [laugh]. Even though I was at risk and I knew that logically and intellectually I was at risk, it's different your head knowing and you feeling. With any sort of disaster or crisis, it's human, it's natural for humans to think that it's not going to happen to them, it's their way of dealing with it, and I don't know that we'll ever really change that. (health-care worker, 32)

Similarly, another woman emphasised the importance of the campaign to others rather than to herself: 'I just think that the 'Grim Reaper' campaign was very good, I think it was excellent, people criticised it, but at least they noticed . . . [but] it didn't make any changes to *my* behaviour, I just thought, 'What a good ad!' (student, 45).

Several other people said that while they initially felt at risk after viewing the 'Grim Reaper' advertisement, they 'turned off' because of the fear they felt. The fear aroused by the advertisement caused them to take notice and to remember it years later, but they did not go on to identify with it: 'I remember the "Grim Reaper", oh yes, I remember that one, it sent shivers through me. But then I thought, "So what?" (tradesman, 47). Another person commented that the advertisement was:

> . . . too emotive, just played on fear, was really dumb . . . I really believe that instead of operating on fear all the time, people should be made to think that they might be a risk to someone else rather than thinking all the time that someone else is going to infect them. (female professional, 35)

For the majority of participants the 'preferred' meaning of the 'Grim Reaper' text—that AIDS is a risk of which all Australians should be aware and against which they should take steps to protect themselves—was generally understood and acknowledged as important.

Few people challenged this function of public health advertisements, particularly in relation to the importance of warning 'others' about HIV/AIDS. This is, perhaps, not surprising, given the currency in western cultures of the discourse around the importance of providing 'information' to citizens concerning health risks and threats. Where interpretations differed was in the extent to which the advertisement was thought to be 'useful' and 'effective' for oneself. As we have shown, in some cases the individuals we interviewed advocated and supported shock tactics such as those used in the 'Grim Reaper' advertisement to frighten people (including themselves) into changing their behaviour to prevent the spread of HIV/AIDS. Others, however, were cynical and critical about the use of such strategies, pointing out that people tend to 'switch off' when fear is involved and that such frightening images may serve to stigmatise people with HIV/AIDS. Still others, while acknowledging the need for advertisements such as the 'Grim Reaper', felt that it did not 'speak to them' personally.

Several of those participants who expressed negative attitudes towards the 'Grim Reaper' advertisement, however, were quite positive about the 'Beds' advertisement. This advertisement, as we explained in chapter 3, depicted a scenario in which a naked couple engaging in a passionate embrace in a bed look up to see around them scores of beds containing couples doing the same. The message of the advertisement was that if one's partner had had other sexual partners, one was vulnerable to contagion from these other partners in a context of exponential spread of infection. The participants who remembered the 'Beds' advertisement said that it had provoked them to reflect upon the number of sexual partners they had had in the past. The advertisement had caused these participants to redefine their sexual past as posing a threat by identifying themselves as the subject of such messages:

> The 'Grim Reaper' first, I suppose, made me think I better go and get tested, just to make sure. And then when I saw the 'Bed' [sic] one I started thinking about sexual partners even more than I had before and I thought, 'Phew!—I identified with that. (unemployed man, aged 21)

> The 'Beds' one definitely has the biggest impact on you, it really hits home, it really is real . . . that's definitely had an effect on my attitude

now, because you just don't know how many other people [one's partners] have slept with. (male technical college student, aged 19)

Interestingly, a study carried out in San Francisco of 37 people's responses to AIDS education advertisements from around the world (including the 'Beds' but not the 'Grim Reaper' advertisement), found that of all the advertisements the 'Beds' one was most liked by participants (Johnson 1994). In these focus group discussions, participants made approving comments similar to our Australian interviewees concerning the 'reality' of the situation portrayed. As one man said, 'I liked that one ['Beds'] . . . you could look at it and say, "Damn, that's real"', while another man noted 'It helps to dispel the notion that [HIV/AIDS] is something that happens to someone else'. A third man commented that this advertisement, 'stuck in my head . . . 'cause you never know how many people that the people you slept with have been with in the past', while a female participant said, 'I remember the one with all the beds. It's something that people should be aware of. Make sure that you ask the person that you're sleeping with, have they slept with someone else?' (Johnson 1994, pp. 121–2 and 130–1).

While AIDS media campaigns designed to shock may have seemed to have provoked anxiety and concern in some of these audience members, such campaigns were only part of a complex interrelationship between perception of personal risk and the decision to change behaviour. The 'Grim Reaper' and the 'Beds' images resonated with a number of participants, particularly in their capacity to arouse fear and, in the case of the latter, to suggest the 'dangers' of having sexual relations with people who have had other partners. Several said that they had been prodded to have an HIV test by one or both of these advertisements. Other participants, however, suggested that this decision was made following a process by which they had already deemed their sexual pasts as 'risky'. As we described in chapter 3, mass media coverage, including AIDS campaigns, has often emphasised the role played by the contaminating Other in transmitting HIV infection. Many participants (most of whom were women) in the HIV test study felt that they had come into contact with such contaminating figures, either through direct sexual contact or via a chain of infection, and felt the need to protect themselves, to establish the integrity of their body boundaries. This, of course, was the central message of both the 'Beds' and the 'Needle Bed' advertisements.

Several participants also made negative judgements concerning their own imputed 'promiscuity', not in terms of morality linked to sexual activities per se, but in terms of placing themselves at risk from contracting a potentially fatal illness. Such individuals were therefore particularly receptive to media campaigns that sought to establish the viewer as the focal point of infection due to sexual activity with a number of partners.

The advertisements, therefore, tended to articulate pre-existing concerns and anxieties about risk which were often half-conscious, half-forgotten, habituated. Yet there were also many other reasons why people began to feel themselves to be at risk; for example, having gay friends or knowing someone who had HIV, experiencing generalised ill-health following a period in which they had had several sexual partners, being offered the test while attending a medical clinic for another reason and having doubts about the 'cleanliness' and sexual or drug-using pasts of their sexual partner/s. Still others in this study who had had an HIV test did so at the request of a sexual partner, to demonstrate their sincerity and commitment to the relationship, or to provide them with reassurance after they had admitted to an infidelity. While they had sought at least one (and sometimes more) HIV test, they never felt particularly at risk from HIV infection (Lupton et al. 1995a, 1995b).

THE AIDS EDUCATION STUDY

The AIDS education study found that at least some participants in all 17 discussion groups remembered the 'Grim Reaper' advertisement, even though they were only 10 or 11 years old when it was shown in 1987. Indeed, some young people commented that viewing the advertisement was their first introduction to the topic of AIDS. The advertisement was particularly memorable for the young people because of its horror-movie iconography, which they said attracted their attention at that age:

> I think when you're young, if you see a monster or something like that on TV, you sort of always remember those sort of scary things.

> . . . Like the 'Grim Reaper', you know, with the sword [sic], bowling down and killing people. (boys group)

That scared me, that commercial. I couldn't watch it. It came on at half-past eight, and I got so scared of it, I went to bed. (girls group)

A significant feature of the discussion of the 'Grim Reaper' in a number of focus groups was its grouping by participants with other highly memorable HIV/AIDS advertisements, so that a 'shock-horror' narrative was constructed. The students would usually begin by mentioning the 'Grim Reaper' advertisement as memorable, and then discuss other advertisements that had stuck in their memories for similar reasons. When, for example, one group was asked about the HIV/AIDS media campaigns they remembered, a discussion of the 'Grim Reaper' television advertisement was followed by references to the 'Beds' and 'Needle Bed' advertisements:

That ad with the bowling ball.

The bowling ball one.

The 'Grim Reaper'.

Yeah, the 'Grim Reaper'.

Interviewer You know the 'Grim Reaper' came out in 1987, so you must have been really young then.

I always remember, I used to always watch it to see all the people standing there going, 'Oh no, not me!.'

Yeah. He used to get the bowling ball and go—

That was a mad—

Interviewer You remember that? [laughter] But you all remember that?

Yeah. That really stuck in my memory.

Seeing a scary figure and then all these other people going, 'Oh no!' And then he wipes them all out with a bowling ball.

That's the first time I heard about AIDS.

Yeah, same here.

And then they stopped it and put—

—those beds. Like, heaps of beds and there's—

Yeah, all the needles.

All the needles, yeah.

Needles, syringes, with a sheet covered over them. (boys group)

Some participants also remembered the controversy incurred by the 'Grim Reaper' advertisement, while remarking that they found it a 'good ad':

> Those ads on television. There was lots of argument about them; like the bowling one and that, because it's offensive and that. But it shouldn't be that way. It should be so . . . society should change. Because it's a controversial issue.
>
> That was a good ad too.
>
> Yeah. (girls group)

> Why did they stop all the AIDS ads? They used to do the 'Grim Reaper' ones . . . They were really good I thought—
>
> —the bowling balls and the beds with the needles.
>
> Yeah, that was like a scare campaign; sort of what they're doing now for speed and alcohol, and they stopped doing AIDS and stuff. (boys group)

Members of one group talked about why they found the advertisement effective, drawing on the imagery used in the 'Grim Reaper' to describe the threat posed by HIV/AIDS to Australians: 'Because like it's entering into reality. This [AIDS] is a big problem and it's happening. We've got to do something about it otherwise we're going to get knocked over by it, sort of thing'. (girls group). Members of a boys group also remarked upon the potential of the shock tactics used in such advertisements to prevent HIV transmission: '. . . they just scare you; sort of scare you into being sort of neurotic about stuff'. 'Yeah, but it might scare you from doing stupid things and catching it.'

Many of these young people, as these comments suggest, approved of the shock tactics and controversial nature of the 'Grim Reaper' and other 'scary' advertisements. This was because such advertisements made the problem of HIV/AIDS 'real' for them, forcing them to consider the implications by scaring them. While most of the participants said that they found the advertisement memorable, however, not all agreed that it was a 'good ad', commenting that scaring audiences is not necessarily an appropriate way to educate them. Some young people commented on the emphasis on 'effect' in the advertisement to the detriment of the 'facts':

The 'Grim Reaper', it showed him bowling, then this voice come over and said something. It just scared you—'Geez, I don't want to get AIDS!' But it still didn't get across what it is or how you don't get it or anything like that—not wanting to get it and I don't think anyone did anyway. It still didn't explain what it was. (boys group)

Other participants made comments concerning the possible stigmatising effect of the association of the spectral figure of the 'Grim Reaper' with HIV/AIDS and those who have it: 'I think it had a detrimental effect, in it sort of scared people off it. Like it's a really sort of scary disease and it, you know, and if you've got it you're really sort of a freak almost because, you know, the Grim Reaper's got you!' (boys group)

These young people had come to sexual maturity in the shadow of AIDS. It is therefore perhaps not surprising that we found in the study that they were very anxious to know the details of AIDS and other STDs. They felt that they had been given a lot of 'superficial' information about AIDS at school and in other contexts, but that very little of it provided the 'in-depth', 'real' and 'nitty-gritty' information concerning the symptoms of HIV infection and the stages of progression from HIV to AIDS that they required. There was little indication that the participants felt unthreatened by the risk of HIV/AIDS or refused to countenance the possibility that they might be at risk. In other words, we found little of the sense of 'invulnerability' which the 'health belief' model focuses on and seeks to penetrate and challenge in relation to risk and HIV/AIDS. On the contrary, the young people were seeking a reflexive knowledge of their sexual bodies in a situation of uncertainty. Advertisements like the 'Grim Reaper', 'Beds' and 'Needle Bed' were considered useful and important by many paticipants because they attracted attention and therefore maintained public awareness of the problem of AIDS. Such advertisements, however, did not tend to satisfy the young people's own desire for 'the facts' and 'details' of HIV infection in the same ways that documentaries of 'real life' stories did (see chapter 11).

These findings suggest that for these young people, where fear-inspiring AIDS advertisements were particularly valued it was in this particular reflexive context of monitoring their own bodies rather than in terms of simple (hypodermic) 'impact' effects. The 'Grim Reaper' advertisement undoubtedly did have a major impact in 1987 in making viewers aware of HIV/AIDS. This is indicated by the fact that six to seven years later these young people (who were young children when they saw the advertisement) still instantly referred to the 'Grim Reaper' as the television AIDS material they remembered most. By 1993–94, when the research was conducted, the 'Grim Reaper' had a rather different inflection in the students' perception. It was now associated with health promotion advertisements that signified 'risk' to the human body, and with a continuing narrative 'lack' that neither television nor school education was filling: 'what happens to your body' when you have HIV/AIDS or other STDs.

CONCLUDING COMMENTS

In this chapter we have looked at the use of interviews and focus group discussions to explore the complex socio-cultural dimension of audience responses to AIDS television advertisements. The findings of our two studies suggest that it is those advertisements that personally strike a chord with viewers in relation to their everyday lives which they find particularly memorable and effective. Audiences are by no means passive or ignorant recipients of such texts. This has been long recognised by commercial advertisers, who construct their advertising with the notion of the critical, selective, media literate and cynical audience member in mind (Nava 1992; Shields 1992). Advertisements like the 'Grim Reaper' draw upon socio-cultural meanings that are already circulating, sometimes combining them in novel ways that attract attention. In particular, the 'Grim Reaper' advertisement drew on key advertising conventions (the 'problem' and 'solution' format) and key action-adventure, suspense and horror conventions.

In many ways, however, the 'Grim Reaper' drew on these conventions in order to subvert them. The emotional power of the iconography of the grim reaper figure itself depended on the fact that in this case science did not have a cure. Thus the mother and baby are not saved in the end, but are smashed to destruction by the reaper's bowling ball. Many audience members responded to the advertisement and to other 'scare-tactics' advertisements such as 'Needle Bed' with a frisson of fear, with a shiver, recognising and responding to these elements in ways that lodged in their memories. In contrast to the horrifying images of the 'Grim Reaper', the 'Beds' advertisement, with its more anodyne (but equally memorable) images of couples romping in bed, directly addressed those members of the audience who had had a number of sexual partners; in the words of a woman in the HIV testing study: 'All those beds and *that was me in the middle*'.

As this suggests, advertisements like 'Grim Reaper', 'Beds' and 'Needle Bed' only work because, like commercial advertisements, they appeal at either the conscious or unconscious level to a lack, a pre-existing desire, or fit into a self-image already at least partially formed or in the process of changing. A felt need to monitor the sexual body, a half-recognised fear that one's partner or oneself has put one at risk—it is these pre-existing desires and recognitions that such AIDS advertisements seem to cue. To achieve any effect advertisements must interpellate audiences, making individuals recognise themselves as the subject of the advertisement and constitute themselves as 'the audience'. For some, the 'Grim Reaper' advertisement did not do this, constituting for them its audience as 'other people who are "at risk"'. But for others (as the rush for HIV tests indicates) it certainly did, encouraging many people to seek desperately the science of testing where a science of cure was not available. Our point here is that even where an apparently direct 'hypodermic effect' seems to have occurred, this was based on pre-existing discourses (for example, those relating to 'science as saviour' and personal risk).

Looking beyond the televisual text/audience relationship, therefore, is integral to understanding the specific and constantly changing context in which people 'make sense' of these texts. Other texts, discourses, emotional responses, embodied experiences and so on will shape the ways in which audience members respond to the meaning constructed in the text. Singling out the quite specific psychological 'effect' of television advertisements in such a complex interplay of personal experience, symbolic meanings, subconscious desires and anxieties is difficult and probably not especially useful. Nor, given the changing nature of subjectivity, 'the multifarious ways in which we constitute ourselves through media consumption' (Ang 1989, p. 110) and the highly contextual nature of any research, can we say with confidence that the opinions these participants espoused at the time would necessarily be the same in a different time and setting.

What we *can* say is that the presence of a television advertisement sponsored by the government on AIDS acts in the first instance as an indicator to audiences that AIDS is a 'problem' about which health authorities are concerned—after all, they have spent time and money in producing and screening such advertisements. Most people, as our research suggests, tend to accept that this use of television is, in itself, 'a good thing', for it is generally assumed that governments should take some responsibility for health education and promotion. In the second instance, features of such advertisements do prove noticeable and memorable for specific audience members (for example, sexually-experienced adults with many partners) in specific contexts. Such advertisements seem to have contributed in significant ways to the construction of personal risk and feelings of vulnerability at some times in some people's personal biographies. It is very unlikely, however, that these advertisements alone will produce such effects. It must also be remembered that the production of meaning in television texts is not one-way. As we have emphasised throughout this book, the producers of television texts (and other media texts) on AIDS draw from, as well as reproduce, many of the same stock of discourses, narratives, metaphors and meanings about the body, responsibility and risk circulating in society around AIDS and sexuality that these respondents are accessing.

READING THE 'TESTIMONIALS' AND 'VOX POP CONDOM'

We have argued that media researchers need to be aware of their complicity in the production of knowledge and the exercise of power, including the multiple forms of discourse that constitute their own subjectivities as researchers. They need to be open to the notion that their research is situated in a cultural context, and to articulate in their methodology what that context is. Consequently in this chapter and the next we use quantitative analysis to address the 'processual' nature of our cultural research. In other words, we try to enter the cultures of television producers and allow their discourses, intertexts and practices to shape the questions on our survey.

Our ethnographic field work within the commercial television industry set out to trace those readings and meanings among the discourses and practices of production. In Part II, we tried to isolate the audience meanings that the producers of AIDS television texts constructed. The processual analysis of chapters 5, 6 and 7 established a number of aims in relation to ideas about what audiences wanted which were progressively worked into the text as AIDS meanings proliferated. These will be our units of meaning for quantification in this and the following chapter. But so too will be some of the dominant discourses (about condoms and romance, about the Other and sexuality, about age and sexuality) that circulate more widely in our broader cultures. Our focus in this chapter will be audience responses to the 1990 Australian 'Testimonial' and 'Vox Pop Condom' advertisements. Chapter 10 also explores the relationship between production and audience meanings, this time focusing on soap opera.

THE 'TESTIMONIALS' AUDIENCE RESEARCH

An audience study was conducted with 893 young people attending government schools in Sydney. This study took place between May and November 1990, shortly after the 'Testimonial' advertisements had screened on national television. The students were chosen equally from schools in working-class and middle-class suburbs of Sydney, and were also balanced in terms of gender: 51 per cent (458) were from working-class suburbs, 49 per cent (435) from middle-class suburbs; 46 per cent (414) were male, 54 per cent (479) were female. All participants were in their penultimate year of secondary schooling (Year 11) during the research program (4 per cent were 15 years old, 52 per cent were 16 years old, 44 per cent were 17 years old). As individuals in their late adolescence and entering early adulthood they consequently constituted a key target audience for the 'Testimonial' campaign which was directed at people aged 24 years and younger.

As we explained in chapter 5, the major intention in designing the 1990 AIDS television campaign, as expressed in government documentation, was to develop a campaign to 'socialise' the use of condoms, dissuade the use of shared needles for injecting drugs and emphasise the risk of 'the second/third wave' of HIV infection; that is, the risk of contracting HIV through having unprotected sex with someone who has shared a needle or who has had a sexual partner who has used injecting drugs. The specific intention of the 'Testimonial' advertisements was to 'personalise' these risks for young heterosexuals by using the narratives of 'real' young people who had contracted HIV.

The participants were shown one of two sets of the 1990 series of television advertisements (each set containing the opening 'Needle Bed' advertisement, three of the 'Testimonial' advertisements, and one version of the 'Vox Pop' advertisements). Immediately after the screening they completed a questionnaire relevant to their particular screening, and some groups participated in focus group discussions. One questionnaire assessed responses to 'Needle Bed', the 'Sarah', 'Chris' and 'Debby' 'Testimonials' and 'Vox Pop Condom (Punk)'; the other questionnaire assessed responses to 'Needle Bed', the 'Laura', 'Emma' and 'Tracy' 'Testimonials' and 'Vox Pop Condom (Granny)'. The questionnaires consisted of closed, pre-coded questions, open-ended questions which were later coded into categories and semantic differentials.

The semantic differential method was used because it is a useful way of quantifying cultural values and relating textual meaning with audience response. The method consists of identifying the values to be investigated and setting these out as binarily-opposed concepts on a five- or seven-point scale. Groups of respondents (differentiated, for example, by gender or class) are then asked to record their reactions on each scale and the results are averaged and groups' responses compared. The method as we used it asked the participants to evaluate each of the six 'Testimonial' characters according to binarily-opposed concepts on a seven-point scale. The eleven pairs of concepts derived partly from earlier research examining violence, 'killers' and victims in fictional and news media (Gerbner 1970; Fiske 1982; Tulloch & Tulloch 1993). They also drew on concepts derived from production workers' comments in relation to the television advertisements that we identified in chapter 3.

We felt that, given the potentially fatal nature of AIDS and the fact that the 'innocent versus guilty AIDS "victim"' representation had been particularly dominant in the Australian news media for some time (Lupton 1994a), a comparison between semantic differential responses to the government advertisements and other 'villain and victim' studies would indicate the degree to which culturally cultivated 'victims' and 'villains' profiles were perceived among people living with HIV/AIDS by our audience groups. So too, we would be able to explore how these 'innocent' and 'guilty' individuals compared with more conventional, fictional 'victims' and 'villains' on attractive/repulsive, usual/unusual, expert/inexpert, and logical/impulsive scales. A number of the closed and the open-ended questions were also designed to assess specific formal and textual features of the AIDS advertisements that were isolated in the production study. The intention, therefore, was to assess the degree of 'message take-out', a category of audience 'effect' that was important to the producers of the advertisements. The survey went further in also assessing audience responses to some of the producers' professional strategies and idiolects, relating, for instance, to matters of camera work and setting.

AIDS advertisements are verbally complex and also, as we have seen in previous chapters, semiotically 'thick'. That is, they convey messages via a cluster of audio and visual sign systems (lighting, set design, characterisation, body language and gesture, music and sound and so on). For example, in one of the 'Vox Pop Condom' advertisements, an Italian–Australian youth gives a hip-thrusting gesture as he shows the condom in his wallet and says that carrying condoms with you is 'good'. Asked what persons in this advertisement they liked best and least, and why, many participants indicated the 'ethnic' (or 'Italian' or 'European' or 'foreigner' or 'wog') as the character they most disliked. The reasons given generally picked up on his body language: 'he thought he was a stud', 'his actions of having sex were disgusting'. All of these particular responses were from female adolescents and it is likely that a mixture of gender and ethnicist (and possibly class-based) attitudes were combining to encourage negative readings of the advertisement at that moment. In this example, audience response to visual gesture helps construct the actor as Other. This response exemplifies the way in which the semiotic 'thickness' of a television text engages with pre-circulating cultural discourses that shape the ways in which audience members respond to the meanings constructed in the text. It was because of their potential to construct either empathy or 'otherness' that two particular visual aspects of the 'Testimonial' advertisements particularly interested us: lighting and set design.

Lighting is a standard means in film and television of conveying mood, establishing risk and threat, constructing villainy, and so on. We observed previously that the individuals who participated in the 'Testimonial' advertisements were lit in silhouette to protect their anonymity. In current affairs television programs, individuals with a 'secret to hide', such as sexual offenders and their victims are customarily lit this way. Consequently, as we suggested in chapter 3, lighting of this kind is conventionally associated with 'social problems', thus visually constructing the interviewee as Other (in contrast to 'normal' young people interviewed in the 'natural' light of street or beach with their faces fully revealed as in the 'Vox Pop Condom' advertisements). As we noted in chapter 5, the silhouette technique was not the original preferred method of lighting the 'Testimonial' subjects. We were interested to what extent the 'personal revelation' silhouettes of the 'Testimonials' would emphasise the meaning of the 'insidious them' or Other from whom the disease spreads in contrast to the 'natural' lighting of the 'Vox Pop Condom' advertisements emphasising 'us' in the everyday world. To assess this, our questionnaires both asked directly about formal features of the advertisements and employed semantic differential scales assessing the participants' feelings, attitudes and emotions towards each of the 'Testimonial' speakers.

Set design can also convey distancing effects unintended by the producers of the television text. A particular 'processual' feature of the 'Testimonial' advertisements quite unintentionally exacerbated this as a problem. The decision to use the silhouette style of lighting, thus obscuring the participants' facial expressions (which are so central to television camera rhetorics), meant that the 'Testimonial' images had to be made visually interesting in other ways. In the 'Testimonials' this was achieved particularly via *mise en scène*, lighting and the background in which the subjects of the advertisements were positioned. All the background settings suggested the homes of the subjects. The 'Laura' advertisement had as a background ocean waves sweeping onto a Sydney beach, 'Emma' had a highly attractive 'conservatory' background with lots of greenery and hanging plants, 'Sarah' had the polished floors, fireplace and bookshelves of the professional middle classes, and even the kitchen in 'Debby' was highly aestheticised via lighting and arrangements of terracotta jars and so on. As we discussed in chapter 7, a conventional professional value among television set designers and lighting technicians is for 'something with a bit of character'. This professional idiolect is very clearly evident in all the 'Testimonial' advertisements; and this aestheticising tendency gives a very middle-class 'feel'.

Research into audience responses to public health media campaigns very seldom takes account of issues of style. However, an earlier evaluation by the British Health Education Authority of an AIDS advertisement set in an 'up-market' flat had indicated that positive responses on the part of audiences to the relevance of the advertisement tended to be from 'the more affluent [English] Southerners'. The evaluation went on to argue that, 'Such a scenario is sufficiently alien to most respondents that an alternative, more down-to-earth setting would be more helpful' (Wellings & Orton 1988, p. 11). Part of the design of our audience study, therefore, was to examine whether respondents perceived the people living with HIV/AIDS in the 'Testimonial' advertisements in terms of their social class, given that they were positioned in rather 'up-market' Australian settings. We also wanted to explore the extent of audience empathy or alienation, if any, this attracted.

Considerations of socio-cultural representation (of being middle-class, white, male/female and so on) are important in cultural studies research, given its criticism of individualist 'effects' studies. As the stylistic intention of the 1990 television campaign was to break through young people's complacency without setting up 'self-protective barriers', how successful in its own terms was this 'psychological' strategy? Would the psychological emphasis itself be a problem, given that cultural differences of social class, gender and ethnicity were not seriously considered in producing the advertisements? For instance, the members of one focus group we ran with senior Sydney school students noted that the characters were unrepresentative, since all of them were Anglo–Celtic and (in all but one instance) young. But how representative was this focus group comment? The members of other groups noted that although most of the characters were young, they were clearly 'over twenty' and thus 'not our generation'. Our audience surveys included questions designed to assess audience understanding and evaluation of both the content (in relation to age, gender and class issues related to the subjects of the advertisements) and the style (for example, the silhouette technique and set design) of the 'Testimonial' advertisements.

Messages

'Audience reach' is a standard quantitative measure used by health departments and their commercial research agencies to evaluate the 'effect' of their public education campaigns. The participants in our study were surveyed between three and six months after the peak of the 1990 television campaign. Their recollection of seeing the individual 'Testimonial' advertisements was as follows: 'Sarah' 78 per cent; 'Chris' 60 per cent; 'Debby' 32 per cent; 'Laura' 72 per cent; 'Emma' 38 per cent; 'Tracy' 57 per cent. In this simple quantitative sense of 'audience reach', most of the 'Testimonials' can be regarded as successful in terms of having reached large numbers in the target group of young Australians. Quantified research is useful in assessing audience reach. But we were also interested in exploring at a far more detailed level how the sample responded to these advertisements in terms of their 'message take-out'. Our audience sample was asked, therefore, to complete an open-ended question asking them 'What was the message?' of each 'Testimonial' advertisement in their own words. Responses were later coded into ten categories. The main responses indicate that all the 'Testimonials' conveyed more than one specific and identifiable message to the audience members, and that in the case of 'Sarah', six messages were identified by the participants.

But which information units were most recalled? Table 9.1 shows the major messages identified by the young people for each advertisement. The 'control your own health' message ('use condoms/don't share needles') was remembered substantially more often than the 'you can't tell by looking who has HIV/AIDS' message. The intended objective of the DCSH was to impress upon audiences that 'anxiety arousal is not enough' because the real task is to encourage long-term prophylactic thinking and behaviour. By this standard, therefore, these television advertisements can be deemed successful in conveying their intended overt messages. We can also see that the specific 'preferred' meanings of the message clusters of each of the 'Testimonials' were quite closely decoded by the audience groups. Thus the greater cluster of messages in the 'Sarah' advertisement compared with the 'Debby'

Table 9.1 Major messages identified for each 'Testimonial' subject

Subject	Message	Percentage of participants identifying message
'Sarah'	'Always use condoms'	25
	'Safe sex'	20
	'Have an HIV test before stopping safe sex'	15
	'Assume partner has HIV/AIDS—trust no-one'	13
	'You can't tell who has the virus, even in long-term relationships'	11
'Chris'	'Don't share needles'	53
	'No way of knowing who has HIV/AIDS: don't trust anyone'	26
'Debby'	'Don't share needles—not even once'	61
	'It takes only one dirty needle to ruin your life'	18
'Laura'	'You can't tell from looking who has HIV/AIDS'	56
	'Don't have sex with anyone unless you know their past sex life'	23
'Emma'	'Don't share needles'	67
	'Casual users can get HIV/AIDS too'	14
	'You are never sure who has HIV/AIDS: you can't trust anyone'	5
'Tracy'	'Use condoms'	67
	'Don't trust your partner'	10
	'You can't tell by looking who has HIV/AIDS'	9
	'You don't have to inject drugs to get HIV/AIDS'	9

advertisement is reflected in the greater number of messages identified by the audience for 'Sarah'.

Further, 'Debby' is the only 'Testimonial' where the 'you can't tell by looking/you can never be sure' message is not specifically promoted, and it is the only one where this response is not given by the audience groups. At the same time, the 'Debby' advertisement is the only one that specifically articulates the 'one occasion of sharing contaminated needles is enough' message, and it is the only one which elicits this specific response from the audience groups we surveyed. Only in the case of 'Laura' was the 'you can't tell by appearances; don't trust anyone' response the major one generated by the audience groups. The other 'Testimonial' advertisements generated responses that emphasised above all the specific 'risky' and 'safe' practices. But unlike these other 'Testimonials', 'Laura' was the only one that did not specifically mention sexual practices (other than in the use of the term 'lover') or needle-sharing, and consequently was the only one which did not talk about 'safe' practices.

Meanings

Clearly, the specific and overt messages of the 'Testimonial' advertisements were quite well comprehended by the young people we surveyed. As Lewis has pointed out, however, 'the strength of quantitative surveys lies . . . upon our ability to interpret the meaning of the replies' (1991, p. 76). So what did the textual narratives actually *mean* to these young people? Were they involved, bored or alienated by these advertisements? Was there any systematic pattern as to which advertisements involved them and which ones turned them off? If so, what did this mean in terms of the participants' responses to the 'real-life' people living with HIV/AIDS they viewed in the advertisements? As we saw from the research findings reported in the previous chapter, fear-inducing appeals to emotion *are* memorable, but this feature does not in itself necessarily lead to the construction of HIV/AIDS as a personal threat. Indeed it may have the opposite effect of inducing derision, cynicism and dissociation from the intended meanings of the advertisement.

In our audience study of the 'Testimonials', we asked the pre-coded question: 'How did you react to the *feel* of this ad? (a) "scary—it could happen to me that way"; (b) "nothing—because I'm not relating with gays, bisexuals or injecting drug users, so it doesn't affect me"; (c) "boring—we've seen it all before"; (d) other reaction—please specify'. The results shown below in Table 9.2 indicated that the participants felt 'scared' and personally involved or, alternatively 'nothing' and 'bored' depending on whether they watched the 'Sarah'/'Laura'/'Tracy' or the 'Chris'/'Debby'/'Emma' advertisements.

For the 'Chris' advertisement (the only one featuring a male subject) there was a statistically significant gender difference in response, with 42 per cent of boys compared with 25 per cent of girls responding to the 'nothing—I don't relate with gays, injecting drug users etc.' category and 11 per cent of boys to 3 per cent of girls finding it 'boring'. For the 'Debby' advertisement, there were again significant gender differences, with 47 per cent of boys compared with 32 per cent of girls responding 'nothing etc', and 13 per cent of boys to 6 per cent of girls responding 'bored'. Notwithstanding this gender difference as Table 9.2 shows there was a general trend in all groups of feeling distant or alienated from the needle-sharers 'Chris', 'Emma' and 'Debby' compared with the other 'Testimonial' subjects who had contracted HIV via sexual activity.

Our data suggest an important qualification to the optimism of a British Health Education Authority study of attitudes to AIDS advertisements which reported that 75 per cent of respondents agreed

Table 9.2 Emotional responses to the 'Testimonial' advertisements

Advertisement	Response	Percentage of participants who experienced response
'Sarah'	'scary—it could happen to me that way'	61
	'nothing', 'bored'	21
'Laura'	'scary etc.'	57
	'nothing', 'bored'	18
'Tracy'	'scary etc.'	50
	'nothing, 'bored'	32
'Chris'	'scary etc.'	23
	'nothing', 'bored'	57
'Debby'	'scary etc.'	25
	'nothing', 'bored'	48
'Emma'	'scary etc'	12
	'nothing', 'bored'	48

that 'you need to use fear to get people to take notice' (Wellings & Orton 1988, p. 8), and to our own findings in chapter 8 that suggested that people tend to endorse the use of 'scare tactics' in AIDS campaigns. The question is, take notice of what? A majority of the young people in our study did feel 'scared' into an evaluation of their personal activities, but only where they sympathised with the 'Testimonial' subjects (as we will demonstrate from the semantic differential test findings described below). The British research evaluated advertisements that dealt only with the risks of sexual transmission. In our study it was the responses to advertisements emphasising sexual transmission ('Sarah', 'Laura' and 'Tracy') that registered high personal involvement percentages. In contrast, agentive needle-sharing messages (that is, where the 'Testimonial' speaker was a needle-sharer) generated relatively low scores on this response, even where they were directly related to the risk of heterosexual sexual transmission (as in the case of 'Chris'). On the other hand, where the speaker was a sexual 'victim' of a needle-sharer, like 'Tracy', the personal involvement response was high.

A second open-ended question designed to examine audience meanings was: 'What were your first thoughts on seeing this ad?'. Responses were later coded into 30 categories. Overall, responses either focused on: i) character (for example, 'I feel sorry for her'); ii) message content (for example, 'anyone can have it'); or iii) message style (for example, 'direct and to the point'). The answers fell largely into two kinds of overall response. The sexually-infected 'Sarah' and 'Laura' subjects drew a similar cluster of responses; as did 'Chris', 'Debby' and 'Emma', but with a differently patterned cluster. For 'Sarah' and 'Laura', positive responses that constructed them as 'innocent victims' (evoking such comments as 'sorry, sad for her personal situation', 'don't trust anyone/anyone can have it', 'sorry—she's innocent') heavily outweighed negative responses ('stupid—she deserves it', 'sorry—but she deserves it'). If we add to the positive side those responses where the respondent empathised with the subject (for example, the responses 'shocked, worried, scared, depressed', 'could happen to me in my own sex life'), the figures are: 'Sarah', positive 50 per cent, negative 15 per cent; 'Laura', positive 56 per cent, negative 12 per cent.

By contrast, for the 'Chris', 'Debby' and 'Emma' subjects, negative responses that constructed them as irresponsible, stupid, careless agents who then inflict further suffering on their 'victims' (for example, the responses 'stupid—s/he deserves it', 'sorry—but s/he deserves it', 'sorry for victim he infected', 'sorry for her kids') heavily outweighed positive or empathetic responses ('sorry, sad for personal situation', 'shocked, worried, scared, depressed'). The figures were: 'Chris', positive 10 per cent, negative 56 per cent; 'Debby', positive 19 per cent, negative 40 per cent; 'Emma', positive 8 per cent, negative 28 per cent. The 'Tracy' subject received the responses of positive 36 per cent, negative 25 per cent, and was therefore closer to the 'Sarah'/'Laura' cluster than to 'Chris'/'Debby'/'Emma'. Unlike these latter subjects, she was not a needle-sharer. It seems for this reason 'Tracy' was regarded, on balance, fairly positively by the young people. Unlike 'Sarah' and 'Laura', however, 'Tracy's' partner *was* identified as a needle-sharer, which may account for a higher 'deserves it' response ('Sarah' 15 per cent, 'Laura' 12 per cent, 'Tracy' 25 per cent) even though it was made clear in the advertisement that 'Tracy' was unaware of her partner's activities until she was infected.

As we have demonstrated, the responses to 'how did you react to the feel of this ad?' clustered in the same two patterns. A major intention of this campaign, as was evident in the official documentation, was to emphasise the relationship between needle-sharing and heterosexual risk. Unprotected sexual activity was to be seen as the 'bridge between the world of "them" (injecting drug users) and "us"'. The 'Chris' subject emphasised the heterosexual nature of the risk to his girlfriend; and 99 per cent of the participants understood the message that his girlfriend may well have contracted HIV from him. Yet 57 per cent of our audience groups responded with 'nothing' or 'boredom' to this advertisement. Less than 25 per cent were sufficiently scared by it to see its personal relevance. In the case of 'Tracy' (the sexually infected partner of a needle-sharer) although 50 per cent of the participants did feel scared that the situation could happen to them, there was still a significantly larger (32 per cent) 'nothing/bored' response than in the case of the other sexually infected 'Testimonial' speakers.

The majority of the young people we surveyed clearly did not identify with, or feel sympathy for, the subjects who were associated with using injecting drugs, positioning them as Other and therefore of little relevance to their own lives. This response was mediated through gender, however. As we noted above, the male 'Chris' subject, who had contracted HIV via needle-sharing but posed a threat to his girlfriend, was of less interest to boys than to girls, and the girls were more empathetic towards 'Laura' and 'Sarah' who had each contracted HIV unknowingly from their infected boyfriends via sexual activity. None of the women in the advertisements was directly constructed as posing a threat to her male partner via sexual activity. It is perhaps for that reason that many of the male audience members did not feel personally interpellated by the texts as 'at risk' from HIV infection.

Semantic differentials

The semantic differential scales we used included many of the binary opposites used in hero/villain/victim research by Gerbner (1970). However, we also used binaries derived from producers' concepts, identified through our ethnographic production research. For example, the item 'someone you sympathise with/someone you don't sympathise with' originated from the view of *ACP*'s executive producer, James Davern, that soap operas are more successful than public health advertisements in conveying health messages because the risk narratives in the former can focus on major characters with whom the audience members sympathise.

Comparison of the semantic differential scales for the 'Sarah', 'Chris', 'Debby', 'Laura', 'Emma' and 'Tracy' subjects revealed marked homogeneity within the scales for each 'Testimonial' text. In other words, differences in response *between* 'Testimonials' were more significant than differences raised by the class or gender of respondents in reacting to any one text. Compare, for instance, responses to the 'Laura' and 'Emma' subjects in Figures 9.1 and 9.2.

Fiske's conclusion, however, that the 'negotiation between text and reader produces a meaning that in the first case is determined more by the reader and in the second by the text' (1982, p. 133) is overly simplistic. A closer analysis of the scales indicates two distinct patterns of graph: those relating to sexually-acquired infection (the 'Sarah', 'Laura' and 'Tracy' subjects) and those relating to infection acquired via injecting drug use ('Chris', 'Debby' and 'Emma'). The graphs for the 'Sarah', 'Laura' and 'Tracy' subjects are remarkably homogeneous, as are the graphs for 'Chris' and 'Emma', while there is a marked variation between these two clusters. The graph for the 'Debby' subject is somewhere between the two, viewed more positively than 'Chris' and 'Emma' but more negatively than 'Sarah',

Figures 9.1 Semantic differentials—'Laura'

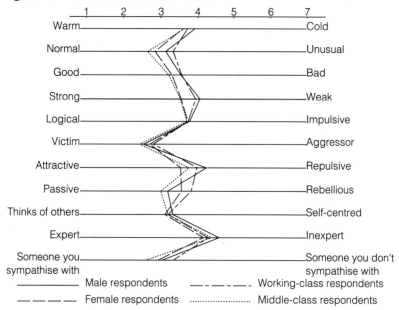

Figure 9.2 Semantic differentials—'Emma'

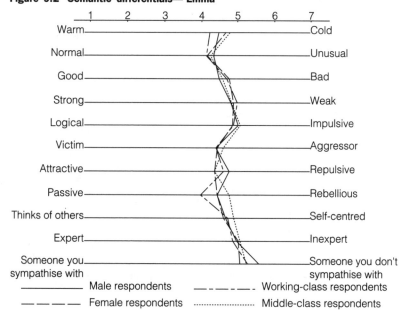

'Laura' and 'Tracy'. The remarkably homogeneous cluster of the 'Sarah', 'Laura' and 'Tracy' characters, however, excludes 'Debby'. The 'Debby' subject only shares a close similarity with these three subjects on the warm/cold scale, while she is much closer to 'Chris' and 'Emma' on the good/bad, strong/weak, victim/aggressor, attractive/repulsive, and sympathetic/unsympathetic scales (see Figure 9.3).

Rather than these two homogeneous clusters of response indicating simple textual influence, the markedly differentiated 'positive'/'sympathy' affiliation with sexually acquired infection and 'negative'/'non-sympathy' affiliations with infection via injecting drug use suggest strongly held cultural views determining the readings. In particular, taken together the responses to the 'feel' of the 'Testimonial' advertisements, the 'first thought' responses and the semantic differential responses powerfully confirm that the young people in our audience study read the casual needle-sharers as Other.

These responses may be compared to the findings of Clift et al. (1990) who asked a sample of 14- to 18-year-old young people living

Figure 9.3 Semantic differentials—all 'Testimonial' subjects

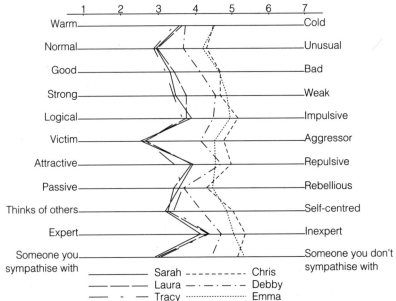

in the south-east of England to write an account of their own views of HIV infection and AIDS. They found that some of the young people were far more judgemental of gay men, drug users, prostitutes and bisexuals infected with HIV than of other people with HIV/AIDS (such as haemophiliacs or children), because of the former groups' status as irresponsible, reckless or 'deviant' in contracting the virus. Extreme statements such as the following by an 18-year-old male were made: 'those who have contracted AIDS through drug abuse, sleeping around or homosexual activity ought to be left to rot because they have caught what they deserve and we should be helping the haemophiliacs and the babies born with AIDS' (quoted in Clift et al. 1990, p. 61).

Audience responses to style

As we argued in chapter 4, the televisual construction of the 'real' person living with HIV/AIDS has tended to represent him or her as sickly and gaunt. This image seems to be prevalent amongst the public. Research conducted with groups of Scots, for example, found that when asked what images they associated with 'AIDS people', the participants gave such replies as 'Someone white and skeletal'; 'Disease-ridden emaciated body sat in a bed'; 'Dying' (Kitzinger 1993, p. 285). Not surprisingly, therefore, there was concern evident in the DCSH's research and development documents about the suitability for television of the silhouetted version of the 'Testimonial' concept, related to the audiences' propensity to 'fill in the faces' with images of illness. This would perhaps contradict a main theme of the advertisements: that 'you can't tell simply by looking who has HIV/AIDS'. To address this issue, we asked the participants to complete an open-ended question: 'Which aspects of the style of this ad did you (a) like, (b) dislike?'. We also asked them, 'If you could see the details of her/his face, do you think she/he would look (a) normal; (b) show some physical signs of AIDS; (c) look terrible—in the final stages of AIDS?'; and 'Did you try to fill out her/his features in your mind while watching the ad?'.

The 'style' responses were later coded into twenty categories. Notably, 74 per cent of respondents to the 'Laura' advertisement who mentioned specific stylistic dislikes commented on the silhouette technique or the 'visually boring' image. Similarly, 66 per cent of respondents to the 'Debby' advertisement, 58 per cent to 'Emma',

58 per cent to 'Tracy', 53 per cent to 'Chris' and 32 per cent to 'Sarah' who had specific stylistic dislikes nominated such aspects as the silhouette technique or the 'visually boring' images or the 'visuals'. On the other hand, 34 per cent of those who mentioned features of style they specifically *liked* in 'Laura' said 'the darkened face', while a further 11 per cent mentioned the setting. For 'Emma', 21 per cent mentioned the 'darkened face' and 8 per cent the setting; for 'Tracy', 37 per cent liked the darkened face and 13 per cent the setting; for 'Debby', 17 per cent liked the darkened face and 15 per cent the 'homely atmosphere'; and 13 per cent of 'Chris' responses and 11 per cent of 'Sarah' responses liked the darkened face. In actual numbers, the participants who specifically mentioned liking or disliking the silhouette technique were roughly equal (like = 78, dislike = 91). As we have seen, the silhouetted face technique did not mean loss of impact: 61 per cent of respondents to 'Sarah' and 57 per cent to 'Laura' nominated the 'scary, it could happen to me that way' response to the advertisements. Further, the silhouette technique did not uniformly construct the 'Testimonial' subjects as Other. As we have seen from the semantic differential measures, degree of 'sympathy' and 'normality' depended not on the visual technique used but on the type of HIV risk activity described by the subjects themselves.

Clearly, the visual style of these advertisements was highly salient to a proportion of the audience group. But what did it *mean* to them? In particular, what did they see 'behind' the silhouette? In response to the question, 'Did you try to fill out her/his features in your mind while watching the ad?', 'yes' was the response for around half of the audience groups for each 'Testimonial'. Interestingly, while about the same proportion of participants (48 to 56 per cent) found themselves filling in the silhouetted features of each of the 'Testimonial' people living with HIV/AIDS, there was a marked halo effect in *what they saw*. As the data in Table 9.3 below show, although a substantial majority of the participants read into the image a 'normal' face, significantly fewer participants saw 'normality' and significantly more saw 'some physical signs of AIDS' in the cases of injecting drug users 'Emma', 'Chris' and 'Debby'.

Far from the participants uniformly projecting into the darkened 'Testimonial' faces the 'terminal image' of AIDS (which the marketing agencies suggested might be the effect of this lighting device), the majority saw a 'normal' face behind the shadow. Consequently, what

Table 9.3 Signs of HIV/AIDS discerned in 'Testimonial' subjects

	'normal' (%)	'some signs of HIV/AIDS' (%)	'final stages of HIV/AIDS' (%)
'Sarah'	78	22	0
'Laura'	70	23	6
'Tracy'	81	19	1
'Chris'	55	38	6
'Debby'	55	34	11
'Emma'	51	45	4

most people 'saw' did not contradict the 'you can't tell by appearances' message of the 'Testimonial' advertisements. To the degree that they saw any signs of AIDS, however, this depended on the particular HIV risk practice in which the subject had engaged. Notably, this same clustering of responses that we have seen earlier ('Sarah'/'Laura'/'Tracy' and 'Chris'/'Debby'/'Emma'), cuts across any obvious 'villain/victim' narrative stereotyping, since, while 'Sarah' and 'Laura' are portrayed as 'victims' and 'Chris' as the agent of infection, the 'Debby' subject infects no-one but herself (although a number of responses emphasised her 'irresponsibility' in allowing herself to be exposed to risk practices while the mother of young children).

Audience perception of social class

We made the point earlier that the 'aestheticising' of the 'Testimonial' images gave them, in most cases, a very 'middle-class' and somewhat 'up-market' feel. Would this 'class' aspect of the settings be perceived by the participants, and would this influence their responses to the advertisements? The participants were asked 'what class of person' they thought that individual 'Testimonial' characters were. The responses are given below in Table 9.4 in terms of overall percentages, and also in terms of the participants' own class positions (determined through suburb of residence and parental occupation).

All 'Testimonial' subjects except 'Chris' and 'Emma' were perceived by most participants as middle-class. 'Sarah' and 'Debby' were seen as middle-class by over 60 per cent. Only 'Laura' was perceived as upper-class by more than 25 per cent of the participants. Judging by the visual evidence of the advertisements, interpretation of the settings seems unlikely to have been the cause of 'Chris' and 'Emma'

Table 9.4   Perceived social class of 'Testimonial' subjects

Subjects	Perceived class of subjects	overall (%)	working-class (%)	middle-class (%)
		Class of respondents		
'Sarah'	working-class	32	28	37
	middle-class	61	66	55
	upper-class	4	6	2
'Chris'	working-class	68	64	72
	middle-class	31	36	25
	upper-class	1	0	3
'Debby'	working-class	27	30	22
	middle-class	61	54	70
	upper-class	11	15	6
'Laura'	working-class	14	13	16
	middle-class	55	52	58
	upper-class	28	34	22
'Emma'	working-class	50	42	58
	middle-class	43	53	32
	upper-class	6	5	6
'Tracy'	working-class	38	44	32
	middle-class	53	47	59
	upper-class	8	7	9

being described as working-class. It is true that whereas other 'Testimonial' subjects have ocean views, cedar and leadlight conservatories or academic-looking book collections in the background, 'Chris' has a more cluttered background with a bicycle propped against the wall. But the background also includes a piano. Further, the 'Emma' advertisement has one of the most 'aesthetic' of backgrounds with polished wood floors, leadlight doors and native fernery. 'Laura', on the other hand, is almost certainly typed middle/upper class because of her background of ocean beaches (a sea view is one of the attributes of prime real estate in Sydney).

We tested these assumptions about class perceptions and setting by asking the participants an open-ended question as to why they thought the particular 'Testimonial' character was working-, middle- or upper-class. Quite systematically, participants ascribed class status mainly by *either* language *or* setting. For instance, 91 per cent of the young people who give reasons for calling 'Laura' upper-class said 'view of the beach behind her'. In the case of 'Emma', 41 per cent of them gave as a reason 'the way she spoke' compared with 15 per cent who gave her 'house, background' as the reason for calling her working-class, while 53 per cent gave her 'house, background' compared with 13 per cent who gave the 'way she spoke' as the reason for calling her middle-class. In the case of 'Chris', 30 per cent of the participants gave as a reason 'the way he spoke' compared with 10 per cent who gave his 'house, background' as the reason for calling him working-class, whereas 22 per cent gave his 'house, background' compared with 13 per cent 'the way he spoke' as the reason for calling him middle-class. These data provide interesting evidence of audiences' ability to manipulate different visual or verbal codes (of the semiotically 'thick' television text) in line with different cultural interpretations. The visual style of the 'Emma' advertisement *mise en scène* would be difficult to decode as 'working-class'. As these responses suggest, however, 'Emma's' voice is more ambiguous in class terms, and is consequently easier to label as 'working-class'.

Perceptions of the class of characters (by language or setting) do not, however, seem to have systematically influenced the young people's identification with them or their sense of 'Otherness'. Both the 'middle-class' 'Debby' and the 'working-class' 'Chris' were regarded unsympathetically by the young people, whereas the 'middle-class' 'Sarah' and the 'middle/upper-class' 'Laura' were viewed sympathetically by working-class and middle-class students alike. It is likely that it was the 'Otherness' of their (needle-sharing) lifestyle rather than direct class factors that primarily accounted for the negative responses to the 'Chris', 'Emma' and 'Debby' subjects. What this indicates is the significance of what Dervin calls 'time-space-bound' as against 'across-time-space' constancies (1992, p. 67). The 'Testimonial' data provide strong evidence that participants were responding primarily in terms of their own time-space-bound self-constructions as 'normal' individuals (in contrast to the stigmatised Other), rather than in terms of social class. This construction of the self versus the drug-using Other is not simply individualistic, but is developed through culture, related to binary oppositions around normal/deviant, clean/dirty, pure/contaminated. For example, as found in a study of crack cocaine users in a United States city, illicit drug users themselves adopt similar dichotomies to present themselves as 'clean' and therefore at low risk of contracting sexually transmitted diseases versus immoral and 'dirty' Others who are deemed more at risk of infection (Balshem et al. 1992).

We should also note, however, that the two most unsympathetic subjects, 'Chris' and 'Emma', were also the only two whom a majority of the study participants judged to be working-class. Given that a greater percentage of middle-class than working-class participants defined 'Chris' and 'Emma' as working-class, it may be that there was a process of out-grouping at work here. That is, 'Testimonial' characters who were primarily seen as Other because of their lifestyle were then redefined as Other in class terms too. Thus, because these characters used injecting drugs, they may have been considered 'working-class' by students who identified as 'middle-class'.

THE 'VOX POP CONDOMS' AUDIENCE RESEARCH

As well as pushing further into quantitative analysis of dominant cultural rhetorics, our 'Vox Pop Condom' research also began to extend our link between quantitative and qualitative methods of audience research. The second stage of the audience study was conducted in 1992 and consisted of showing the 'Condom Vox Pop (Granny)' advertisement to nearly 100 Year 11 Sydney school students (again chosen to give equal weight to gender and class). This screening was followed by three different measures of audience response: i) a qualitative measure which asked the participants first to summarise 'in three or four sentences what the ad was about'; ii) a short questionnaire about the advertisement; iii) finally, the participants were interviewed about their responses to the advertisement (this third measure of audience response will not be discussed in detail here for reasons of space, except illustratively).

Many studies have reported the largely negative meanings that inhere to condoms in the context of AIDS. In the area of 'faithful heterosex', for example, Kippax et al. (1990) point to dominant discourses among young Australians which frequently preclude the discussion of condom use at all. First, there is a major emphasis on the supposed 'normality' of heterosexual penetrative sex (in fact a practice dominated by male-dominant discourse). Second, heterosexuality is understood as involving romance, love and fidelity. The introduction of a condom into this scenario challenges these ideals, and it is therefore unlikely that condoms are introduced into 'regular' partnerships for condoms signify 'distrust'. Another study of young British people also found that condoms were more likely to be used in short-term relationships or for 'casual sex' as longer-term relationships involved issues of trust and faith that do not square well with using condoms to protect against HIV (Stephenson et al. 1993).

While government-sponsored AIDS advertisements have warned viewers to 'use condoms always', other media representations have swung from portraying condoms as 'life-savers' by protecting against the spread of HIV, to also showing them as embarrassing and risible (Lupton 1994a, pp. 72–7).

Given that the major intention of the DCSH and its advertising consultants in devising the 'Vox Pop Condom' advertisements was to 'socialise' condoms and make them 'fun' and 'normal', we were interested in exploring the ways in which young audiences responded to these advertisements. Just as there is an 'invisibility of heterosex' (Crawford et al. 1992, pp. 52 ff), so too there is an equally notable invisibility of discussion about older people's sexuality in western society. 'Condom Vox Pop (Granny)' did, albeit very briefly, focus on an older person's sexuality (though through events in her past). We were interested to see to what extent young people's representations of the advertisement derived from this 'sexuality in the past' (when she was younger) discourse, or whether they transformed the original text via a 'sexuality in the present' reading.

The summaries

In asking 'What was the ad about?' we were asking participants for 'topics of discourse'. The topic of discourse is a semantic representation that summarises the gist of a narrative and provides a text, at the macro level, with overall coherence from the respondent's point of view (van Dijk 1991, p. 72). Any text, whether written, audio or audio-visual, establishes 'macrostructural' propositions that hierarchically organise its various lower level propositions. For instance, a 1990 DCSH document argued that the 'Vox Pop Condom' advertisements addressed four key issues regarding condoms: buying them, carrying them, using them and parental endorsement. Thus, 'parental endorsement' is a macroproposition of the text, in the view of its producers. This organises the meaning and significance of lower level propositions like 'my mum found one in the wash'.

One of the main cognitive functions of textual macrostructures is the organising in memory of complex semantic information (van Dijk 1991, p. 72). The DCSH consultants may have seen 'Vox Pop Condom' as a simple, 'clear' and 'direct' (rather than 'subtle') public health advertisement. In fact, despite its brevity, it is a complex message form containing a wide range of semantic information, conveyed by different age and character types, a variety of gestures and emotions (from the 'stud' gestures of the Italian–Australian youth to the embarrassment of the girl because her 'mum might be watching'), and, as we noted above, four separate 'key issues' or messages. The topics of discourse are macrostructural in the sense that they reduce the complexity of the audio-visual text and thus facilitate memory ('this ad is about not being embarrassed to buy condoms', or 'this ad tells you that using condoms can be fun'). Topics of discourse are, in other words, entailed by the text-in-full, yet are at the same time (in our summaries) audience categories of information reduction that assisted memory.

By asking our respondents to write summaries of the advertisement prior to answering our survey questions, we were trying to establish what the salient units of information were for the audience. Our 'topic of discourse' measure was examining the differences in processing and memorising that 'text-in-full' by young people of different gender and class background. Each participant's choice of discourse topic indicated the main meaning of the text's detailed information for her/him. It was therefore important for this measure to be completed first before the questionnaire refocused their memories and meanings. This qualitative measure could then, of course, be quantified and compared to the DCSH's own stated 'key issues'.

Examples of the advertisement summaries provided by the young people are as follows:

> It's about condoms. They asked the people have you used them, and it's not embarrassing to buy them any more. Condoms are a natural part of life when before it wasn't.

> I think this ad was about condoms and the advantages of condoms. The ad shows the reactions that people have towards condoms and also the population that use them. It shows the fun that can be had with condoms and also what people know about them. It basically tells the public not to be so shy or embarrassed about using and purchasing them.

This 'topic of discourse' measure could draw out responses to the focus and form of the advertisement ('it's about different people's opinions about condoms') and its audience focus ('it is aimed mainly at the youth of the audience'). It could also elicit evaluations of this advertisement compared with other forms of public AIDS education: 'just other people's views on condoms—but it wasn't a very educational or explanitory [sic] advert for people who don't know nothing'; 'it's good to see that many people of old and young approve of them and think that they are good'; 'I think it is good that people are so open about it and now it can be used in a comical way but at the same time be serious'. In addition, the summaries gave the opportunity for young people to call up their own intertexts and push the 'comical way' subversively further—as in one participant's cartoon responses: 'Ronald McDonald uses pink condoms!', and 'Conelle [sic] Sanders from KFC uses edible condoms: "finger lickin' good"' (see Figure 9.4). Sometimes a single 'qualitative' response (as in these cartoons) can summarise an entire group's attitude and mood; the young people responded extremely positively to 'Vox Pop Condom'.

Figure 9.4 One student's suggested AIDS images

Table 9.5 Topics of discourse in the 'Vox Pop Condom' advertisement

	Gender of respondents		Class of respondents		
Topic	girls	boys	working-class	middle-class	total
The ad was about . . .	%	%	%	%	%
buying condoms	26	14	23	17	20
carrying condoms	14	25	26	15	20
using condoms for safer sex	84	59	63	77	71
safe sex is fun	35	23	9	42	29

Table 9.5 shows the 'topics of discourse' responses by class and gender, revealing that girls had a higher response to all the 'key issues' of the message take-out except for 'carrying condoms'. There are also statistically significant class differences in relation to the 'safe sex is fun' responses, with 42 per cent of middle-class but only 9 per cent of working-class students including this as a topic of discourse.

The questionnaire

According to the results of our 1990 survey, the 'Vox Pop Condom' advertisements had reached large numbers of the sample group when they were screened during the course of that year: 71 per cent of the participants recalled seeing the 'Condom Vox Pop' on air and 90 per cent of these had seen the 'Granny' version. Overall, 95 per cent of the participants who responded agreed 'with what they say about condoms in the ad', citing as their main reasons: 'safe sex is important' (59 per cent), 'sex is fun/ condoms are not a problem' (34 per cent), 'cool—seems to be the trend' (7 per cent) and 'shouldn't be ashamed of them/everyone should use them' (2 per cent). The few students who disagreed with the advertisements cited as their reasons 'condoms are a hassle', 'they are safe but don't feel as good', 'boring after a while, the pill is better with a regular partner', 'I don't like how they are slimy' and 'no sex before marriage'.

To address the ageist and racist representations that we had noted in open-ended responses to the 1990 post-screening questionnaire, we began the 1992 'Vox Pop Condom' questionnaire by asking, 'Which person in this condom ad did you like best? Say why?', and 'Which person did you like least? Say why?'. In addition, the participants were later asked specifically, 'Was it a good or bad idea having the older lady in the ad? Say why?'. Overall, the young people chose the older woman as the 'most liked' character (26 per cent), followed closely by the Italian–Australian youth (25 per cent) and the lifesaver character (25 per cent). The 'most liked' character differed substantially according to gender. Boys chose the Italian–Australian youth first (39 per cent), followed by the older woman (36 per cent), the two girls on the beach (8 per cent) and the lifesaver (8 per cent). Girls chose the lifesaver first (41 per cent), followed by the older woman (16 per cent), the 'other guy on the beach' (13 per cent), the Italian–Australian youth (11 per cent), the woman embarrassed that her mum might be watching (11 per cent), and the two girls on the beach (9 per cent).

The Italian–Australian youth (44 per cent) and the older woman (29 per cent) were also the most disliked overall, confirming our impressions from the 1990 post-screening questionnaire that these two characters generated strong pro and anti attitudes. Whereas girls were virtually unanimous in their reasons for liking the lifesaver best ('good looking', 'his body'), their reasons for liking or disliking the Italian–Australian youth and the older woman differed markedly. Girls easily disliked the youth most (56 per cent), followed a long way behind by the older woman (19 per cent). Boys disliked the older woman most (40 per cent), followed by the youth (30 per cent). Responses as to why they disliked these characters did reveal a degree of ageism and racism. In relation to the older lady, 53 per cent of the responses were either of the 'no-one would have sex with her/she made me sick' variety or else 'not appealing to my age group/didn't suit the topic of sex/looked out of place, odd'. The fact that all of these responses were from boys also indicates a degree of sexism here in addition to ageism. Responses as to why the participants disliked the Italian–Australian youth revealed 25 per cent of responses of the 'the wog loves himself, thinks he's a stud' variety, plus 12 per cent who said 'he looked a liar' or 'didn't speak good English'. There were, however, also a number of responses about this character condemning his attitude towards sex (34 per cent), almost entirely from the girls: 'has sex for fun, not caring', 'acts like he uses girls for one thing only', 'makes sex look dirty' and so on.

Responses to the question, 'Was it a good idea having the older lady in the ad?' revealed that the vast majority of the young people liked her role. Even a number of those who disliked her personally wanted her in the advertisement: 88 per cent thought it was a good idea. Analysis as to why they thought it was good to have an older person in the advertisement revealed a surprise: 47 per cent of those who responded (41 per cent of the total sample) to the open-ended question argued that, 'It shows that old people have sex too, and all generations need to use condoms'. These reasons situated the older woman's sexuality very clearly in the present, not the past (for example, the answers 'shows that sex isn't just for younger people', 'shows that older women, men still have sex'), despite the fact that in the advertisement the woman discusses her past, not her current sexual activity. Of the other responses, 33 per cent positioned her sexuality in the past (25 per cent said 'shows that condoms have been around for a while, weren't invented yesterday'; and 8 per cent said 'older people are wiser, have had more sexual experiences'); 12 per cent gave 'endorsement' reasons ('shows older people are not embarrassed by/accept condoms—views from all sides'); and 5 per cent found her 'funny'. Responses as to why it was a 'bad idea' including the older woman in the advertisement again revealed a degree of ageism, as in such comments as 'sex is for teenagers', 'you can't imagine old people using condoms', 'doesn't relate to our generation', 'gives a sense of disbelief'. Six out of the ten negative responses were of this kind (though this was only 7 per cent of the total sample).

CONCLUDING COMMENTS

In this chapter we have brought quantitative and qualitative approaches together in analysing young people's responses to key advertisements in the 1990 AIDS television campaign. As we said at the beginning of the chapter, our quantitative surveys were largely determined by the discourses and meanings circulating at the bureaucratic/commercial interface where these advertisements were made, and also in wider society. Throughout the chapter we have referred to 'the major message of the documentation', 'the major intention of the DCSH' and so on, because it is the relationship between their meanings and those of the young audiences that we were quantifying. At the same time, of course, we were relating young people's understandings to some of the meanings and discourses about AIDS, sexuality and injecting drug use that have been generated by cultural research on issues of gender, class, age, romance, notions of self and Other and so on.

It was within these already existing commercial/bureaucratic and societal discourses that the 1990 advertisements inevitably inserted themselves. Hence we can now extend our analysis in chapter 8 to argue that the 'effectiveness' of a television AIDS education campaign can be assessed in at least three significantly different ways: i) the 'economic' and quantitative measure of 'audience reach'; ii) the degree to which the 'message take-out' designed by the producers of the campaign is recognised as equally salient by its audiences; and iii) the relationship of the campaign to dominant discourses and meanings circulating among the audiences for AIDS advertisements. While it was apparent from our research that the audience members were easily able to identify the key messages of these advertisements, and seemed largely positive about them, there was strong evidence of an 'us/them' separation of *'clean' and 'dirty' sub-cultures*. The women in the 'Testimonial' advertisements who had contracted the virus sexually were constructed as 'victims' and 'like us', whereas there was evidence of a strong 'blaming the stigmatised Other' response in relation to the characters who had contracted HIV through sharing needles to inject drugs. In the next chapter we go on to discuss how the characters in the *ACP* 'Sophie' episodes were viewed by young people.

READING 'SOPHIE'

In chapter 2, we made a number of criticisms of conventional quantitative analysis in the field of health communication. We argued that qualitative work, particularly ethnographic analysis, is situated analysis. That is, it works out inductively from the cultural group in question. This approach, rather than analysis inwards via sampling procedures and statistical techniques, is the focus of ethnographic research because 'variables' cannot be isolated until cultural meanings are. Our ethnographic study of the production of the *ACP* 'Sophie' episodes did give us access to meaning and professional practice in the time-space coordinates of producing a popular, peak-viewing soap opera.

In this chapter we will look at young people's responses to these episodes in the context of the intentions of the production team that we explored in chapters 6 and 7. These include their concerns with young people's awareness about 'the second wave', concerns about the AIDS-related risks of 'shooting up once at a party', suggestions that heroin should be legalised, the intention of changing young people's perception of the class basis of heroin use, and so on. By using these insights into the meanings and preferences of the producers as a basis for our questionnaire, we do not entirely avoid the inflexibilities of survey research that we described earlier, but we do base our quantification on the notions of audience meaning established among the production team and revealed during the ethnographic part of the research. The actual construction of what might otherwise look like a 'laboratory-style' survey method, moreover, where we showed audience groups differently edited versions of 'Sophie', was itself determined by production house-style concerns.

MEASURING RESPONSES TO PRODUCTION MEANINGS

Writer Tony Morphett had expressed concern to us about the house-style of *ACP*. According to *ACP*'s 'older sort of storytelling on screen', writers have to cut away from stories involving any one set of characters if there is a scene shift: for naturalistic reasons, 'you must give them "time to get across town"'. Morphett commented that:

> As a screen writer, it's probably the most awkward convention in *A Country Practice* . . . Very often you find that you have to put one story aside and do a scene somewhere else about something totally different, and then come back to your story, instead of driving forward with your main story. It's an impact problem—you're losing momentum. Now this may, in fact, make *A Country Practice* less threatening viewing. It may be that it creates a sense of audience relief from a heavy story.

Here there is a perceived contradiction between commercial television's primary concern with keeping viewer attention ('driving on with your main story . . . an impact problem . . . losing momentum') and the specific program ideology of consensus and 'happy endings' ('a sense of audience relief from a heavy story'). As a central part of the rhetorical strategies of making *ACP*, this is an important practical concern that threads itself through all stages of the production process, not just the writing. It has, in other words, production *effect*. As we described earlier, producer Forrest Redlich adopted the strategy of 'thematically balancing stories' (for instance the contrast between the 'kids off the rails' and 'exploited kids' stories, the latter including the 'parallel' between the 'Terence abandons child Sophie' back-story and the 'father abandons kids' sub-plot). This was one way of doing 'a scene somewhere else about something totally different' without losing the thematic focus of the episode.

THE 1990 AUDIENCE RESEARCH

To explore this production concern about audience 'impact' further, in the 1990 school students project we described in chapter 9, we showed different student groups (of similar age, class and gender composition) three differently edited versions of 'Sophie'. One contained the parallel 'father abandons kids' balancing story, while the other two were 'impact' versions, containing only the central AIDS 'health message' story. In quantifying audience responses to these processual meanings, we wanted to avoid some of our own criticisms about conventional quantitative work in health communication and health promotion (see chapter 2). Rather than using traditional researcher-led coding categories like 'predominant message appeal', we used, as noted in the previous chapter, stylistic aspects of the television text that were significant to production goals. Similarly, in this chapter we use specific 'message intent' discourses drawn from the production team. We are, in other words, accepting up-front that the preconstruction of coding categories is a subjective task and is contextually based (in this case in the time/space coordinates of commercial television).

In this research we were concerned with audience 'meanings' as well as with Tony Morphett's sense of audience 'impact'. By using the same research procedures for audience responses both to the 1990 AIDS advertising campaign (chapter 9) and to the 'Sophie' episodes we could begin to probe generic differences in audience meanings as well. We were interested also in the audience meanings generated by production discourses associated with the 'semiotically thick' television text. As we discussed in chapter 7, a 'pastoral' country versus city opposition was constructed in the 'Sophie' episodes particularly through the use of lighting and sound. Again there was a potential production contradiction here: between the 'bit of a rebel' teenager Paul with whom the executive producer James Davern hoped young viewers would empathise, and Paul as the 'deviant Other' from the city, marked in particular by the ominous bell-tree music 'heroin' sound. One problem with Jim Davern's preference for the sympathetic construction of Paul's character was that it focused on only one characteristic, whereas a character who is represented over nearly four hours of narrative is inevitably complex, conveying many potential meanings to an audience. Our quantitative methodology needed to be able to assess more complex dimensions of positive and negative responses towards Paul around this 'bit of a rebel' characterisation.

To attempt to address these issues, in our research design one version of 'Sophie' (tape one) contained the parallel 'failure of communication' story of the father who deserts his children, two versions did not. Of the two versions of 'Sophie' that excluded this 'balancing story', one (tape two) contained the sequence where Paul comes to Terence and Alex's house with Rhys Rees' ominous 'heroin' score playing, and one (tape three) omitted this scene. These differently edited versions of 'Sophie' were designed to examine; a) the influence of the parallel 'balancing story' on audience impact and meanings; and b) the influence of the Paul scene with menacing sound score on audience impact and meanings. As such, one variation in the process of transformation (writing) and one variation in the process of transcodification (audio) were examined. Clearly it is impossible to experimentally isolate audio codes when researching to-air programs. Other aspects of the characterisation of Paul in this scene, such as Sophie choosing to leave her father's house to join Paul, may well have been significant in influencing audience readings. In this very short sequence, however, the musical score was especially dominant.

The 'Sophie' audience research was part of a broader project that included the 'Testimonials' and 'Vox Pop Condom' audience study. This was conducted (as explained in chapter 9) with nearly 900 students balanced in terms of class background and gender. In this study we wanted to go beyond simple survey questions about needle-sharing awareness. We wanted to try to compare the effectiveness and the meaning of government AIDS advertisements with soap opera. Further, we wanted to try to examine the 'impact' of different kinds of soap opera narrative, following Tony Morphett's concern with narratives that 'cut away' from the main AIDS-related action. We were, of course, manipulating the 'Sophie' episodes; we were not screening the 'real', to-air four-episode 'Sophie' sequence. All research, however, is 'manipulated' in some way and in this case our manipulation was determined by production discourses.

Three kinds of comparison were made possible by the audience research plan for this study: i) 'before' and 'after' comparisons of responses to specific health messages: for example, about legalising heroin, the risks of needle sharing and so on; ii) 'balancing story' and transcodification comparisons as between responses to three different 'Sophie' narratives; iii) generic comparisons between responses to the soap opera and the government AIDS advertisements.

'Before' and 'after' comparisons

Wayside Chapel social worker, Virginia Foster, had persuaded the *ACP* production team to do a 'second wave' story (that is, that needle sharing was a conduit for HIV infection) to get across the message: 'HIV/AIDS is not just a homosexual disease, it belongs to everybody'. The question, 'Do you think you are at risk from AIDS?' was asked in both the pre- and post-screening 'Sophie' questionnaires, ranked on a five-point scale from 'very high risk' to 'no risk'. For the groups as a whole, there was a significant shift between pre- and post-screening responses, but in the direction of even less perception of self-risk. Students felt *less* that the risk of AIDS 'belonged to everybody' after seeing the *ACP* needle-sharing story. This was particularly the case for girls, whose 'no risk' response increased from 37 per cent to 45 per cent after seeing 'Sophie', and working-class students whose 'no risk' response increased from 39 per cent to 48 per cent.

Because of the minimal emphasis in 'Sophie' on Paul and Sophie's sexual relations, and given, too (as we will see from the semantic differential data), the general reading of Paul and Sophie as Other, the needle-sharing message in 'Sophie' seems to have been received by these young people, but read as someone else's problem. Focus group discussions with the young people indicated that most students did not know anyone who used heroin, and that they tended to see injecting drug use as something done in some other place. Their responses included such comments as: 'maybe closer to the city', 'most of them around here are too smart to do it. But down the Cross is a higher sort of risk area to hang around in our age group'. The young people also tended to describe injecting drug use as an activity of other groups of young people: 'most of them [injecting drug users] drop out of school before year 10', 'most of them are older and have left school'. While, for this reason, they felt that they were more at risk personally from sexual contact, many students believed that things were relatively under control in that area: they felt they knew a lot about protection, and moreover that they and their friends mostly 'were careful' and used condoms. They recognised that safer sex did not always happen, but compared with the very high risk of needle infection among other communities, they felt relatively less at risk.

Consequently, the focus in 'Sophie' on AIDS risk, emphasising the problems associated with needle sharing rather than with Sophie and Paul's sexual activities, may actually have distanced the risk rather than making it seem to 'belong to everybody'. Hence the generally lower personal 'risk' responses post-screening. This does not explain, however, why viewers of tape two did not feel less at risk after seeing 'Sophie'. We will return to this later.

In one scene from 'Sophie', Terence Elliott discusses the economy of heroin use with Matron Sloan and suggests that many of the problems Sophie faced would have disappeared if heroin were legalised. While initially plotting this as something of a time-filler, director Leigh Spence had changed his mind and taken extra care with this scene after hearing a radio program about legalising heroin. Spence was a director who rarely deviated from his pre-planned camera positions (a style of directing associated, in the view of producers, with 'BBC/ABC' directing conventions). But after watching the scene being shot, Spence did what for him was unusual, and changed his camera positions. What Spence now called 'an important scene', was reshot more expressively, with Terence more often in full-face rather than in profile (as the scene was blocked originally). This was the only scene in the four episodes where legalising heroin was raised as an issue. What impact would this message (with its intertextually influenced camera style) have on the students?

The question 'Do you think heroin should be legalised?' was asked in both the pre- and post-screening questionnaire. In the pre-screening questionnaire, 25 per cent of the sample agreed (boys 29 per cent, girls 21 per cent, working-class respondents 18 per cent, middle-class respondents 30 per cent). This response increased markedly in the post-screening questionnaire with 44 per cent of the sample responding agreeing to this question (boys 50 per cent, girls 39 per cent, working-class respondents 37 per cent, middle-class respondents 51 per cent). These findings reveal there were statistically significant changes in all gender and class categories in favour of legalising heroin. This response, however, does not tell us *why* the participants changed their minds.

Our methodology enabled us to trace these changes in more detail. In both the pre- and post-test surveys we asked students the reasons why they thought that heroin should or should not be legalised. By comparing these with the reasons given by Terence for legalising heroin, we could trace the degree to which his arguments appeared for the first time among students who changed their minds to saying 'yes' to legalising heroin. The reasons given by Terence in the 'legalise heroin' scene were: by prescribing heroin there would be more control and benefits for society; it would stop the violence and crime associated with the illegal heroin sub-cultures; it would save on police activity and reduce the black market in heroin; it would improve health conditions among injecting drug users, both in terms of better nutrition and lifestyle (since heroin itself would be cheaper) and in ensuring clean heroin and needles; and it would end the making of profit out of users' misfortune.

When we examined post-screening reasons given for 'yes' responses to legalising heroin, we found that 73 per cent of the participants gave one or more of Terence's reasons, and 27 per cent gave other reasons (for example, 'it would be less fun if it was legal, so less people would do it', 'there would be less spread of heroin'). We could, however, be even more precise than this. Because we had coded individual pre- and post-screening responses, we were able to trace the reasons given by those students who changed their minds about legalising heroin and compare these with their earlier reasons as well as with agreement with Terence's reasons or 'other' reasons. Of the students who changed their minds, 87 per cent did so from 'no' (or uncertain) to 'yes', 6 per cent from 'yes' to 'no', and 7 per cent from 'no' to 'yes/no' (uncertain). Of those who changed their mind from 'no' to 'yes' (77 per cent), 'uncertain' to 'yes' (10 per cent) and 'no' to 'yes/no' (8 per cent), 94 per cent gave Terence's reasons for this change, and 6 per cent gave 'other' reasons. We can then say with some confidence that the script editor's extra scene may well have had some effect on changing attitudes to the issue of legalising heroin (bearing in mind that a major weakness of this kind of before/after research is that it only measures attitude change in the very short term).

We have to remember that 50 per cent of the boys and 61 per cent of the girls still said 'no' to legalising heroin even after seeing this scene. Significant numbers of students, however, did change their minds to a 'yes' response to legalising heroin, and for these Terence's arguments seem to have been persuasive. Why? It may be that, despite the paralleling of Sophie's and Terence's drug/alcohol addiction and the indirect suggestion that Terence's alcoholism had started Sophie on her road to disaster, the character of Terence was sufficiently empathised with for the 'legalise heroin' message to get through. Our data support this empathy with Terence. When asked, 'whom do you sympathise with more in this story, Sophie or Terence?', 78 per cent of participants nominated Terence and only 15 per cent nominated Sophie. In the focus group interviews, too, students were generally unsympathetic to Sophie because 'she brought it on herself', whereas in the case of Terence all students were sympathetic, and some said they felt most sorry for him (out of all the characters) because he had made mistakes with his children in the past and was now living with the fatal consequences. In this situation, where it seems that no-one felt hostile to Terence, James Davern's contention that soap opera is less distancing than health education advertisements because of audiences' involvement with the characters and thus 'the message is much, much stronger' seems to have been supported. This may well have had a significant effect on the changes in attitude to legalising heroin.

The overt message of 'Sophie' intended by its producers was 'don't share needles'. When we conducted the research, the government campaign that emphasised the danger of needle sharing in the 'Testimonials' and 'Needle Bed' advertisements was screening. We asked in both pre- and post-screening questionnaires: 'What types of things do people have to do to get AIDS? Please list these in order of risk as you perceive it.' Although the participants were knowledgeable about needle sharing before viewing 'Sophie', their ranking of it 'in order of risk' was significantly higher post-screening. In the pre-screening questionnaire data, all the nominated sexual risk activities ('sex', 'unsafe sex', 'sex without protection with infected person', 'casual sex') accounted for 46 per cent of the students' first ranked 'risk practice' choices, and all the nominated needle risk activities ('using needles', 'sharing needles', 'contaminated needles', 'dirty syringes') accounted for 34 per cent of the students' first choices. After viewing 'Sophie', sexual risk activities accounted for 28 per cent and needle risk activities for 63 per cent of the students' first choices.

To some extent this change was the result of the students re-ordering their ranking of risk: needle risk activities dropped from 49 per cent to 29 per cent as second choice 'risk' practices between pre- and post-screening questionnaires, as they climbed from 34 per cent to 63 per cent as first choice 'risk' practices. Nonetheless, the overall shift is also the result of more students ranking needle risk activities for the first time: 90 per cent of all students mentioned 'sharing needles' as either first, second or third most risky activity after seeing 'Sophie', whereas only 64 per cent mentioned 'sharing needles' before seeing 'Sophie'. This increase was matched in all groups: boys increased their mentions of 'sharing needles' from 61 per cent to 86 per cent; girls from 67 per cent to 94 per cent; working-class students from 67 per cent to 90 per cent; and middle-class students from 62 per cent to 90 per cent.

In the post-screening questionnaire, the young people were asked a question that related to James Davern's concerns about casual drug use as an HIV risk: 'How much risk is there of getting AIDS from sharing needles once at a party?'. Their responses were as follows: very high risk (66 per cent); high risk (27 per cent); moderate risk (5 per cent); low risk (1 per cent); no risk (1 per cent). This question was not asked in the pre-screening questionnaire in order not to cue the 'What things do people have to do to get AIDS?' question. The post-screening result, however, taken in conjunction with the already reported decrease in the participant's level of perceived risk of HIV/AIDS, indicates that they saw themselves as highly unlikely to share needles. Those individuals who did share needles (for example, Sophie and Paul) were thus likely to be seen by these young people as different, distant and Other.

As we saw earlier, the focus group interviews supported this interpretation. What was clear from the focus group discussions is that when asked which is a higher risk activity, needle sharing or sex, some participants said needle sharing 'because the blood's going straight into the bloodstream', and some said sex because they knew a lot of people who were sexually active while they knew virtually no injecting drug users. In other words, these young people's interpretation of general current risk depended on whether they adopted a direct physical reading of the question, which is probably how they responded to the 'shooting up once at a party' question, or a reading based on personal experience. In neither case did these students see needle sharing as a risk for themselves or for their immediate social group. As participants in one focus group commented of people they knew:

> Sure, a couple of them will try marijuana and stuff like that, but—
> Yeah, but nobody seems to get into needles.

'Balancing story' and transcodification comparisons

Tony Morphett had told us that he was uncertain whether the *ACP* convention of swapping between characters and scenes instead of 'driving the narrative forward' was lessening the impact of his AIDS message in 'Sophie', or alternatively was simply encouraging the audience to keep watching. We have already seen that the responses of the young people differed significantly between pre- and post-screening, and that this shift was in the direction of feeling less at risk. When responses were analysed according to the tape the participants watched, however, statistically significant differences emerged.

Students who watched tape two (the ominous music version) retained almost the same level of 'at-risk' self-perception after seeing 'Sophie', while the 'at-risk' responses of tape one students were significantly reduced after seeing 'Sophie'. Twenty-one per cent of the participants who watched tape two, compared with 12 per cent who watched tape one, felt themselves to be at moderate to very high risk from AIDS. Was it the case (as Tony Morphett speculated) that 'going somewhere else for a minute or two and then coming back' created 'a sense of audience relief from the heavy story'? Certainly these viewers of *ACP*'s regular pattern of 'balancing stories' felt less threatened after seeing it. But then, so too did the viewers of tape three, which did not cut away to a balancing story. Moreover, if, as we suggested earlier, it was the perception of injecting drug users as Other that explains the generally lower 'at-risk' self-perception of students after seeing 'Sophie', why did viewers of tape two differ in this? In fact, as we will see, tape two viewers differed significantly from tape one and three viewers in a number of ways, which we can examine using both quantitative and qualitative methods.

Quantitative measures

We measured Tony Morphett's 'impact problem' in two ways:

i)   by asking students who had seen the different tapes to compare this episode 'with any other TV material about AIDS you have seen (e.g. the "Grim Reaper" ad., *The Flying Doctors* episode on AIDS, *Suzi's Story*, *GP*, the most recent AIDS ads, etc.)' in terms of 'which did you feel was most effective in getting its message across?'
ii) by asking the same students 'what was the main message' of the episode? (How effectively, in other words, did the different tapes get the needle-sharing message across?)

The most noticeable response here was the major increase in the perceived effectiveness of 'Sophie' compared with the pre-screening questionnaire. All groups now nominated *ACP* as the 'most effective' television material about AIDS (46 per cent), followed by the documentary-drama *Suzi's Story* (30 per cent), the 'Grim Reaper' advertisement (14 per cent), all other AIDS advertisements (6 per cent), *GP* (2 per cent), the Canadian youth drama *21 Jump St* and documentaries (each with 1 per cent). As before, clear gender differences were found in regard to students' preferences. This 'impact' shift for *ACP* could, of course, simply be an effect of the students just having watched the *ACP* tape. Indeed, in our other school-based research we found that students overall do not find soap opera very useful in helping them deal with specific HIV-related risks. In our 1994 AIDS education study, when participants were asked what type of media they would find helpful to provide information on safer sex techniques, they placed the response 'A TV drama/soapie like *Melrose Place* that discusses using condoms' last, while favouring 'shock/horror' television advertisements.

The 'most effective' measure revealed no differences in perceived impact between the different tapes of 'Sophie'. Nonetheless, the 'main message' measure did produce significant differences between the audiences of the different tapes. Responses were later coded into 37 categories, of which easily the most frequent overall was: 'needle sharing and AIDS spread' (31 per cent). This response was followed by 'heroin message' (12 per cent); 'effects of drug use on self, family, life' (11 per cent), 'cautionary message about drug use' (7 per cent); 'reality of addict's life' (5 per cent); and 'interrelationship of drugs and AIDS' (5 per cent). However, 41 per cent of students who had seen the 'ominous music' tape two compared with only 27 per cent of students who had watched tape one gave the 'needle-sharing and AIDS spread' response (a similar pattern emerged in relation to the weaker 'interrelationship of drugs and AIDS' response). One likely explanation for this, that there were more messages overall in the longer tape one containing its additional narrative strand, is invalidated by the fact that tape three (the shortest tape, without the parallel story) also generated only 27 per cent who saw 'needle sharing' as the main message. The only difference between tapes two and three was the scene with Paul coming to 'Camelot' and demanding of Alex that he should see Sophie.

In other words, according to this measure, there was no lessening of the impact of Tony Morphett's main message between the story which 'goes somewhere else' (tape one) and the story which 'drives the narrative on' without the distraction of 'balancing stories' (tape three). There is, however, a greater needle-sharing message impact in the story that establishes Paul as a greater threat by way of the ominous 'heroin' music (tape two). If, as it appears from these different measures, there was a difference of impact (especially between tapes one and two), what did this difference of impact mean?

What meaning did these different tapes about Sophie and Paul's addiction convey to the audience? And how might these differences of meaning relate to our unresolved question as to why viewers of tape two felt more personally at risk after seeing 'Sophie' than viewers of tapes one and three, and also extracted a stronger 'needle-sharing' message? To address these questions, in our survey we asked the question: 'Is heroin addiction, do you think, mainly the result of: i) psychological problems (eg, personality disorders); ii) social reasons (eg, family breakdown, peer group pressure etc); iii) personal choice (eg, 'we are in control of what we do'); iv) moral reasons (eg, junkies are innately bad, immoral etc)?'. The 'Sophie' narrative had particularly emphasised both personal choice and social reasons (in particular, family breakdown), but the tape one edited version that we showed carried an additional family breakdown 'balancing story' (involving characters other than those related to the 'Sophie' plot) while the others did not.

Overall, social reasons were seen as the cause of Sophie's addiction by most students. Their major responses were as follows: i) psychological problems (9 per cent); ii) social reasons (58 per cent); iii) personal choice (20 per cent); and iv) moral reasons (2 per cent). Although there were no statistically significant class or gender differences here, there were significant variations according to which tape students watched, with, again, viewers of tape two showing the most marked variation from the overall response pattern. Whereas 61 per cent of tape one viewers and 68 per cent of tape three viewers chose 'social reasons', only 43 per cent of tape two viewers did so. In contrast, 37 per cent of tape two viewers, but only 15 per cent of tape one viewers and 13 per cent of tape three viewers emphasised 'personal choice' as the cause of heroin addiction.

The additional scene that was included in tape two but not in tape three was of Paul coming to Alex's door, being sent away by Alex, but being overheard by Sophie who chases after Paul and (ignoring Alex's desperate pleas) joins him, ending in her fatal overdose. This scene is also included in tape one, but is offset there by the parallel story which underpins the 'parental responsibility/family breakdown' message of the Sophie/Terence story. There is some indication of this underpinning function of the 'balancing story' in the responses to a further question: 'Why do you think that Sophie became a street junkie?': 36 per cent of tape one viewers responded with a 'family breakdown' answer in comparison with 29 per cent of tape three viewers and 27 per cent of tape two viewers.

In the absence of the parallel story, the scene in tape two of the 'villainous' Paul (accompanied by the ominous music) resisted by Alex, but followed by Sophie (who thus chooses her fate) seems to have had some influence on the meaning that students took away from the episode. In emphasising 'personal choice', the tendency was for the young people to view HIV infection as caused by personal choice rather than by social pressures. Again, the semantic differentials data confirm differences in response to the three 'Sophie' tapes (See Figure 10.1).

A discriminant function analysis (which enables us to identify characteristics that differentiate between tapes) indicates that Paul was seen as significantly stronger, more aggressive, rebellious and unsympathetic by tape two viewers than by tape one viewers. The 'bit of a rebel' characterisation which James Davern hoped would attract young audiences to Paul in fact needs to be seen as part of an overall negative cluster of characteristics (cold, aggressive, unsympathetic, rebellious)—particularly for viewers of tape two. Perhaps tape one viewers were more able to equate Paul with the unruly boy abandoned by his father in the parallel story included in the 'Sophie' episodes.

As the survey demonstrated, tape two viewers were also significantly less likely to see 'social causes' as the reason for heroin addiction (Paul, like Sophie, was to some extent the victim of family breakdown). Comparison of responses to the three tapes does seem to suggest that removal of the 'balancing story' could lead to greater 'impact' of the HIV/AIDS message on the young audience members (in terms at least of a greater self-perception of HIV/AIDS risk, and a stronger needle-sharing message). The kind of message that tape one viewers received was more sympathetic than that received by tape two viewers, in the sense that HIV infection was understood as the result of social causes rather than personal motivation. In contrast, viewers of tape two (which 'villainised' Paul by way of ominous music) were significantly less inclined to social explanation, and, as a corollary, saw Paul as personally more agentive (stronger, more aggressive, and much less a victim) in his own destiny and that of others.

In addition, we used regression analysis to reveal the perceptions of Paul which prompted sympathy for him among our audience. The more sympathetic viewers were those who saw Paul as a 'victim',

Figure 10.1 Semantic differentials—'Paul' by different 'Sophie' tapes

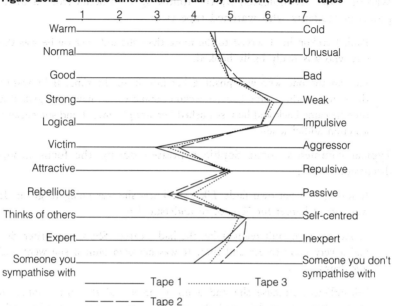

	1	2	3	4	5	6	7	
Warm								Cold
Normal								Unusual
Good								Bad
Strong								Weak
Logical								Impulsive
Victim								Aggressor
Attractive								Repulsive
Rebellious								Passive
Thinks of others								Self-centred
Expert								Inexpert
Someone you sympathise with								Someone you don't sympathise with

——————— Tape 1 ···················· Tape 3

— — — — — Tape 2

'good', 'thinks of others' and 'warm'. Only on the scale victim/aggressor, however, was Paul even slightly on the positive side of the semantic differential scale—and then only for girls and middle-class students. Presumably, these participants were responding to his deprived background. There is also evidence that the 'Paul at Alex's door with ominous music over' scene worked significantly against reading Paul as 'us' rather than Other in the finding that viewers of tape two found Paul more aggressive and less of a victim than viewers of other tapes.

Qualitative measures

Thus far we have drawn only on the quantitative data to examine the different 'impacts' and 'meanings' of the different tapes. This was primarily a quantitative study, but we did conduct some focus group discussions with young people who had viewed tape two or tape three in order to tease out a little further the different readings of Paul and Sophie. The significant impact of the scene of Paul returning to

Wandin Valley is indicated by the following comments from a focus group of students who watched tape two:

> Paul, I reckon he deserved to die more than she did because he was the one who was really badly hooked.

> He was the one who was pushing her into it all the time. If he wasn't there, if he didn't come back, I reckon Sophie would have changed. But then he came back and he just pushed her straight into it and she became a heroin addict again.

Typical comments about Sophie expressed during the focus group discussions were:

> It was sort of her own fault. Like, she knew she was going to get it. It was sort of harder for Terence to understand it.

> It was her own fault really. Like, she had a career. She was a writer. She had a very good career and that. It was her own fault if she went and got drugs.

> Self-inflicted. Because she had a good career and she just wanted to change her path in life, and she just went the wrong way. She could have changed it if she wanted to bad enough, but didn't.

This 'self inflicted/she had the choice' interpretation, however, was inflected in different ways in different groups. A focus group that had viewed tape two was hostile to Paul, ascribing his actions to 'mental problems or something':

> Well, you don't know much about Paul's background. We just know that she saw him shooting up, and that kind of attracted her—his honesty was what attracted her to him. It's hard for just anyone to understand that.
>
> *Interviewer* So did you sympathise with him at all?
>
> Not really—there's nothing much to sympathise with—like he might have mental problems or something. So there's nothing much—there's not much you can, like, sympathise with.

In contrast, a focus group comprised of young people who had viewed tape three, while also emphasising their lack of sympathy, immediately adopted a more frustrated than rejecting position:

> I don't sympathise with them, because they had their choice.

It's more frustrating than anything.

Yeah, I know.

That it's getting bigger. It's not as if it's getting any better. Just more people getting lost.

It's unbelievable. You try and talk about it, but you can't—you don't—there's nothing to say.

You can't say what you feel.

Like, you feel everything. You feel emotion and, like, frustration and anger and that, but still you can't say anything. You can't express yourself properly, because it's just so overwhelming.

The way in which they know it finishes in a dead-end, their lives. And they do it—there's no way out.

In this focus group, the young people's familiar emphasis on 'they had their choice' seemed to lead to fatalism rather than to anger and rejection; or at least to 'feeling everything' but saying nothing because 'it's just so overwhelming'. These students had no purchase on what to do about heroin addiction or HIV infection, or even what to say about those who are affected. Nevertheless, this did not prevent these students from using the 'Sophie' text to try and understand and evaluate Sophie and Paul's actions:

Interviewer Why do you think Sophie became a junkie?

Because of her boyfriend, wasn't it?

Wasn't it just casual? Casual drug taking?

It was coming to terms with herself.

That's what she said.

Yeah.

Yeah, when she saw that boy.

Prioritise.

Had his priorities.

I didn't really know why she had to because she was a journalist.

Mmm. Maybe she was trying to rebel against her father.

To me she had her priorities set, before she met him.

Interviewer What do you think she meant by 'priorities'?

[Long pause]

Maybe—if she was straight and she'd become a journo, you never know what's around the corner. But now that she's a junkie, she knows—what's going to happen to her.

She may have just wanted to express her freedom of choice.

Yeah. The light—it's just clear, you know—you know what's going to happen. I think she was trying to say that even if you're a junkie, like a real second-class citizen or something, you've still got priorities. And priorities are normally—if you have priorities, you're normally a person that knows what's—oh, you know, you're realistic. You know what's going on, and I don't know, like priorities for a person, like a doctor might be to do his job properly, and I don't know, keeping his house tidy or something. But, still, drug addicts have priorities too. But theirs are less—

There's not much of a choice in that.

Yeah—forced upon them.

Interviewer How about Paul? What did you think of him?

I don't know—the picture he put across was more like it was his own fault.

I felt sorry for him in a way. They—as Sophie said, if it wasn't for her he still might have been living.

I felt more sorry for Paul than Sophie though, because Paul was in it and like most young drug addicts you feel sorry for them because they can't get out of that sort of circle. But Sophie didn't seem to mind. She seemed to like the idea of the whole thing.

And she had a better choice too in the lifestyle she leads.

Like he wanted to be a mechanic and she was a journalist.

He was more—you can't be forced, but that's—

He had it harder.

Yeah. That's the only word I can think of.

People like that they get in the situation where they think they've got no choice and just find themselves with a group that do that sort of thing.

He was not getting nowhere near as much money as she was.

With her job she could have a really rich lifestyle, comfortable—but she chose to live in a squat.

What we're trying to say is that we feel more sympathy for Paul, because he had it hard all along, like he got kicked out of home—

There's still no excuse but I see what you mean.

There's no excuse but, he sort of had a reason to turn to drugs. But Sophie—she didn't. She just—probably if you're rich—a little rich rebellious type of thing.

These students who say, 'You try and talk about it, but you can't— you don't—there's nothing to say', in fact do talk, even though they do so at times with hesitation, difficulty and some long pauses. The focus group transcript indicates how they grapple with very specific details of the text—Sophie's talk about 'prioritising' and 'coming to terms with' her life, her doctor father's disgust with her squalid and untidy living conditions in Kings Cross, the back-story of her casual drug taking as a journalist, Paul's account of wanting to be a mechanic and being kicked out of home by his father—in order to make sense of this 'so overwhelming' AIDS narrative.

Quantitative data aside, what we can say by looking at the focus group discussions is that different versions of 'Sophie' gave students different narratives for their explanation of 'what went wrong'. Depending upon which particular narrative they foregrounded in their explanation, the 'self-inflicted' evaluation of Sophie and Paul was weighted in different ways. The 'ominous music' scene of Paul seeking out Sophie was clearly a strong narrative for those students who saw it. In the two focus groups that we conducted with viewers of tape two, this narrative helped to motivate the 'he deserved to die the most' and 'had mental problems' readings. In contrast, perhaps it is not a coincidence that the most sympathetic discussion of Paul took place among viewers of tape three, the only version that did not show the 'Paul arrives/ominous music' scene. Among these students, the narrative about Paul's past enabled a sympathetic reading, and in contrast it was Sophie's privileged class background that was mobilised against her.

We have to be aware of the limitations of both quantitative and qualitative approaches in this particular study. The major quantitative weakness is that our school-based design made it impossible to randomise our sample. So although we were careful to balance our survey groups in terms of the cultural categories of class and gender, it is still possible that some factor other than tape difference accounted for the significant disparities between viewers of tape two and other respondents. The major qualitative weakness was that we conducted too few focus groups (two each with tape two and tape three students) to make any strong claims about our interpretations. But even these few focus group interviews indicate how careful one must be in interpreting quantitative data. All we can say for certain is that television audiences are offered narratives as logics for social and personal explanation and evaluation. When the 'villainised' scene of Paul's arrival at 'Camelot' was shown in the absence of parallel 'family breakdown' narratives, it seems to have been more readily appropriated for interpreting Paul and Sophie (and evaluating their choices of action) than other narrative logics that were available (such as Paul's deprived background). This may be an explanation for the significantly more negative cluster of values associated with Paul by the tape two semantic differentials, as well as the significantly stronger 'personal choice' than 'social causes' interpretation by tape two viewers than tape one or tape three viewers. It may also be the reason for a significantly larger percentage of tape two viewers than tape one or tape three viewers extracting the 'needle-sharing' rather than 'effects of drug use on self, family, life' message from the 'Sophie' texts.

Perhaps, too, it was the greater emphasis on this 'softer' family-context meaning than on the 'harder' aggressive-Paul meanings that left viewers of tapes one and three feeling less personally 'at-risk' than viewers of tape two. Paul was certainly read more as Other by tape two students. However, he was also viewed as more of a 'villain' who penetrates 'our' homes, leading to the death of Sophie when she is trying to be most like 'us'. We should also note that, when giving reasons for 'legalising heroin', 44 per cent of students overall who changed their minds gave crimes like breaking and entering as the reason, whereas 55 per cent of tape two students gave this reason. Perhaps it was the Paul who aggressively confronted Alex at her own home to take Sophie away who made students feel more at risk after seeing the episode. Here was an Other who broke into the very core of the 'normal' heterosexual family. We need to be clear about this, however. We are not suggesting that the 'Paul at door/ominous music' scene had a determinant effect in some kind of 'hypodermic' way. Rather, we are saying that audiences always actively choose among the narrative explanations which they are offered. When the 'villainous Paul' scene *was* offered, it may have had a more powerful influence than some of the other narrative logics on offer.

Figure 10.2 Semantic differentials—'Sophie'

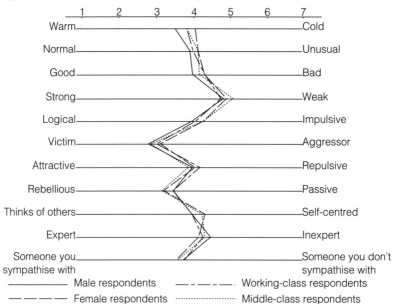

	1	2	3	4	5	6	7	
Warm								Cold
Normal								Unusual
Good								Bad
Strong								Weak
Logical								Impulsive
Victim								Aggressor
Attractive								Repulsive
Rebellious								Passive
Thinks of others								Self-centred
Expert								Inexpert
Someone you sympathise with								Someone you don't sympathise with

———————— Male respondents —— - —— - —— Working-class respondents

— — — — Female respondents ·················· Middle-class respondents

Generic comparisons

Finally in this 1990 study, we were interested to compare the relative impact and meanings associated with needle-sharing messages inserted in soap opera ('Sophie') and government-sponsored AIDS advertisements (the 'Testimonials') in order to assess *ACP* executive producer James Davern's view that soap operas are more effective than public health advertisements in getting health messages across.

Semantic differential measures assessing the Sophie and Paul characters from *ACP* and the 'Sarah', 'Chris' and 'Debby' subjects from the 'Testimonial' advertisements were compared. What was immediately clear was that graphs of responses (by gender and class) for each of the five characters were remarkably homogeneous, and that each character graph differed substantially from the others. Results for Sophie and 'Debby' (both injecting drug users) illustrate this point. See Figures 10.2 and 10.3.

Figure 10.3 Semantic differentials—'Debby'

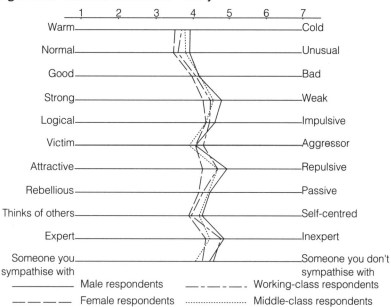

It is notable that we found relatively few gender and class differences of significance in this research in relation to characterisation. Differences between responses to different tape versions have generally been more striking. The similarity within characters (by class and gender) and the contrast between soap opera and AIDS advertisements is clearer visually if we superimpose the gender responses to the *ACP* character Paul and the 'Testimonial' character 'Chris' on the same graph (the responses from all groups to Paul were quite homogeneous, as they were to 'Chris').

Though Paul was seen as less good, more self-centred, more impulsive and considerably weaker than 'Chris', all groups found him more sympathetic than 'Chris', and more of a victim (See Figure 10.4). If, in contrast, we compare group graphs for Sophie and 'Sarah' (see chapter 9) we find a substantially more positive response to 'Sarah' for all groups on nearly all measures. All groups rated Sophie as less normal, less good, weaker, less of a victim, more self-centred, more inexpert, less warm (except for the boys) and much less sympathetic

Figure 10.4 Semantic differentials—'Paul' and 'Chris'

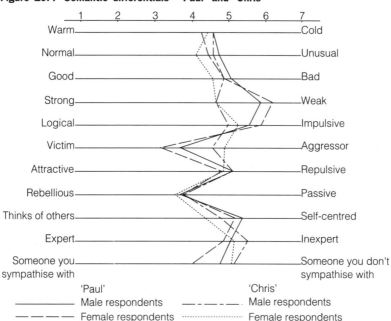

'Paul'
—————— Male respondents
— — — — Female respondents

'Chris'
— · — · — · Male respondents
···················· Female respondents

than 'Sarah'. 'Sarah', however, was understood as a sexual 'victim' of HIV, and Sophie as a needle-sharing 'victim', whereas both Paul and 'Chris' were injecting drug users. If we compare the graphs of two female injecting drug users, Sophie and the 'Testimonial' character 'Debby', we see that Sophie was regarded as more sympathetic and much more of a 'victim' than was 'Debby'. Thus where a 'Testimonial' character, like 'Sarah', was thought to be a 'victim' of sexually induced infection, the students were more sympathetic than to the drug-using characters Sophie and 'Debby'. In the cases of both the male and female characters, however, the 'Testimonial' injecting drug users were in general viewed less sympathetically than the injecting drug-using soap opera characters. Primarily, route of infection, and secondarily, type of text, exerted a stronger influence on audience identification and sympathy than the gender or class of the audience members.

This is not to say, however, that there were no statistically significant gender and class differences in semantic differential responses to individual characters. Boys were significantly more positive about Sophie than girls, girls significantly more positive about Paul. There were also significant gender differences for 'Sarah' on the good/bad, attractive/repulsive, and sympathetic/unsympathetic scales, with girls being more positive than boys in each case. The gender differences indicated in responses to Sophie and 'Sarah' indicate how complex a matter it is to assess the differences between short forms like advertisements (lasting, in some cases, less than one minute) and extended genres like soap operas. Girls tend to respond more favourably to soap operas (like *ACP*) and dramatised documentaries (like *Suzi's Story*) than boys, while the latter (according to the pre-screening responses at least) find AIDS advertisements 'more effective' than the longer genres.

Yet if the aim of using soap opera rather than advertisements is to achieve, in James Davern's words, 'a much stronger message' because of 'emotional involvement' with 'long-time, familiar' characters, then our data suggest that this may often fail precisely because 'social problems' like HIV/AIDS are inserted as closed-off weekly events into the longer-term serial narratives of the regular characters. This may particularly be the case where the weekly 'problems' are conveyed by new (for example, Paul) or non-regular (for example, Sophie) characters. Despite the opportunity afforded by soap opera to weave health issues into emotional involvements with much-loved characters, and despite the narrative space it has to sketch in back-stories and contexts (Sophie's desertion by Terence as a child, for instance), the semantic differential data indicate that there was less involvement with Sophie as a character among young audience members than there was with 'Sarah', who appears for less than a minute on the screen. Despite James Davern's view that 'you have no experience' with the people who feature in public health advertisements, it is not necessarily the case that people become less 'empathetic' and so less 'emotionally involved with them'.

Arguably, this could be an effect of the fictional nature of Sophie, whereas 'Sarah' is a 'real' person who really is HIV positive. Our data, however, do not support this supposition. First choice 'why is this effective' responses to both *Suzi's Story* and *ACP* commented that they were 'about real people, real situations'. A major reason for the difference in sympathy relates to the causes of these individuals' infection. The cause of 'Sarah's' infection is (supposedly) sexual, that of Sophie unknown but implied by the text to possibly be needle sharing (and, as we found, several students also blamed her for wasting her privileged opportunities in becoming a junkie). However the focus group discussions consistently revealed that the difference in sympathy and involvement between Sophie and 'Sarah' was also the result of the self-same 'emotional involvement' with other main characters in the soap opera that resulted from 'character-determined' storylines. Whereas 'Sarah' only has time in her narrative to appear as a 'victim' of her boyfriend, Sophie is also an aggressor in relation to another female character, Alex, whose home and marriage she threatens; she is a source of tragedy for the much-liked Terence; and she is the source of HIV infection for Paul (albeit unwittingly).

When asked whether they found 'Sophie' 'effective' and 'what its message was', one focus group comprised of students who had viewed tape two responded:

> It really showed how hard it is to be an AIDS sufferer or even the parent of an AIDS sufferer.

> It was pretty effective because it showed how hard it was to cope and how hard it was for parents to cope as well.

Asked which of the characters they sympathised with, these students were quite clear:

> Alex, because where she was, Terence was her husband and that was his daughter. She felt left out in her own home because the daughter started taking over, so I really felt sorry for her.

> Terence, because he just—showed how hard it was to come to terms with what it did to a teenage person.

> Terence because he only just, like, found [Sophie] again after a couple of years since he saw her. Then he found out what she was doing and all that, and she went and died on him.

It is evident that the soap genre which encourages narrative investment in the emotional interactions of regular characters also encouraged this reading of 'message effectiveness'. In that context, Davern's emphasis on emotional identification with long-term characters worked against Sophie and Paul, since it was Terence and Alex who were the regulars and who attracted sympathy.

With a generic influence already at work in this way, audiences could then use the specific narrative issues of 'Sophie' (such as Sophie's choice to 'prioritise' her life by becoming a 'junkie') to further negative effect, as in the following responses by a group of students (who had viewed tape three) to the same question. We should note the way in which the narratively foregrounded issue of 'Sophie's choice' is woven into the positive evaluation of Terence and Alex who are seen as having no choice:

> I felt sorry for Alex because she had no choice to be in what was going on and it was wrecking her life. Sophie did make a choice to wreck her life and Terence had to because he was her father. But Alex she had no choice—she only just married him.

> Terence really had it hard too. There was no choice for him. He wanted to make it a better life for her. It was just as bad for him to see her die as if he'd died.

> I don't think there's anything worse than seeing your child dying.

> And he was stuck between his wife and his daughter.

Here the second marriage story that Tony Morphett and Forrest Redlich inserted for commercial 'audience aggregating' reasons may have worked against the 'emotional involvement' that James Davern wanted for his needle-sharing message. The greater hostility felt by girls compared with boys to the Sophie character can probably be traced to this triangular (Sophie/Alex/Terence) relationship. When asked whether they 'strongly agree', 'agree', 'disagree' or 'strongly disagree' with Alex's (very hostile) attitude to Sophie, 46 per cent of students strongly agreed or agreed, while 49 per cent disagreed or strongly disagreed. There were gender differences, however, with 50 per cent of girls compared with 42 per cent of boys strongly agreeing or agreeing with Alex.

Taken together, the findings that viewers of *ACP*'s 'balancing story' perceive themselves less 'at-risk' than before seeing 'Sophie', less 'at-risk' than viewers of the 'villainous Paul' tape two, more inclined to social rather than personal explanation of heroin addiction, and more sympathetic to Paul (who was seen as significantly less bad, less aggressive and more of a victim), do indicate a pattern of audience variation and change. But this is not change in the simplistic sense of 'behaviour change' in relation to needle sharing (few of these students felt themselves 'at-risk' because of 'needle sharing' or 'drug use', either before or after seeing 'Sophie'). Rather it is change in the sense that HIV/AIDS is understood more as a social problem than one of villains and victims, and consequently a problem which (like family problems) can be engaged with and changed. Whereas *ACP*'s policy of 'balancing stories' may, as Morphett suggests, be less threatening and have 'less impact' on audiences, it may, on the other hand, encourage a more context-based, less personalised and stereotyped understanding of the problem (as Forrest Redlich in fact intended). It may well be that other understandings of the social context of HIV/AIDS (for instance, gender power, sexual negotiation and 'safe sex') could be successfully conveyed by soap opera via similar 'balancing' narrative forms.

There is, however, very little evidence that any of the tape versions of 'Sophie' led students to be sympathetic and understanding of the economy of street 'junkies' (which is what Terence was trying to describe in his 'legalise heroin' speech). Although 20 per cent of the students said (in an open-ended question about 'what they particularly liked in the episode') that they liked the realistic view of street life, only 1 per cent responded unprompted that they liked the 'legalise heroin' message, and only 1 per cent tied the problem of street life into issues of social background or class. Indeed the semantic differential measures indicate less sympathy for Sophie than for a shadowy figure who appears for less than 60 seconds on a government AIDS advertisement.

CONCLUDING COMMENTS

In this chapter we have focused primarily on television workers' understanding of how they are using their particular program, genre and production strategies to reach young audiences with public health messages. By examining young people's responses to these professional understandings, we have begun the task of chipping away at the boundaries of cultural authority and 'expertise' on which we first focused in the Introduction. The issues here are extremely complex. Nevertheless, it is these complex relationships between 'effective impact' and 'cultural meaning' that need to be teased out much further before we can better understand the effect of television in conveying public health messages to what some commentators have called its 'mass reach' audience.

11

RESPONSE IN CONTEXT: TELEVISION AND AIDS EDUCATION

Thus far in our empirical research, we have focused on the ways that audiences have responded to specific television AIDS texts. This research has provided useful insights into the response to these texts of the groups we studied, but has not been able to go much beyond this narrow focus. As we have emphasised throughout the book, however, culturally informed research should also seek to explore the broader context in which audiences respond to AIDS television texts. Neither public health advertisements nor television drama are the only sources of information available to people about HIV/AIDS and risk. Other sources include media such as newspapers, radio and magazines, personal experience, interactions with medical workers or sexual health counsellors and formal education. Just as in the case of television professionals, there are many intertexts, many other narratives that negotiate young people's understanding of HIV/AIDS.

To begin to address this question of how AIDS television is viewed and evaluated in relation to the diversity of other sources of information on HIV/AIDS and risk, we now turn to our most recent research, addressing young people's responses to school-based and other forms of education about AIDS and other sexually transmissible diseases (STDs). In this research we were interested in exploring what young people thought of the HIV/AIDS and STDs education they received at school compared with the other sources of information available to them, particularly the mass media. (Some findings from this research have already been discussed in chapter 8.) We also attempted to deal with the methodological and theoretical problems of television research that we identified in chapter 2, informed by our experiences in the previous set of projects we had undertaken that addressed issues of individuals' responses to AIDS television.

THE COMMUNICATION CONTEXT OF HIV/AIDS EDUCATION

Our research on the communication context of HIV/AIDS education for young people, designed in 1992 and conducted in 1993–94, reflected a growing feeling in the field of HIV/AIDS risk and sexuality research that 'the time is ripe to move beyond conceptually limiting paradigms of thought to engage constructively with the expressed needs of young people themselves' (Aggleton 1991, p. 263). Yet it was also important for us to avoid the romantic tendency of identifying young people's experience (as an underprivileged group) with 'authenticity'.

This research project immediately followed one author's involvement in the development research for a heterosexual men's HIV/AIDS education campaign sponsored by the New South Wales Family Planning Association. In this research, focus groups interviews were held with builders' labourers to establish the time/space coordinates of these men's sexual contacts and behaviour so that a campaign could be based on this 'experience'. The apparent consensus among these men was that the best place for sexual contacts was at football clubs or pubs. They argued that given the difficulty of raising issues about condoms in the 'dance floor pick-up' situation, the best mode of safer-sex communication was humorous beer coasters left on tables in the bar, which could raise the issue of using condoms in a lighthearted and non-didactic way. The subsequent campaign drew on the experience of this group of working-class men, within their own preferred leisure space/time patterns. Certainly, the views about using beer coasters early in the archetypical 'pick-up' sexual narrative which the men constructed in the interviews seemed fairly consensual among the focus groups. But because we did not do any quantitative research (nor focus groups of other sub-cultures who used those same clubs) we could not know how broadly based this consensus was.

The HIV/AIDS and school-based education project was designed with this omission in mind. In the first, qualitative phase of this project, 17 single-sex discussion groups were carried out in nine government schools in Sydney and the Blue Mountains and Central West areas of New South Wales, with a total of 138 young people participating: 65 girls and 73 boys. All students were at the end of their penultimate year of secondary schooling (Year 11), and were 16 or 17 years of age. We used the focus groups to establish what appeared to be consensus positions on issues to do with HIV/AIDS education and the mass media. We then adopted these focus group statements as a basis for developing questionnaires administered in the second, quantitative phase of the research to 1005 Year 12 students in 21 government schools in the same metropolitan and rural regions.

In this project we attempted to deal with the kinds of methodological issues we raised in chapter 2 in several different ways. First, we used an experienced sexual health counsellor (rather than an academic or research assistant) as the focus discussion leader with the assumption that young people would feel more comfortable talking with her; and also to enable them to relate to her in her professional capacity as well, asking her questions about things they did not know in the 'de-briefing' following the group discussion. In other words we rejected from the start the myth of the 'objective' interviewer as itself a feature of hierarchical relations, preferring to be reflexively aware of the different discursive moves that the interviewer was making as both interviewer and sexual health counsellor. (For an elaboration of this approach, see Tulloch & Jenkins 1995, ch. 7.) We also felt that this situation was ethically appropriate in trying to avoid using the young people as 'exotic others' (Ang 1989, p. 104) to plunder for data without giving anything in return, as well as much more likely to generate open discussion.

Second, young people were involved in monitoring, adjusting and altering the trial questionnaire. For example, we had avoided a 'strongly agree to strongly disagree' five-point scale in the trial questionnaire because young people both in focus groups and in personal conversation had complained about school HIV/AIDS education programs which made them tick 'strongly agree, agree, disagree' boxes. The trial school students who piloted the questionnaire, however, felt strongly that a simple agree/disagree response to the statements gave them too little scope for gradations of opinion. On their advice, the scale was restored for the final questionnaire. Our response here, as well as allowing the young people to add their own questions to the questionnaire, was to try and meet the kind of criticism raised about questionnaires by cultural studies researchers like Justin Lewis, when he argues that 'Regardless of the conversation respondents would like to have, they are forced to follow the remorseless inner logic of the pre-designed questionnaire . . . Our answers will then be squeezed into the appropriate box so that they can be counted and evaluated' (1991, p. 78). It is interesting that Lewis' criticism is similar to that of the young people themselves. In this case, however, the questionnaire did appear to represent the conversation respondents seemed to 'like to have', based as it was on approximately 40 verbatim statements made by the participants in the focus group discussions.

Our third methodological emphasis addressed the issue of the precise meaning of our survey questions. Lewis, while supporting the need for quantitative audience research in contemporary culture, argues that 'the strength of quantitative surveys lies in the precision of the questions being asked, and upon our ability to interpret the meaning of the replies' (1991, p. 76). In our questionnaire, to try to be more precise and to access young people's meanings, we only used statements made by the young people that made a single point based on their specific logic-in-use in relation to that particular information source. Such statements included, 'Magazines are good sources of information about HIV/AIDS because you can look things up again if you need to'; 'I like radio, personally. If you ring up and ask questions about sex or AIDS, they don't ask your name. So it's a really confidential way of learning more about AIDS and other STDs. I prefer that'; 'I think that they should be able to get on television and say syphilis looks like this'; 'We really need to learn about the symptoms of STDs, what to look for and that kind of thing'. Our intention here was to base our quantitative analysis on the young people's own methods of ordering their world, in terms of which particular information strategy they apply to which particular gaps in their understanding of HIV/AIDS and STDs. In other words, rather than impose our own categories onto the data, we were attempting to use young people's own gap-bridging concepts and language.

BRIDGING THE INFORMATION GAP

In designing this project we drew on Brenda Dervin's sense-making method for analysing the discussion group transcripts as a theoretically appropriate 'below-up' approach which, at the same time, was based on theory-building rather than 'deep mutual understanding' (Silverman 1993, p. 95) with the participants. For Dervin, sense-making is a constructionist approach which denies that information is a simple transmission question, 'flowing' transparently from source via transmitter to receiver according to the traditional communication 'effects' model. Rather, it emphasises the constructive human use of information, in the sense that information must be conceptualised as behaviours—what Dervin calls the 'step-takings that human beings undertake to construct sense of their worlds' (1992, p. 65). Her emphasis here is on linkages between structure and individual agency. Thus a transmission question like, 'Was the information the individual received accurate?' is replaced by a construction question like, 'What strategy did the individual apply that led to rejecting information that another might call accurate?'. The core assumption on which sense-making theory rests is the assumption of discontinuity:

> Sense must be made because the world is in a constant state of change, and people are moving through it. Yesterday's sense is inadequate for the new situation of today . . . A given Sense-Making instance is defined as a situation in which one's movement is blocked . . . a gap which must be bridged. (Dworkin & Dervin 1985, pp. 13–14)

In this respect, Dervin's approach is similar to the constructionist social psychology of Shotter (1984), who argues that an action problem occurs when an individual's experience calls into question social validities. For Shotter, the contradiction within an action problem generates the offering of an account. For Dervin, a discontinuity (for example, between what school AIDS education offers and what students perceive as their needs) generates recognition of a 'gap' and tactical moves to bridge the gap. Dervin's methodological focus in examining information systems is thus based on what she calls 'the sense-making triangle': how the actor saw the situation, the gap, and the help he or she wanted: 'the individual has a mandate—to construct sense of the world in order to move through it. Sense is not seen as being "out there" but rather as something the individual constructs' (Dervin et al. 1980, p. 593). This perspective addresses the contingency of individual action over time and in different contexts.

Clearly, this approach can be applied not only to information needs (for example, about how to engage in safer sex techniques) but also to interpersonal needs (for example, about sexual negotiation and using condoms). As we were not permitted by the relevant authorities to ask specific questions about sexual behaviour in our school-based research, the sense-making approach could only be used in an indirect way in that area, by using hypothetical scenarios rather than asking the young people about their own sexual activities. In this particular research context it was more useful, however, in identifying discursive units in the young people's discussion of information gaps. In particular, two 'gaps' were identified as recurring consistently in all focus group discussions. One was a gap in information/knowledge about sexuality and the body, and the other was a gap about trust and communication. These discursive units were the building blocks for more general themes based on pairs of opposites (as defined by the young people): opposition, for example, between 'basic', 'to the point', 'down-to-earth' information and regulatory 'exam'-type information; and opposition between 'open', 'face-to-face' communication and embarrassed secrecy. The students were quite adamant about their desire for 'openness' about sexual issues and their frustrations that school-based AIDS education was often too indirect and repetitive.

This was the case with groups from both upper-middle-class and working-class metropolitan areas, as well as from country areas. As one girls' discussion group observed:

> You just hear about the main [STDs], like herpes and all those things; not any of the—
>
> And they're not *really* talked about.
>
> They don't tell you, you know, like—
>
> Especially at school.
>
> I wouldn't know if I had one.
>
> Yeah, they don't tell you all the symptoms and stuff.
>
> You wouldn't know if you had one.
>
> No. Unless you looked it up in a booklet or something.
>
> Magazines mostly, have—all the girls' magazines.
>
> Yeah.
>
> Like *Dolly* and stuff.
>
> And *Cleo*.
>
> *Cosmo*.
>
> *Looks, Girlfriend*—
>
> They don't say enough about AIDS and all the information you get is what it is, how you can get it and how you can stop it. But nothing about what actually happens to *you* when you've got AIDS—

I don't know anything–

I know the names of what you can get.

Know the names.

Wouldn't know if I had one.

No—

You still don't know if you have one because some of the symptoms are just like normal symptoms of anything. You wouldn't know that you have an STD—

A lot of people don't know when they have them because they don't get enough information.

So you wouldn't have a clue if you've got it or not.

You only know about like chlamydia and all those other ones, but I still wouldn't know what they were.

I know the *names*.

Chlamydia, but you don't know what it actually *is*.

This discussion is marked by rhetorical moves evident in most of the focus group tapes; where a gap, a dissatisfaction with schools not '*really* talking' about AIDS and STDs, is identified by repetition ('I know the names', 'I wouldn't know if I had one'), and enumeration (of the names of other STDs, and of other places to find out about the symptoms of STDs, such as the magazines *Dolly, Cleo, Cosmopolitan, Girlfriend*). The climax of this search of the media for what the school does not supply is itself, however, marked by repetition: 'wouldn't have a clue whether you've got it or not'. So that whereas in 'scientific' AIDS discourse, repetition, enumeration and climax are often rhetorical moves designed to establish the speaker as authoritative source of a discourse of expertise (Tulloch & Chapman 1992, p. 457), here the interview narrative circles back to what is seen as the 'gap' that neither school nor (in the end) magazines have filled: 'what actually happens to *you*', 'what it does to your body'. Whereas, as discourse theorist Teun van Dijk has argued, the rhetorical operations of repetition, enumeration and climax are 'geared towards the optimal presentation of the self or the accomplishment of an effective story or argument' (van Dijk 1991, p. 141), here, in these young women's accounts, repetition and enumeration have no climax other than an *uncertainty* about the self: 'wouldn't have a clue whether you've got it or not'. Tactical strategies (such as seeking the information in magazines) are suggested to bridge the gap in information, but the rhetorical repetition and circularity suggests that the gap remains.

Many students who participated in the groups expressed opinions privileging a more 'experiential' and explicit understanding of HIV/AIDS and sexuality. Several said that they would like to know more about what actually happens physically when someone contracts HIV or STDs and from whom they could seek more information if they needed it. It is this lack of reflexive knowledge about sexuality, STDs and the body that underpins the young people's constant reference in the focus groups to the tendency of school-based education to 'beat around the bush', 'not get down-to-earth', 'not get to the point' and gloss over issues without 'exploring them in depth'. This is what they mean by bringing sexuality education 'back to basics'. This kind of information helps us understand the high consensus among respondents to our questionnaire over the statement: 'I think the information (about HIV/STDs) has to be down-to-earth, otherwise we lose interest' (79 per cent of girls and 77 per cent of boys agreed).

In contrast to school-based HIV/AIDS education, the focus group discussions suggested that the school students find mass media portrayals of HIV/AIDS important for a number of reasons. One is the sheer visibility offered by television and other visual media such as magazines. Such representations, unlike much of the education they received at school, are able to show how HIV/AIDS and other STDS 'affect the body'. Most of these young people still have had no contact with someone they know to be infected and therefore derived their understanding of the experience from media representations. They argued that providing the full, explicit details of how HIV/AIDS affects the body is important to shock people into the awareness of the dangers of not protecting oneself from infection. If they can read about people who have HIV/AIDS in magazines or see their bodies deteriorate on television documentaries, then the horrific images will make the threat seem 'real'. As the participants in one boys group commented, such documentaries 'really grab you' by making one confront the implications of HIV infection:

Everyone thinks, you know, I'll never get it.

It won't happen to me.

But when you see people that's got [HIV/AIDS], and they thought the same thing, you know.

The quantitative data supported these findings. Overall, the students ranked television as their single most important source of information about HIV/AIDS, followed by school, magazines, and friends, with doctors, family members, newspapers and sexual health centres ranked the least important. The vast majority of students (85 per cent) agreed that television is a better medium for HIV/AIDS education, because it uses visual images, than radio where 'you can only listen'. In response to the statement, 'The stuff you learn in school about AIDS you've already learnt about from TV. All it does is reinforce it.' 50 per cent of the participants agreed and 33 per cent disagreed. So the students themselves would not have rated the schools' HIV/AIDS program highly on this measure.

The most endorsed statement of all among school students in the survey was the following: 'We really need to learn about the symptoms of STDs; what to look for and that kind of thing'. Total agreement among girls was 95 per cent, among boys 89 per cent; total disagreement among girls was 2 per cent, among boys 3 per cent. This result was replicated by other data in the survey. When asked the question, 'What kinds of things about sexuality and HIV/AIDS do you think you do *not* know enough about and would like to learn more about?', both girls and boys very clearly placed 'What happens when you get other sexually transmitted diseases?' first, and 'What happens when someone gets HIV/AIDS?' second. In contrast, 'transmission' education questions like 'How HIV/AIDS is spread' (girls eighth, boys seventh) and 'How to use condoms' (girls seventh, boys eighth) were positioned as much less important.

If they do not get enough information about AIDS and STDs in school, nor do students feel they get sufficient information on television about the symptoms related to AIDS and STDs. Overall, 70 per cent of the students agreed that television does not show in enough detail 'what STDs really look like'. Further, as regards the importance of showing graphic visual material about STDs in schools, 59 per cent of students agreed with the statement made in one of the focus groups that, 'School videos can be good where they show pictures of genital warts and herpes and stuff. That's valuable', while only 17 per cent disagreed. The students argued that school education has tended to repeat television information in its more regulatory aspects ('use a condom', 'no needle sharing'). On the other hand, however, it has the potential for allowing questions, talk and more in-depth discussion which television and many other mass media forms cannot offer. The female students in particular preferred the opportunity to engage in such 'face-to-face' discussions when dealing with issues of sexuality and HIV/AIDS risk. This type of discussion was clearly a potential (and sometimes actualised) bridge for the young women to the 'getting back to basics/to the point' information about AIDS, STDs and the body that they felt they needed. Television was valued in so far as it could give detailed visual access to the infected body. Other media were valued for quite different reasons. For example, the survey data confirmed that radio was liked because it provided a confidential way of learning more about AIDS and other STDs (58 per cent agreed/15 per cent disagreed); and that magazines were liked (especially by girls) as 'good sources of information about AIDS and STDs because you can look things up again if you need to' (77 per cent agreed/10 per cent disagreed).

We argued in chapter 8 that many of the young people who participated in our AIDS education study were approving of the 'scare tactics' of the 'Grim Reaper' advertisement. To determine the extent to which a larger sample of young people shared such views, in the quantitative phase of the AIDS education study we included a questionnaire survey based primarily on statements made by the participants in the initial focus group study. Thus we incorporated the following statement to which members of the larger sample were asked to indicate the extent of their agreement: 'We need scary ads, like the "Grim Reaper" ad, and like that cigarette with the hook that went through her lip. You sit there going yuck! But that's what we need'. The intertext for the 'Grim Reaper' advertisement in this statement was another advertisement that emphasised risk and harm to the human body using 'scare tactics'. This anti-smoking advertisement showed an adolescent girl putting a cigarette to her lips. A vicious looking fishhook suddenly emerges from the end of the cigarette, cutting through her lower lip. The intention of the advertisement was to demonstrate the addictive nature of smoking, the message being 'Don't get hooked'. In the quantitative survey, the statement supporting 'scare tactics' was strongly endorsed: total agreement (strongly agree/agree) among girls was 76 per cent, among boys 73 per cent, while total disagreement (disagree/strongly disagree) among girls was 14 per cent and among boys 13 per cent.

An earlier anti-smoking television advertisement used similarly shocking visual imagery to compare a smoker's lungs with a horribly polluted and discoloured sponge. One of the participants in the focus groups made another analogy comparing this advertisement with the types needed to prevent the spread of STDs: 'I think that they should be able to get on television and say syphilis looks like this. They get in there and said, this is what a smoker's lungs look like—like a green sponge. So why shouldn't they get on TV and show you what STDs really look like?'

Again we used the statement in the quantitative survey, finding similar strong endorsement of such a strategy. Total agreement among girls with this statement was 72 per cent, among boys 69 per cent; total disagreement among girls was only 11 per cent and among boys 14 per cent. These quantitative data suggest that information about 'what happens to your body' in relation to AIDS and other STDS is valued very highly by this population of young people, who indicate strongly that they are not getting the information they need in this area.

Over a number of questions, then, the young people emphasised the importance of a detailed emphasis on HIV/AIDS and STDs and what these do to the body rather than the 'seen it all before' regulatory discourses of 'always use condoms'. Different media forms were considered different bridges to different meaning gaps: pertaining to issues of reflexively monitoring the body, to finding out about intimate information in privacy, and to the ready availability of information in one's own time–space. But *no* source—media, school or interpersonal—provided a wholly adequate bridge to the infected body for these young people.

In this project, drawing on theoretical models (like sense-making) to analyse and understand our 'below-up' qualitative data did help us avoid the romantic 'authentic insight into people's experiences' approach criticised by David Silverman (1993). Our own theoretical preconceptions, however, were also challenged by the research process. These young people were acutely aware of regulatory, simplistic and formulaic AIDS education, and rejected it whether on television or in school. Their responses, therefore, suggested a more complex and agentive model of students' differentiated use of the media than we had anticipated when planning the research. As regards education about AIDS, STDs and the conduct of sexual relationships, what the young people said they needed in this situation were not more 'tick the box' warnings about using condoms and so on (transmission questions), but the development of sexual health skills that went beyond simply naming STDs and the risk factors and symptoms related to HIV/AIDS (construction questions).

These findings suggest that the young people in our study were looking for an education that made them skilled in monitoring their bodies' sexual health. Given the all-pervasive presence of discourses on risk in late-modern societies, and the continual need to present one's body in its most favourable light to win social and sexual approval, the project of the body is a never-ending reflexive enterprise. To that end, all sources of information and knowledges about HIV/AIDS and STDs—whether media, school or interpersonal—are constantly and actively negotiated in order to bridge the variety of gaps that the discourses of body maintenance and risk generate for these young people.

CONCLUDING COMMENTS

In this chapter we have explored some of the problems associated with both quantitative and qualitative approaches to analysing television; and we have responded by way of a case study to the calls of Morley, Lewis, Silverman and others for research that draws on the strengths of both enumeration and interpretation. Because space has been short, we have not been able to elaborate the connections between qualitative and quantitative methods in this study (see Lupton & Tulloch 1996a, 1996b for more details of our findings). But it is important, in conclusion, to ask to what extent this research met our own criticisms of these methods.

As regards our critique of quantitative methods, we addressed the problem of over-reliance on 'science' by recognising from the beginning that the questionnaire items were not 'neutral' but based on the subjectivity of the students themselves. Since selecting pre-coding categories is always, in part, subjective, we made that 'below-up' approach an articulated part of the research method. By working backwards and forwards between focus group interview tapes and survey data, we could avoid some of the rigidity of structured surveys in dealing with sensitive and complex issues. This was especially so because our use of a sexual health counsellor who did not talk down to the students and who also had the experience that the students wanted (in terms of access to knowledge of the body) offered the students something in return for their frank talk. It is noteworthy that in a number of the focus groups, when the students were asked what kind of format they would like for school-based HIV education, they said 'Just like this'. Because we could observe the students embed both preferred media genres and school teaching formats in their own constructions of risk and the sexual body, we were not counting separated 'bits' of texts (as in content analysis), but attending to the relationship between the students' own narratives and those in the media and classroom. As a result, even though we did concentrate on methodology, we feel we were at least as concerned with explanatory and theoretical issues. So too, our use of Dervin's sense-making approach began to focus on meaning as individual constructs rather than simply 'out there'.

As regards the problems we stated earlier with qualitative methodology, clearly our basing of questionnaires on what appeared to be strong focus group consensus (as well as strong differences) of view did enable us to explore the reliability of our qualitative data, and generalise our findings across a large sample (for example, that students want more education about 'other STDs'). At the same time, questionnaires allowed students an anonymity of response that was not present in the focus groups. But what Silverman calls the 'ethnographic romantic' tendency (of believing that the voices of our participants are somehow transparently 'authentic') was especially a potential for us, given our methodological emphasis on below-up, subjective responses. We countered by strongly theorising our method (for example, the building-in of Dervin's sense-making approach to the analysis of the focus groups *and* to the construction of the survey questions). On the other hand, the opposite problem in qualitative research of preconceived concepts and theory also had to be addressed. Students' responses in both focus groups and surveys indicated that young people did not distinguish between 'school' and 'media' discourses in relation to a 'good AIDS education'. Rather, they emphasised the importance (in either forum) of particular content (more on other STDs), particular audio-visual emphases (more visuals of the infected body), particular modes of address (more equal and 'open', less jargon), as well as the different roles different media performed in bridging their different 'gaps'.

As well as this last point raising the issue of an individual's multiple subjectivities in relation to 'AIDS education', these findings forced us back to our own research plan where we noted that the preconception of an opposition between school and media discourses on HIV/AIDS was built into our original grant application. Our data contradicted this 'opposition', and theoretical rethinking had to follow. Nevertheless, we were both aware of the degree to which the preconceived 'opposition' between school and media discourses was *also* tactical in our research application, given that this was already a significant assumption among key members of the Department of School Education and we needed the approval of their committee to get access to schools for our research. This Department had recently refused such permission to a major national research project on HIV education in schools. We were always aware, in other words, that our research was shaped by power relations, politics and professional concerns, and that both the research plan itself and the data produced are culturally situated (in this case, there were quite specific kinds of questions that we could not ask). The relationship between tactical strategies and one's own (career-path) theoretical assumptions is, of course, another issue for reflexivity. The situating of a research grant application within many other academic subjectivities is not always conducive of instant self-awareness in this matter. At the very least, though, the combining of qualitative and quantitative methods in our research did lead us further into issues of theory and reflexivity, and this seems to us a research bonus.

◼ CONCLUSION

In this book we have explored the ways in which television texts about AIDS are produced and interpreted. Our emphasis has been on how individuals in their daily practices of making and 'reading' television understand the phenomenon of HIV/AIDS and the risks associated with it. We have done so using a variety of research methods, seeking to explore and highlight their strengths and weaknesses through a reflexive discussion of our own empirical research. In response to our criticism about the paucity of socio-cultural theory in mainstream health communication research, we have also sought to theorise our findings in relation to the text/audience relationship in the context of notions of health, disease, risk, the body, the self and the Other in western societies.

We have argued throughout the book that television texts on AIDS contribute to the ways in which risks related to HIV infection and the 'AIDS body' are understood and experienced. Television provides a 'window on risk', a means of working through the complexities of human relationships and of demonstrating the ills to which human bodies may become prey. The television texts we have analysed here have drawn from and reproduced a generalised mood in western societies concerning the fear of risk and the importance of preserving one's bodily boundaries. They underline the anxieties circulating around the relationship between contagion and activities that are proscribed as 'deviant' such as injecting drug use, homosexuality and non-monogamous sexuality. Representations of HIV/AIDS on television have made frequent use of powerful binary oppositions to define certain people, social groups and spaces as either threatening or threatened: for example, clean/dirty, active/passive, rural/urban, controlled/unruly, innocent/guilty. Whether meanings about HIV/AIDS and risk have been presented in television drama or public health advertisements, they share a concern for defining and portraying the types of people or social groups that are deemed to be 'at risk' from

HIV/AIDS. Often this definition implies not only that such individuals pose a threat to themselves, but also that they threaten others through their lack of self-control, their participation in 'deviant' activities or their passivity. Those 'at risk' of illnesses or disease are frequently portrayed as ignorant, lacking self-discipline and requiring better self-control. It is only fair to note as well here that television drama has also often portrayed 'society' as an ignorant, uncontrolled oppressor of people living with HIV/AIDS. In fact, the very first major portrayal of the HIV/AIDS issue on Australian television drama—an episode of *The Flying Doctors* which covered victimisation of gay sexuality—was of this kind. Despite this, AIDS television texts do quite clearly serve to construct idealised notions of the body: the body that is self-contained, well regulated and protects its health rather than allows itself to succumb to desire.

In television drama, the gay man (particularly in the early 1980s) and the young woman (from the late 1980s onwards) have been singled out and cast as the primary 'victims' of HIV infection. Notable by their absence have been heterosexual men, injecting drug users (with the exception of the 'Sophie' *ACP* episodes) and older women and men. In contrast, AIDS advertisements produced for government-sponsored media campaigns have focused on heterosexuals (both male and female), albeit younger rather than older, and injecting drug users, virtually ignoring gay or bisexual men. This difference in representation of the 'at-risk body' is partly related to the differing cultures of production.

Television drama, as we have shown, is strongly shaped by the commercial imperative, the need to attract and maintain audiences, to work around commercial breaks, to avoid alienating commercial sponsors, to keep a dramatic edge while simultaneously maintaining the integrity of regular characters, as well as constructing a convincing portrayal of a public health issue such as HIV/AIDS. A focus on a pair of gay lovers against the community (as in *The Flying Doctors* episode) provides this dramatic conflict while testing the integrity of the regular characters. In contrast, television public health campaigns have somewhat different objectives. They are also intended to attract audience attention, but in relation to a specific 'target' audience deemed to be 'at risk' from a defined health threat. Their primary objective is to convey one or more discrete health messages and to attempt to change attitudes and behaviours using a text that is far shorter than episodic drama, and conflictual only in a more cataclysmic sense—as in the horrendous bowling balls mowing down people like ten-pins in the 'Grim Reaper' advertisement, or the frightening shadow of the reaper rearing over the young couple in the 'Russian Roulette' advertisement. Government-sponsored television campaigns also serve the institutional objective of being a highly public means of demonstrating that government public health authorities are acting on a particular health issue. Thus the logo of the grim reaper itself became a sign of 'dynamic' and continuing activity by the government in the years following its first appearance in 1987.

Both genres of television, however, have drawn upon similar discourses, knowledge bases and other texts. They have both used dramatic representations of risk to attract audiences' attention and relied upon 'expert' knowledges in relation to changing opinions about which practices were 'risky' and which social groups were considered to be 'at risk' from HIV/AIDS. For example, the focus in Australian AIDS campaigns on heterosexuals and injecting drug use was, as we have shown, strongly linked to government policy around the designation of the social groups considered to be at risk of HIV/AIDS in the mid to late 1980s via the 'second' and 'third waves' of HIV infection. So too, the decision of the television workers producing *ACP* to focus a series of four self-contained episodes on the 'second/third wave' of infection, involving injecting drug use, was related to 'expert' advice and news texts reporting the existence of this threat, as well as to commercial imperatives.

The two different television genres we have analysed have also shared similar taboos in relation to the absence of certain HIV risk practices. As in other Anglophone countries, Australian television campaigns have shied away from discussing homosexuality. One reason for this is the difficulties related to discussing gay sexual practices on commercial television. Indeed, original plans to include at least eight gay male couples embracing in the 'Beds' television advertisement had to be dropped because of objections raised by the Federation of Australian Commercial Television Stations, which failed to approve the concept because some members found it offensive. These objections are mirrored in mainstream television drama, where portrayals of gay sexuality rarely appear. While the gay man with HIV/AIDS has become a familiar figure on commercial television, even such anodyne gestures as touching, hugging or kissing between men tend to be treated gingerly. If they *are* shown, such scenes are often subject to controversy. A 1994 episode of the Australian medical drama *GP*, for example, that showed two gay men lying in bed together was subject to numerous complaints by viewers. Another reason, advanced by some critics, is that gay men were simply not conceptualised as a 'mass audience' suitable as a target for television advertising because of their status as a stigmatised minority group. Governments did not see the need to provide resources for advertising campaigns while AIDS was viewed as limited to that group. As this suggests, decisions about which public health risks 'deserve' government-sponsored media campaigns, and which social groups are considered to be 'at risk', both reflect and reproduce broader cultural understandings. These understandings include what types of behaviours are deemed to be 'risky' and how such risks should best be dealt with.

In this book we have confined our analysis to portrayals of AIDS and people living with HIV/AIDS in mainstream popular television. There have, of course, been a number of efforts on the part of activist cultural producers to construct alternative images and narratives for television. Goldstein (1990, pp. 298–9) argues that popular media representations have tended to portray an 'immune' perspective, presenting the viewpoint of those who consider themselves to be not personally at risk from HIV infection. By contrast, representations of people living with HIV/AIDS and the AIDS epidemic by cultural activists in the arts have tended to tell the 'story' of HIV/AIDS from the 'implicated' perspective: that is, the perspective of those deemed to be 'at risk' or who are already infected with HIV. The imperative for this type of cultural production, therefore, goes far beyond the intention of many mainstream media workers to produce a text with an HIV/AIDS 'message' that is sympathetic to people living with HIV/AIDS or is 'educational' for a mass audience. While the producers of television texts for a mainstream audience tend not to be personally involved with the epidemic, or have the syndrome themselves, the reverse is true of cultural activists. Such representations have an overtly political activist rather than commercial intention, seeking to critique socio-cultural response to HIV/AIDS. These portrayals have difficulties gaining screen time because of their confrontational nature, their explicitness and therefore their potential to cause controversy and moral outrage. They tend to be screened, if at all, late at night on channels such as the British Channel 4 and Australia's SBS which have relatively small audiences (see Treichler 1993, p. 190, for a list of some of these productions).

It was evident from our research that many individuals have a consciously reflexive approach to both assessing and interpreting media in relation to health risks such as AIDS. The intended meanings of television are mediated through audience members' personal biographies and lived constructions of risk. We found, for example, that the participants involved in our audience studies, most of whom were young people in their mid to late adolescence, were highly aware of the risks associated with HIV/AIDS, and favoured television portrayals that provided details on the 'AIDS body' so as to better view and understand how HIV infection is expressed. This desire was not simply a matter of voyeurism or prurience, but emerged from their need to monitor and interpret AIDS risk as it related to themselves. These audience members varied in their assessment of different types of media which was often associated with their judgement of how 'shocking' or 'realistic' the portrayal of AIDS risk was. Self-identification with AIDS risk was phrased through their understandings and moral judgements made about the evident degree of 'innocence' or 'normality' of people living with HIV/AIDS.

Our findings therefore suggested that central moral meanings around HIV/AIDS, risk and the body are shared not only by the people who produce television but also their audiences. Individuals who injected drugs were considered far less sympathetically than were others living with HIV/AIDS, and the audience members tended not to identify with them. The subjects of the 'Testimonial' advertisements who had become infected through using injecting drugs, for example, were subject to more negative responses. So too, the characters of Paul and Sophie in the *ACP* episodes were viewed by many as deserving their fate, as drug users who had 'voluntarily' put themselves at risk of HIV infection and death, despite a heavy emphasis in the verbal narrative (and indeed in specific questionnaire audience responses) on the social reasons why young people use drugs. Thus the 'knowledge' of an individual's risky undertaking is central to the way in which that person is considered by others, as 'passive' or 'active', as 'victim' or 'villain', as 'innocent' or 'guilty'.

In 'risk society', in which there is a heightened sense of the threats to one's health, it is all too easy to imagine oneself as 'victim', falling prey to the duplicity of others, although this is mediated by gender, age, social class, sexual experience and identity and so on. Such a role does not contravene images of oneself as responsible and civilised, and therefore susceptible to blame if illness strikes, but rather presents the self as trusting and innocent, free of guilt and not deserving of one's fate. By contrast, the 'irresponsible' act of apparently taking risks voluntarily—of engaging in homosexual activities, 'promiscuous' heterosexual activities or injecting drugs, for example—attracts moral judgement and blame, placing that individual on the 'outside' of normality. It is such a person who is conceptualised as posing a risk to 'us', or those on the conceptual 'inside'.

We suggest that it is the social-psychological dominance of this insider/outsider dichotomy—paired with other tendencies to polarise, as in the city equals depravity/abnormality:country equals purity/normality of the *A Country Practice* pastoral genre—that makes 'real life' disasters like the mass shootings at Dunblane and Port Arthur so extraordinarily traumatic. A key feature of people's apparently widespread inability to cope with these killings, as represented in the media, was the fact that not only did they occur in 'rural', 'quiet' parts of Scotland and Australia (and not, as many people emphasised, in the world's big cities), but also that the gunmen came from *inside* these rural communities. Consequently a great deal of public and media rhetoric in the ensuing weeks had to work hard to reposition these men in terms of a discourse that would restore somehow that purity and sense of safety.

This example takes us further into the links between the cultural, the unconscious and concepts of the body and risk than this book has been able to go. Our research suggests that responses to media representations of health risks such as HIV/AIDS do not only involve the hierarchical steps of 'attracting attention', 'understanding the message', 'identifying with the message' or 'assessing personal relevance' that are so often identified in the health communication literature (for example, by Atkin & Freimuth 1989). What is left out of this formulation of response are the embodied rationalities and irrationalities of Otherness, desire, the emotions and the unconscious, which have their own, often non-linear, momentum and logic. A televisual text on a risk like HIV/AIDS may be partly responded to on a subliminal level, involving 'message involvement' at a level of complexity that audience members may find difficult to articulate. So too, the producers of television texts, while inhabiting professional cultures that shape their decisions in constructing the discursive elements of the text, also operate at a sub- or unconscious level when making their choices. We ourselves, as members of the broader society and more specifically as academic interpreters of television texts, including the texts of interviews and survey data, are responding to these data in ways that inevitably involve the unconscious, which is itself shaped through the socio-cultural context.

This question of the psychoanalytic dimension of developing and responding to meanings about risk and the body on television and other media texts is an intriguing one that we have not had the space to further develop in this book. The dominant discourses on risk, reflexivity and health tend to privilege the notion of the rational actor, the mind in full control of the body. There is less recognition of the ways that the emotions, desires and fantasies are engaged and con-structed through the mass media, and how the identification of certain individuals or social groups as 'risky' or 'unhealthy' provides a way of dislocating and externalising central anxieties from the self by projecting them onto the Other (Figlio 1989). As Robert Crawford argues, when the self or the body appear to be threatened:

> the individual's fear of loss of control and loss of life engenders a defense: a perception of the afflicted as *particularly* susceptible due to their distinctive behaviours, emotional predispositions, social or geographical environment, or unexplained susceptibilities believed to be the properties of groups. Death is kept distant, far from the 'natural' or 'normal' vitality of the healthy self. Projection is a tactic of self-reassurance. (1994, p. 1355, original emphasis)

It is this emotional and often unconscious response to bodily risk as it is represented in the media and other forums, involving such unconscious strategies as projection, externalisation and the return of the repressed, that may explain why advertisements such as the 'Grim Reaper' attracted so much attention when first screened and remain lodged in people's memories (see Williamson 1989). It may also at least partly explain why, as we found in our research, the intentions of the producers of texts like the 'Testimonial' advertisements and the 'Sophie' episodes to 'personalise HIV/AIDS risk' for their young target audiences were not achieved for many of these viewers, because of their tendency to construct the 'Testimonial' subjects and the Sophie and Paul characters as the contaminated Other. These questions of the psychodynamics of the interrelationship between risk, media and the body, which we have been able only to begin to speculate upon here, suggest a whole area of research that as yet remains rather underdeveloped in cultural and media studies and the sociology of health and illness as well as in health communication research.

To conclude, the production and reception of meanings in relation to television AIDS texts are inevitably embedded in social and cultural processes. These include the cultures of production that work to shape the content of such texts, such as the understandings of health promotion and media among public health bureaucrats and their marketing research and advertising consultants, as well as the professional objectives, intertexts, concerns and constraints of television workers in making television drama. So too, the ways in which diverse audience members respond to these texts are shaped by the prior experiences, beliefs, understandings and unconscious meanings they bring to the text as well as by the directive closures of the texts themselves. As this suggests, the production of AIDS 'messages' on television does not 'come first' (as 'source') in any simple, linear sense, but is the result of a continuous negotiation between production rhetorics, institutional values and constraints and intertexts. The same is true of audience reception of these AIDS 'messages'. Whether we think of the interpreters of AIDS texts as production 'workers' (in terms of contributing to the production of meaning) or as simply their audiences, the meanings they make out of these texts are culturally determined, and so require methods of inquiry that recognise the importance of culture in constructing meaning.

REFERENCES

Aggleton, P. (1991) 'When will they ever learn? Young people, health promotion and HIV/AIDS social research', *AIDS Care*, 3(3), 259–64

Alcalay, R. and Taplin, S. (1989) 'Community health campaigns: from theory to action', in Rice, R. and Atkin, C. (eds), *Public Communication Campaigns* (2nd ed.), Newbury Park, CA: Sage, pp. 105–31

Alcorn, K. (1989) 'AIDS in the public sphere: how a broadcasting system in crisis dealt with an epidemic', in Carter, E. and Watney, S. (eds), *Taking Liberties: AIDS and Cultural Politics*, London: Serpent's Tail

Ang, I. (1985) *Watching Dallas: Soap Opera and the Melodramatic Imagination*, London: Methuen

——(1989) 'Wanted: Audiences. On the politics of empirical audience studies', in Seiter, E., Borchers, H., Kreutzner, G. and Warth, E.-M. (eds), *Remote Control: Television, Audiences, and Cultural Power*, London: Routledge

Atkin, C. and Freimuth, V. (1989) 'Formative evaluation research in campaign design', in Rice, R. and Atkin, C. (eds), *Public Communication Campaigns* (2nd ed.), Newbury Park, CA: Sage

Austin, S. (1990) 'AIDS and Africa: United States media and racist fantasy', *Cultural Critique*, 14, 129–41

Backer, T., Rogers, E. and Sopory, P. (1992) *Designing Health Communication Campaigns: What Works?*, Newbury Park, CA: Sage

Balshem, M., Oxman, G., van Rooyen, D. and Girod, K. (1992) 'Syphilis, sex and crack cocaine: images of risk and morality', *Social Science & Medicine*, 35(2), 147–60

Beck, U. (1992) *Risk Society: Towards a New Modernity*, London: Sage

Beharrell, P. (1993) 'AIDS and the British press', in Eldridge, J. (ed.), *Getting the Message*, London: Routledge

Bennett, T. and Woollacott, J. (1987) *Bond and Beyond*, Basingstoke: Macmillan

Bray, F. and Chapman, S. (1991) 'Community knowledge, attitudes and media recall about AIDS, Sydney 1988 and 1989', *Australian Journal of Public Health*, 15(2), 107–13

Brown, J., Waszak, C. and Childers, K. (1989) 'Family planning, abortion and AIDS: sexuality and communication campaigns', in Salmon, C. (ed.),

Information Campaigns: Balancing Social Values and Social Change, Newbury Park, CA: Sage

Bush, A. and Boller, G. (1991) 'Rethinking the role of television advertising during health crises: a rhetorical analysis of the Federal AIDS campaigns', *Journal of Advertising*, 20(1), 28–37

Carr, A. (1987) 'The Grim Reaper: bowling ball or boomerang?', *Australian Society*, July, 28–30

Clift, S., Stears, D., Legg, S., Memon, A. and Ryan, L. (1990) 'Blame and young people's moral judgements about AIDS', in Aggleton, P., Davies, P. and Hart, G. (eds), *AIDS: Individual, Cultural and Policy Dimensions*, London: Falmer

Commonwealth Department of Community Services and Health (1988) *AIDS: A Time to Care, A Time to Act: Towards a Strategy for Australians*, Canberra: Australian Government Publishing Service

Crawford, J., Kippax, S. and Tulloch, J. (1992) *Appraisal of the National AIDS Education Campaign*, Canberra: Department of Health, Housing and Community Services

Crawford, R. (1994) 'The boundaries of the self and the unhealthy other: reflections on health, culture and AIDS', *Social Science & Medicine*, 38(10), 1347–65

Dan, B. (1987) 'The National AIDS Information Campaign: once upon a time in America', *Journal of the American Medical Association*, 258(14), 1942

Dervin, B. (1992) 'From the mind's eye of the user: the sense-making qualitative–quantitative methodology', in Glazier, J. and Powell, R. (eds), *Qualitative Research in Information Management*, Englewood, CO: Libraries Unlimited

Dervin, B., Harlock, S., Attwood, R. and Garzona, C. (1980) 'The human side of information: an exploration in a health communication context', in Nimmo, D. (ed.), *Communication Yearbook 4*, New Brunswick, NJ: Transaction Books

Douglas, M. (1992) *Risk and Blame: Essays in Cultural Theory*, London: Routledge

Dworkin, M. and Dervin, B. with Fraser, B. and Chul Sim, J. (1985) 'A perspective on the convergence of two paradigms: British cultural studies and uses and gratifications', paper presented at the International Communication Association conference, Hawaii, May

Edelman, L. (1993) 'The mirror and the tank: "AIDS", subjectivity, and the rhetoric of activism', in Murphy, T. and Poirier, S. (eds), *Writing AIDS: Gay Literature, Language, and Analysis*, New York: Columbia University Press

Elam, K. (1980) *The Semiotics of Theatre and Drama*, London: Methuen

Elias, N. (1978) *The Civilizing Process*, New York: Urizen

Fairclough, N. (1992) *Discourse and Social Change*, Cambridge: Polity

Featherstone, M., Hepworth, M. and Turner, B. (eds) (1991) *The Body: Social Process and Cultural Theory*, London: Sage

Figlio, K. (1989) 'Unconscious aspects of health and the public sphere', in Richards, B. (ed.), *Crises of the Self: Further Essays on Psychoanalysis and Politics*, London: Free Association Books

Fiske, J. (1982) *Introduction to Communication Studies*, London: Routledge

Flora, J. and Thoresen, C. (1988) 'Reducing the risk of AIDS in adolescents', *American Psychologist*, 43, 965–70

Foucault, M. (1984) 'Truth and power', in Rabinow, P. (ed.), *The Foucault Reader*, New York: Pantheon Books

Fuqua, J. (1995) '"There's a queer in my soap!": the homophobia/AIDS story-line of *One Life to Live*', in Allen, R. (ed.), *To Be Continued . . . Soap Operas Around the World*, London: Routledge

Geraghty, C. (1995) 'Social issues and realist soaps: a study of British soap operas in the 1980s/1990s', in Allen, R. (ed.), *To Be Continued . . . Soap Operas Around the World*, London: Routledge

Gerbner, G. (1970) 'Cultural indicators: the case of violence in television drama', *Annals of the American Association of Political and Social Science*, 338, 69–81

Giddens, A. (1986) *The Constitution of Society: Outline of the Theory of Structuration*, Cambridge: Polity

Giddens, A. (1991) *Modernity and Self-Identity*, Cambridge: Polity

Gilman, S. (1995) *Health and Illness: Images of Difference*, London: Reaktion Books

Goldstein, R. (1990) 'The implicated and the immune: cultural responses to AIDS', *The Milbank Quarterly*, 68 (suppl. 2), 295–319

Gross, L. (1989) 'Out of the mainstream: sexual minorities and the mass media', in Seiter, E., Borchers, H., Kreutzner, G. and Warth, E.-M. (eds), *Remote Control: Television, Audiences, and Cultural Power*, London: Routledge

Grover, J. (1992) 'Visible lesions: images of the PWA in America', in Miller, J. (ed.), *Fluid Exchanges: Artists and Critics in the AIDS Crisis*, Toronto: University of Toronto Press

Hart, G. (1993) 'Safer sex: a paradigm revisited', in Aggleton, P., Davies, P. and Hart, G. (eds), *AIDS: facing the Second Decade*, London: Falmer Press

Jenks, C. (1993) 'Introduction: the analytic bases of cultural reproduction theory', in Jenks, C. (ed.), *Cultural Reproduction*, London: Routledge

Jensen, K. (1991) 'Introduction: the qualitative turn', in Jensen, K. and Jankowski, N. (eds), *A Handbook of Qualitative Methodologies for Mass Communication Research*, London: Routledge

Johnson, D. (1994) 'The effect of information load on cognitive responses to HIV/AIDS television PSAs', unpublished doctoral dissertation, Department of Communication, Stanford University

Johnson, D. and Rimal, R. (1994) 'Analysis of HIV/AIDS television public service announcements around the world', paper presented at the International Communication Association conference, Sydney, July

Jones, J. (1992) 'Discourses on and of AIDS in West Germany, 1986–90', *Journal of the History of Sexuality*, 2(3), 439–68

——(1993) 'Refusing the name: the absence of AIDS in recent American gay male fiction', in Murphy, T. and Poirier, S. (eds), *Writing AIDS: Gay Literature, Language, and Analysis*, New York: Columbia University Press

Juhasz, A. (1990) 'The contained threat: women in mainstream AIDS documentary', *Journal of Sex Research*, 27(1), 25–46

King, S. (1993) 'The politics of the body and the body politic: Magic Johnson and the ideology of AIDS', *Sociology of Sport Journal*, 10, 270–85

Kippax, S., Crawford, J., Waldby, C. and Benton, P. (1990) 'Women negotiating heterosex: implications for AIDS prevention', *Women's Studies International Forum*, 13(6), 533–42

Kitzinger, J. (1993) 'Understanding AIDS: researching audience perceptions of Acquired Immune Deficiency Syndrome', in Eldridge, J. (ed.), *Getting the Message: News, Truth and Power*, London: Routledge

Kreps, G. (1989) 'Setting the agenda for health communication research and development: scholarship that can make a difference', *Health Communication*, 1(1), 11–15

Lash, S., Szerszynski, B. and Wynne, B. (eds) (1996) *Risk, Environment and Modernity: Towards a New Ecology*, London: Sage

Lewis, J. (1991) *The Ideological Octopus: An Exploration of Television and its Audience*, New York: Routledge

Lievrouw, L. (1994) 'Health communication research reconsidered: reading the signs', *Journal of Communication*, 44(1), 90–9

Ling, J. (1989) 'New communicable diseases: a communication challenge', *Health Communication*, 1(4), 253–60

Lupton, D. (1994a) *Moral Threats and Dangerous Desires: AIDS in the News Media*, London: Taylor & Francis

——(1994b) 'Talking about sex: sexology, sexual difference and confessional talk shows', *Genders*, 20, 45–65

——(1995) *The Imperative of Health: Public Health and the Regulated Body*, London: Sage

——(1996) 'The feminine "AIDS body" in television drama', *Media International Australia*, 80, 99–109

Lupton, D., McCarthy, S. and Chapman, S. (1995a) '"Panic bodies": discourses on risk and HIV testing', *Sociology of Health and Illness*, 17(1), 89–108

——(1995b) '"Doing the right thing": the symbolic meanings and experiences of having an HIV antibody test', *Social Science & Medicine*, 41(2), 173–80

Lupton, D. and Tulloch, J. (1996a) '"All red in the face": students' views on school-based HIV/AIDS and sexuality education', *Sociological Review*, 44(2), 252–71

Lupton, D. and Tulloch, J. (1996b) '"Bringing home the reality of it": senior school students' responses to mass media portrayals of HIV/AIDS', *Australian Journal of Communication*, 23(1), 31–45

McGrath, R. (1992) 'Dangerous liaisons: health, disease and representation', in Boffin, T. and Gupta, S. (eds), *Ecstatic Antibodies: Resisting the AIDS Mythology*, London: Rivers Oram Press

McGuire, W. (1989) 'Theoretical foundations of campaigns', in Rice, E. and Atkin, C. (eds), *Public Communication Campaigns*, Newbury Park, CA: Sage

Montgomery, K. (1990) 'Promoting health through entertainment television', in Atkin, C. and Wallack, L. (eds), *Mass Communication and Public Health: Complexities and Conflicts*, Newbury Park, CA: Sage

Morgan Gallup (1987) *Poll Report: AIDS of Greater Concern in 1987*, Sydney: Morgan Gallup Ltd

Morlet, A., Guinan, J., Diefenthaler, I. and Gold, J. (1988) 'The impact of the "Grim Reaper" national AIDS educational campaign on the Albion Street (AIDS) Centre and the AIDS hotline', *Medical Journal of Australia*, 148, 282–6

Morley, D. (1992) *Television, Audiences and Cultural Studies*, London: Routledge

Morley, D. and Silverstone, R. (1991) 'Communication and context: ethnographic perspectives on the media audience', in Jensen, K. and Janowski, N. (eds), *A Handbook of Qualitative Methodologies for Mass Communication Research*, London: Routledge

Murray, J. (1991) 'Bad press: representations of AIDS in the media', *Cultural Studies from Birmingham*, 1, 29–51

Nava, M. (1992) *Changing Cultures: Feminism, Youth and Consumerism*, London: Sage

Patton, C. (1990) *Inventing AIDS*, London: Routledge

Petersen, A. and Lupton, D. (1996) *The New Public Health: Health and Self in the Age of Risk*, London and Sydney: Sage and Allen & Unwin

Rhodes, T. and Shaughnessy, R. (1990) 'Compulsory screening: advertising AIDS in Britain, 1986–89', *Policy and Politics*, 18(1), 55–61

Ross, M., Rigby, K., Rosser, B., Anangnostou, P. and Brown, M. (1990) 'The effect of a national campaign on attitudes toward AIDS', *AIDS Care*, 2(4), 339–46

Rosser, B. (1988) 'Reaping the grim results' (letter), *Medical Journal of Australia*, 148, 368

Scott, S. and Morgan, D. (eds) (1993) *Body Matters: Essays on the Sociology of the Body*, London: Taylor & Francis

Scott, S. and Freeman, R. (1995) 'Prevention as a problem of modernity: the example of HIV and AIDS', in Gabe, J. (ed.), *Medicine, Health and Risk*, Oxford: Blackwell

Sherry, M. (1993) 'The language of war in AIDS discourse', in Murphy, T. and Poirier, S. (eds), *Writing AIDS: Gay Literature, Language, and Analysis*, New York: Columbia University Press

Shotter, J. (1984) *Social Accountability and Selfhood*, Oxford: Blackwell

Shields, R. (1992) 'Spaces for the subject of consumption', in Shields, R. (ed.), *Lifestyle Shopping: the Subject of Consumption*, Routledge, London

Silverman, D. (1993) *Interpreting Qualitative Data*, London: Sage

Smith, D. (1990) *The Conceptual Practices of Power: A Feminist Sociology of Knowledge*, Boston: Northeastern University Press

Sontag, S. (1989) *Illness as Metaphor/AIDS and Its Metaphors*, New York: Anchor

Stephenson, N., Breakwell, G. and Fife-Schaw, C. (1993) 'Anchoring social representations of HIV protection: the significance of individual biographies', in Aggleton, P., Davies, P. and Hart, G. (eds), *AIDS: Facing the Second Decade*, London: Falmer

Taylor, B. (1987) *NACAIDS Campaign: Three Months On*, Canberra: Commonwealth Department of Community Services and Health

ten Brummelhuis, H. and Herdt, G. (1995) 'Introduction—anthropology in the context of AIDS', in ten Brummelhuis, H. and Herdt, G. (eds), *Culture and Sexual Risk: Anthropological Perspectives on AIDS*, Amsterdam: OPA

Treichler, P. (1992) 'Seduced and terrorised: AIDS and network television', in Klusacek, A. and Morrison, K. (ed.), *A Leap in the Dark: AIDS, Art and Contemporary Cultures*, Montreal: Véhicule Press

——(1993) 'AIDS narratives on television: whose story?', in Murphy, T. and Poirier, S. (eds), *Writing AIDS: Gay Literature, Language, and Analysis*, New York: Columbia University Press

Tulloch, J. and Chapman, S. (1992) 'Experts in crisis: the framing of radio debate about the risk of AIDS to heterosexuals', *Discourse & Society*, 3(4), 437–68

Tulloch, J. and Jenkins, H. (1995) *Science Fiction Audiences*, London: Routledge

Tulloch, J. and Moran, A. (1986) *A Country Practice: 'Quality Soap'*, Sydney: Currency Press

Tulloch, J. and Tulloch, M. (1993) 'Discourses about violence: critical theory and the "TV violence" debate', *Text*, 12(2), 183–231

Turner, B. (1992) *Regulating Bodies: Essays in Medical Sociology*, London: Routledge

van Dijk, T. (1991) *Racism and the Press: Critical Studies in Racism and Migration*, London: Routledge

Waldby, C. (1993) 'Biomedicine and the body politic', paper presented at the Sex/Gender in Techno-Science Worlds conference, Melbourne, June–July

Waldby, C., Kippax, S. and Crawford, J. (1993) *Cordon sanitaire:* "clean" and "unclean" women in the AIDS discourse of your heterosexual men', in Aggleton, P., Davies, P. and Hart, G. (eds), *AIDS: Facing the Second Decade*, London: Falmer Press

Walkerdine, V. (1986) 'Video replay: families, films and fantasy', in Burgin, V., Donald, J. and Kaplan, C. (eds), *Formations of Fantasy*, London: Methuen

Wallack, L. (1989) 'Mass communication and health promotion: a critical perspective', in Rice, R. and Atkin, C. (eds), *Public Communication Campaigns* (2nd ed.), Newbury Park, CA: Sage

Watney, S. (1987) *Policing Desire: Pornography, AIDS and the Media*, London: Comedia

———(1989) 'The spectacle of AIDS', in Crimp, D. (ed.), *AIDS: Cultural Analysis, Cultural Activism*, Cambridge, MA: MIT Press

———(1992) 'Short-term companions: AIDS as popular entertainment', in Klusacek, A. and Morrison, K. (eds), *A Leap in the Dark: AIDS, Art and Contemporary Cultures*, Montreal: Véhicule Press

———(1993) 'Emergent sexual identities and HIV/AIDS', in Aggleton, P., Davies, P. and Hart, G. (eds), *AIDS: Facing the Second Decade*, London: Falmer Press

Wellings, K. and Orton, S. (1988) *Evaluation of the HEA Public Education Campaigns, February–June 1988*, London: Health Education Authority

Williamson, J. (1989) 'Every virus tells a story', in Carter, E. and Watney, S. (eds), *Taking Liberties: AIDS and Cultural Politics*, London: Serpent's Tail

INDEX

'active' audience model (of
   communication), 14, 19, 84
age, 14, 21, 82, 154, 177, 221;
   sexuality, and, 149
ageing, sociology of, ix
ageism, 172–3
AIDS as cultural phenomena, 9
AIDS body, 49, 50–71 *passim*,
   216, 220; AIDS body, female,
   53; AIDS body, gay, 56; AIDS
   education, 137, 203–15 *passim*;
AIDS public education/media
   campaigns, ix, 7, 31–4 *passim*,
   39, 70, 77–82, 141, 171, 185
AIDS Task Force, 84
AIDS television advertising, viii–ix
   passim, 12, 13, 22, 25–6, 29–49
   passim, 74–94, 133–74, 178,
   198, 201; health promotion
   advertisements, 12, 39, 81, 146;
   pedagogic function of, 15, 30,
   52, 59, 106, 128; San Francisco
   study, 141; 'target'
   groups/audience/ cultures, 82,
   83, 94, 150, 217; *see also* health
   promotion
AIDS 'waves' of infection, 98–106
   passim, 113, 114, 123; 'first
   wave', 98, 102; 'second wave',
   102, 176, 179; 'second/third
   waves', 102–5, 122, 123, 150
Alcoholics Anonymous (AA),
   109–10
All My Children, 53

'America Responds to AIDS'
   (American advertising
   campaign), 35–6, 37
An Early Frost (American television
   drama), 52
Another World, 53
Anti-Discrimination advertisements
   (Australian campaign), 43
*Appraisal of the National AIDS
   Education Campaign*, 78–9
As the World Turns, 54
audience research, ix, 177–9;
   impact, 178–9; meanings,
   176–9; reach, 154, 175
audience response, 12, 13, 58,
   123, 133, 149, 150, 177
audience sub-cultures, 12
Australian Medical Association
   (AMA)
AZT (azidothymidine), 57

'Beds' (Australian advertising
   campaign), 43, 45, 140–7,
   passim 218
Beverly Hills 90210, 54
Black Death, 41
Blue Mountains, 4, 203
body, the, ix, 10, 11, 24, 37, 41,
   51, 55, 69–70, 141, 146, 148,
   207–9, 211–14 *passim*, 216,
   222; addicted body, 69;
   'animalistic' behaviour, and,
   32–3; 'civilised' , 11, 32–4
   passim, 49, 70; 'clean', 11;

'disciplined', 11; diseased, 41, 163; emaciated, 37; experiences and sensations, 11; 'grotesque' 34; 'healthy', 11, 70; idealised notions of, 217; infected body, 212, 214; media, and, 223; 'normal', 11, 52; 'risky bodies', 70; risk, and, 214, 217, 221, 223; sexual, 147, 214; sociology of, ix; *see also* embodiment; AIDS body, the
Brady Bunch, The, 107, 108
British Health Education Authority, *see* Health Education Authority (Britain)
Brookside (British television drama), 54, 58

Cagney and Lacey, 54
censorship, 38
Centers for Disease Control, 35
Chernobyl, 5
city, 59, 60, 65–6, 117, 118, 120–3, 178, 180, 221
'civilised' body, the, *see* body, the
class, 4, 14, 21, 34, 92, 113, 151, 152, 154, 160, 167–75, *passim*, 176, 177, 179, 181, 193, 195–7, 201, 221; middle-, 109, 110, 114, 150, 153, 165–8, 172, 181, 183, 189, 207; working- 150, 166–8, 172, 181, 183, 187, 203, 207; upper-, 165–7, 207
Commonwealth Department of Community Services and Health (DCSH), 39, 75, 77–8, 80–91, 134, 136 *passim*, 155, 170, 174
communication, models of, 13; constructionist, 80, 205–6; 'effects', 14–18, *passim* 25, 79, 80, 85, 94, 128, 206; 'hypodermic', 14, 16, 86, 87,

106, 145, 147, 194; 'Morin model' of behaviour change, 85, 89, 91; 'noise' (semantic) the concept of in, 79–81, 92; 'process', 17, 21; Knowledge-Attitude-Behaviour (KAB), 17–18, 76, 79, 85–6, 92, 94–5; linear, 97; transmission, 80; *see also* health communication
communities, professional, viii
condoms, 4, 38–47 *passim*, 88–93, 149, 103, 150, 151, 155, 168–74, 170, 180, 186, 230, 210; eroticising the, 47
country, 59–60, 64–5 117–23, 207, 221
Country Practice, A, 13, 50, 58–69, 96–112, *passim* 175–201, 217–21 *passim*; 'Sophie' episodes, 60–9, 96, 98–113, 175–201, 217, 222
Cultural [and media] Studies, vii–ix, 7–10, 14–16 *passim* 19, 21, 25, 29, 82, 223; British, 79
cultural reproduction, 19
cultural theory, 16, 18
culture, vii, 3, 9–11, 13, 15, 19, 51, 79, 93, 94, 167, 223; dominant, 4
cultures, 82; expert/professional, 11, 75, 81, 90, 95, 105, 128; of health promotion, 76; of production, 13, 76, 223; audience, 128; commercial, 128

Dallas, 59, 100
Denton, Andrew, 47
death, vii, x, 6, 9, 38, 40–1, 42, 51, 55, 68, 69, 98, 99, 222; as *memento mori,* 40; representation of, 51, 56; Sophie, of, 122, 194

Department of Human Services and Health, *see* Commonwealth Department of Community Services and Health

Department of School Education, 215

'deviant', 4, 5, 11, 48, 163, 178; sexual desires, 9, 70; sexuality, 51, 216, 217

discourse(s), vii, 8, 10–12 *passim*, 18, 22, 24, 29–31, 37, 50, 51, 69, 71, 78, 81, 87, 97, 105, 140–9, 175, 204, 207 *passim*, 168, 174–5; AIDS, 11, 208; body maintenance, 213; 'expertise', 113, 208; health, 76, 82; medical discourses, 9, 11, 215; production, 178, 170; risk, 6, 213; technologisation of, 30, 31, 75, 78, 80, 134; topics of, 169–72

'Disco' advertisement, *see* Health Education Authority (Britain)

discriminant function analysis, 188

disease, 15, 16, 31, 33, 51, 69, 86, 92, 103, 136, 179, 216

Donahue, 53

'Don't Die of Ignorance' (British advertising campaign), 36, 39, 42

Dunblane (Scotland), 5, 221

EastEnders (British television drama), 54, 55, 57

embodiment, vii, viii, 7, 95; embodied experience/sensations, 9, 12, 24; embodied rationalities and irrationalities, 214; culture as embodied, 10; *see also* body, the

ethnicity, 10, 21, 82, 83, 92, 154; ethnic, 14, 83, 91, 152

ethnography, vii–ix, 21–2, 95; of production, 96–8, 160;

ethnographic research/analysis, 8, 14, 21–4, 176 passim, 58, 77, 97; space and time coordinates, 96–7, 124, 128, 176, 178; *see also* research, qualitative and quantitative

families, heterosexual, 194

'Feet' (Australian advertising campaign), 43–4

Flying Doctors, The, 56, 102, 104

focus groups, 12, 20–2, 23, 133, 137, 141, 143, 146, 150, 154, 180, 184, 189–93, *passim* 194, 199, 203–9, 211, 213, 214

gay community, 34, 37, 83, 36; plague, 53, 54

gay man/men, 20, 37, 39, 44, 49; and AIDS, 34, 42, 51, 52, 53, 54–6, 57, 70, 89, 102, 105, 134, 156, 157, 163, 218

gender, 10, 14, 21, 83–4, 91, 92, 150–4, *passim*, 157, 160, 168, 170, 172–5 *passim*, 177, 179, 181, 185, 187, 193, 195–201, 221

genre, vii, ix, 21, 30, 41, 210, 218; *film noir*, 42, 45; gothic, 41, 42; horror, 49, 102; media, 214

GP, 57, 58

'Grim Reaper' (Australian advertising campaign) 3–4, 39–42, 44, 49, 56, 77, 78, 82, 84–9, 93, 94, 96, 102, 133–47, 185, 211, 218, 222

haemophiliacs, 163

'health belief' model of behaviour, 17, 145; *see also* health communication

health communication, viii, ix, 11, 29–34 *passim*, 79, 176; models

of behaviour, 6, 17; campaigns,
viii, 8, 14, 16, 29–37 *passim*,
71, 75, 76, 78, 105, 128, 140,
153–4, 160, 170, 195, 198,
202, 216, 217;
cultural/ethnographic models of,
79, 95; literature, 15, 16, 32,
221; messages (public), ix, 11,
16, 18, 29, 70; research, 8–26
passim 216, 223; theories, ix; *see
also* AIDS advertising; health
promotion
Health Education Authority
(Britain) 37, 75, 157, 153;
'Disco' advertisement, 37; 'Stay'
advertisement, 37; *see also* AIDS
advertising
health promotion, 12, 16–18,
31–4 *passim*, 76–7, 79, 105,
177, 223; literature, 15
health related behaviour, models,
of, 17–18
heroin addiction, 60–9, 98–113
passim, 122, 176, 187–93
heroin legalisation, 180–2, 187–8,
201
heterosexual community, 93, 104
heterosexual men, 46, 54–5, 70,
136, 203, 217
heterosexuality, 44, 76, 93, 123
heterosexuals and AIDS
advertisements/campaigns, 34,
39, 43–7, 53–5, 83, 88, 90–4,
123, 136, 150, 218
heterosexuals and the media,
53–7, 102, 103, 123, 134
HIV, 17, 38, 46, 87
HIV/AIDS *see* AIDS
homosexuality, 50, 52, 54, 56, 60,
86, 101, 163, 216, 218
homosexual community, 98

hypodermic (model of
communication) *see*
communication, models of

idiolects, 123, 124, 128, 151
injecting drug use(rs), 9, 12, 34,
107, 162, 175, 216; advertising,
and, 36–49 *passim*, 89, 90,
92–4, 134, 156–64, 195, 197;
drama, and, 98, 217, 218;
second/third wave, and, 102,
103; soap opera, and, 50, 58,
67, 70, 83, 180, 181, 184–5
intertextuality, vii–viii, 12, 18, 42,
78, 105, 114, 128; intertexts,
97, 106, 113, 124, 128, 149,
171, 202, 211, 223
interviews, 12, 20–4, 98, 133,
137, 146, 158, 172
Intimate Contact, 55

Kaposi's sarcoma, 37, 51
Knowledge-Attitude-Behaviour
(KAB) model (of
communication), *see*
communication, models of
knowledge(s), vii, viii, 4, 7, 8, 10,
84, 214, 218, 220; AIDS, of,
86; attitudes/beliefs/behaviour,
and, 17–18, 86, 129;
expert(s)/professional, 5, 6, 25,
81, 199, 105, 123, 218; 'lay'
25; medical and public health,
6; production of, 149; public
health field, in, 32

lighting (use in soap opera),
115–20 *passim*

magazines and STD information,
208
Melrose Place, 55, 59, 186
Midnight Caller (American
television drama), 53

National Advisory Committee on AIDS (NACAIDS), 39, 42, 80–7, 134, 135
National Campaign Against Drug Abuse, 42
'Needle Bed' (Australian campaign), 44–5, 49, 78, 88, 92, 93, 141–7, *passim*, 150, 183
New South Wales Family Planning Association, 203
noise (semantic) *see* communication, models of

Other, the, 5, 11, 37, 42, 69, 117, 119, 123, 141, 149, 152, 162, 167–8, 175, 175, 178, 180, 184–5, 189, 194, 204, 216, 221–3

pastoral, 114, 116, 121, 123, 126, 178; genre, 221; myth, 64–65; *see also* country
participant observation, 12, 22, 97
Port Arthur (Australia), 5, 204
'process' model (of Communication), *see* communication, models of
processual (poetics of production), 23, 149, 153; *see also* transcodification and transformation
prostitutes/prostitution, 102–4, 163

questionnaire(s), 24, 176, 204, 209, 214; post-screening, 150, 152, 168, 170–3, 181–4; pre-screening, 181–184; self-administered, 12, 20, 23; survey, 20, 21
'Q' ratings, 99
quantitative research methods, viii, ix, 8, 14, 19–25 *passim*, 134, 137, 149, 154, 174–5, 176,

178, 185–9, 193–4, 203–5, 210–12, 215
qualitative research methods, ix, 14, 19–25 *passim*, 85, 133, 134, 137, 168, 170, 174, 176, 185, 189–94, 203, 212–15

'rational actor' and risk, 4, 32, 222
reading formation, vii, 114
reflexivity, 7–8, 97, 145, 204, 215, 216, 220, 222; see also subjectivity
regression analysis, 188
research methods, see quantitative research methods, and qualitative research methods
risk as a cultural concept, 4–9 passim, 25–6, 216–23
risk, class and gender, 6
risk groups/categories, 83, 94, 185, 200, 217
risk society, 5, 221
'Russian Roulette' (Australian advertising campaign), 42, 218

safe(r) sex, 16, 18, 39, 44, 54, 56, 85, 88, 93, 172, 201, 203, 206
safe practices, 156
'second/third wave' of HIV infection, see narrative
semantic differentials, 150–2, 158, 60, 164, 180, 188, 194–201
semiotic density/'thickness', 22, 115, 116, 119, 151–2, 167, 178
sense-making method (for analysing group discussion) 205–6, 214
sexuality, 7, 11, 12, 36, 38, 39, 49, 51, 148, 175, 203, 209–11; age, and, 149, 169, 174; behaviour, and, 4, 38, 82, 85, 203, 206; body, the and, 207; codes in AIDS advertising, and,

39, 76; ; Other, the, and, 149;
gay, 9, 69, 217, 218
Sexually Transmitted Diseases
(STDs), 38, 145, 146, 202,
205, 207–14 passim; chlamydia,
208; clinics, 135; education,
202; genital warts, 210; herpes,
210; syphilis, 205
Shakespeare, 108; *Othello*, 108
soap opera, viii-ix, 12, 13, 49–71
passim, 102–3, 106, 149, 160,
179, 183, 186, 195–9 *passim*; see
also genre
'Sophie' see *Country Practice, A*
sound (use in soap opera), 120–3
passim; heroin music, and, 178,
186
space/time coordinates, see
ethnography
Stanislavsky Method, 108
'Stay' see Health Education
Authority (Britain)
subjectivity, vii, 24, 147; multiple,
67, 95; researcher and
researched, of, 8, 149; students,
of, 213
Suzi's Story, 57, 71

'Testimonial' (Australian
advertising campaign), 45–6,
48, 78–9, 89–93, 134, 149–68,

175, 179, 183, 195–9, 220,
222, 223
textual analysis, vii, 8, 10, 12, 50,
94, 97
textual practice, vii–ix *passim*
'third wave' of HIV infection *see*
narrative
time/space coordinates, *see*
ethnography
transcodification, 23, 75, 98, 113,
114–5, 179; transcodified text,
123; *see also* processual poetics
transformation (intertextual), 75,
98, 106, 108, 113, 114, 179;
see also processual poetics
21 Jump St, 54

United States Department of
Health and Human Services, 35

'Vox Pop Condoms' (Australian
advertising campaign), 47, 79,
89, 91, 93, 134, 149–51,
168–74, 179; 'Vox Pop
Condoms' (Granny), 150,
168–9, 172; 'Vox Pop Condoms'
(Punk), 150

women, representations of 44,
53–7, 175, 217, 220;
heterosexual, 57, 70; older, 47,
174; 'passive victims', as, 46,
57; 'target groups', as, 83

Young and the Restless, The, 53